Capitalism, Institutions and Social Orders

Capitalism, Institutions and Social Orders develops a novel political economy approach by establishing a dialogue between the Social Structures of Accumulation (SSA) theory and Ernesto Laclau's post-Marxism theory. Using this synthesis, it provides an in-depth analysis of Spain's recent socio-economic evolution since the early 1990s.

The book develops a theoretical framework capable of appraising capitalist dynamics together with their relationship to the institutional environment surrounding and structuring them. This is in order to explore the interrelation between the historical development of the capitalist mode of production, on the one hand, and the various co-existing social processes, social consensuses and political identities, on the other. Contemporary Spain provides an interesting case study: until the onset of the Great Recession, Spain had an impressive macroeconomic record supported by several contradictory social processes, such as a massive real estate bubble, an upsurge in private indebtedness and a deteriorating manufacturing sector. However, the accumulation of internal imbalances during those years led inevitably to the sudden disintegration of this institutional and social environment in the years after 2008, thus resulting in a breakdown of capitalist activity accompanied by widespread social contestation. The book also explores the ensuing political scenario, including the emergence of the 'indignados' movement and the anti-austerity party Podemos.

This work is of significant interest to critical political economy and discourse-theory scholars, critical theorists in general, and social scientists concerned with the recent Spanish experience.

Pedro M. Rey-Araújo is a Researcher at the University of Santiago de Compostela, Spain.

Routledge Frontiers of Political Economy

Understanding Financial Crises
Ensar Yılmaz

The Political Economy of Populism
An Introduction
Petar Stankov

Capitalism, Institutions and Social Orders
The Case of Contemporary Spain
Pedro M. Rey-Araújo

Power and Influence of Economists
Contributions to the Social Studies of Economics
Edited by Jens Maesse, Stephan Pühringer, Thierry Rossier and Pierre Benz

Rent-Seeking and Human Capital
How the Hunt for Rents is Changing Our Economic and Political Landscape
Kurt von Seekamm Jr.

The Political Economy of State Intervention
Conserving Capital over the West's Long Depression
Gavin Poynter

Intangible Flow Theory in Economics
Human Participation in Economic and Societal Production
Tiago Cardao-Pito

Foundations of Post-Schumpeterian Economics
Innovation, Institutions and Finance
Beniamino Callegari

Distributive Justice and Taxation
Jørgen Pedersen

For more information about this series, please visit: www.routledge.com/books/series/SE0345

Capitalism, Institutions and Social Orders

The Case of Contemporary Spain

Pedro M. Rey-Araújo

Routledge
Taylor & Francis Group
LONDON AND NEW YORK

First published 2021
by Routledge
2 Park Square, Milton Park, Abingdon, Oxon OX14 4RN

and by Routledge
605 Third Avenue, New York, NY 10017

First issued in paperback 2022

Routledge is an imprint of the Taylor & Francis Group, an informa business

British Library Cataloguing in Publication Data
A catalogue record for this book is available from the British Library

Library of Congress Cataloging-in-Publication Data
A catalog record has been requested for this book

ISBN: 978-0-367-56722-4 (pbk)
ISBN: 978-0-367-48066-0 (hbk)
ISBN: 978-1-003-03781-1 (ebk)

DOI: 10.4324/9781003037811

Typeset in Bembo
by Taylor & Francis Books

A Bego.

Contents

Illustrations

Figures

Tables

Acknowledgments

I would like to express my gratitude to Melchor Fernández and Alberto Meixide, who supervised the PhD dissertation from which this book partly springs; to Ramón Máiz, for remaining an indispensable source of support, guidance, and inspiration at home; to Luis Buendía, without whose continuous support and involvement this book would not have come out; to Lina Gálvez, for having supported this project when it was most needed; to Terry McDonough, to whom whichever merits this book might have owe a great deal; to José Manuel Naredo, whose work and generosity remain an ethical and intellectual reference for these pages; and, of course, to my family and friends, for everything.

Preface

This book represents the culmination of the research project I initiated back in 2014, when I began my doctoral studies at Santiago de Compostela, Spain. Back then, the Spanish economy was just starting to recover from a deep recession with utterly dramatic social consequences. On the one hand, the Great Recession had dealt a fatal blow to Spanish capitalism, as manifested in astonishingly high levels of unemployment, widening social inequalities, and thousands of people being evicted from their homes. The success story of Spanish capitalism, which had consistently received multiple laudatory appraisals prior to the onset of the Great Recession, had now turned into a collective nightmare. On the other hand, political and economic elites were by then plunged into an unheard-of crisis of legitimacy, while social contestation in the streets had been on the rise since 2011, when the so-called 'indignados' movement managed to turn upside down the then-dominant social consensuses regarding the causes and culprits of the economic crisis. As the wave of mobilizations thereby initiated was gradually dying down, a new political party emerged, Podemos, which attempted to bring such a climate of social contestation into the State institutions. Those events sparked a multitude of new theoretical concerns. How did the abruptness and intensity of the economic breakdown relate, in the last instance, to the success story of Spanish capitalism I lived through in my youth? What relation, if any, did the Great Recession have with the proliferation of populist movements in the years that followed? What scope was there for radical social transformation in a Southern European state with arguably few sovereign capacities? Hence, the present book represents both a personal endeavor to provide some valid answers to those pressing questions, as well as an attempt to develop a theoretical framework through which those same questions could be appropriately posed in the first instance. The two separate blocks this book consists of, one strictly theoretical, the other offering an empirical application of the aforementioned framework to the study of contemporary Spain, thus respond to the same theoretical problematic and to the same historical conjuncture. Two separate lines of inquiry converged in the present enterprise.

Firstly, I found myself at the intersection of two separate theoretical traditions. On the one hand, while I understood that having recourse to political economy analyses was fundamental to discern the causes and consequences of the Great Recession, as well as the various scenarios its provisional resolution might have given rise to, I was not content with the deterministic, reductionist, and over-simplistic approach to politics more often than not espoused by the literature. On the other hand, there were several authors in the post-Althusserian tradition, such as Ernesto Laclau, Jacques Rancière, or Slavoj Žižek, who offered stimulating theoretical categories to interrogate ongoing socio-political action in a non-deterministic and non-reductionist fashion. Nonetheless, the role played by capitalist dynamics in affecting the very social field where socio-political action was undertaken was, in their works, either overlooked or, at best, deemed to be a secondary enterprise. Could a 'middle ground' position be found between both approaches, that is, one which properly acknowledged the role played by capitalist dynamics in conditioning the terrain where socio-political interactions take place, without deriving the latter from the nature of the former?

Secondly, I was eager to understand what it was that had so dramatically changed in Spain with the onset of the Great Recession. Prior to 2008, it looked like the whole country was sharing the benefits of a well-established parliamentary democracy, finally leaving behind the anguishing memories of a not-so-distant fascist past; it seemed that arguably old-fashioned narratives of class cleavages had eventually been superseded by a generalized 'middle-class' status which promised not to leave anyone behind; while the specters of the Civil War were once and for all, or so it seemed, left behind an amnesic veil. A nominally social-democratic government could simultaneously enjoy the support of both bankers and trade unionists, constituting itself as the main employment creator within the European Union while, simultaneously, advancing a civil rights agenda whose progressiveness equally surpassed European standards. However, the scenario one would encounter by 2014 was a radically distinct one. The generalized euphoria of the past had given way, all of a sudden, to widespread confusion and desperation; instead of booming employment opportunities, one could only observe mounting unemployment and perfidious precariousness everywhere; widespread de-proletarianization in the guise of rising housing prices had given way to thousands of families being evicted from their primary homes; previous 'middle-class' consensuses had been shown deceitful by thousands of citizens camping in squares all over the country; class cleavages were suddenly coming to the fore as a widening gulf between rulers and ruled was made violently apparent to anyone trying to secure their own subsistence; and the European Union was no longer a symbol of modernity and progress, but took the shape, instead, of foreign men wearing black suits indiscriminately curtailing everyone's social rights. How to make sense of all of it?

As noted above, this book consists of two separate blocks. The core objective of the first block is to develop a dialogue between two distinct theoretical traditions, namely Social Structures of Accumulation (SSA) theory and Ernesto Laclau's post-Marxism. It is our view that, while the former excels in appraising capitalist dynamics, it nonetheless suffers from an under-developed account of socio-political interactions. Conversely, Laclau's post-Marxism's very nuanced account of political interactions suffers from a marked disregard of the role played by capitalist social processes within the social formations it is concerned with. It is our core contention that the various shortcomings identified in each can be successfully corrected and/or ameliorated through, precisely, their joint consideration. Building upon key insights from the two above-mentioned schools of thought, a theoretical synthesis is developed in order to explore how the historical development of the capitalist mode of production related, on the one hand, to the various non-capitalist social processes which act as the former's ultimate conditions of possibility and, on the other hand, to existing social consensuses and political identities. Moreover, various theoretical insights drawn from poststructuralist social theory and Marxist political economy are deployed together in order to develop a notion of 'social orders' from a political economy perspective. This way, it is argued, a better grasp can be obtained of how capitalist dynamics shape the uneven terrain where social struggles are conducted, as well as how the latter, in turn, both relate and respond to the historical development of the former.

The second block takes Spain's recent socio-economic evolution as its case study. Contemporary Spain is an interesting case in point insofar as the very impressive macroeconomic performance it recorded until the onset of the Great Recession, on the one hand, and the wide-raging social consensuses it secured, on the other, were ultimately supported by several self-defeating dynamics, such as a massive real estate bubble, an impressive upsurge in private indebtedness, and a deteriorating productive structure. Moreover, systemic reproduction was crucially dependent upon several other processes mostly neglected by standard political economy analyses, such as the role played by women's unpaid household work, or the proliferation of atypical rents derived from asset prices' self-revaluation. Besides such an atypical process of economic expansion, wide-ranging social consensuses were definitely attained during those years. While, on the one hand, the above-mentioned unsustainable trends attenuated the worst social effects derived from each – thanks, precisely, to their joint occurrence – existing lines of political segmentation left the main institutional processes governing the economic expansion virtually untouched. However, the accumulation of internal imbalances throughout the period fostered a sudden process of disintegration of such an institutional environment from 2008 onwards, which, in turn, could not but undo existing social consensuses and agreements. That is, a systemic crisis was immediately translated into an organic one. To that extent, an analysis of the timing and patterns of the economic breakdown is supplemented by a detailed account of the ensuing political scenario, paying singular attention to the various measures adopted by political-economic elites and to the emergence of various oppositional movements intimately related to the above-mentioned internal contradictions, ranging from the 'indignados' movement springing up in 2011, to the emergence of the anti-austerity party Podemos.

Part I

Capitalism, institutions and social orders

1 Dancing over the 'middle ground'

Social heterogeneity and capitalism

Our societies are not simply societies in the abstract but, rather, capitalist societies or, more accurately, social formations where capitalism is the dominant mode of production. These same societies are nonetheless irreducibly plural, in the sense that their phenomenal diversity cannot be reduced to any single common denominator. Starting from this dual recognition, we aim to develop a social theory that enables us to grasp the various social determinants of historical development at play in a given conjuncture, together with the various social tensions and conflicts coterminous with the former. In our opinion, theorizing capitalist societies from a holistic perspective requires, at one and the same time, to study the internal dynamics of the capitalist mode of production (i.e. the internal evolution of its constituent elements as well as the various relations existing among them at a given time and place), as well as the various processes through which people make sense of the social conditions in which they are immersed (i.e. how people react, contest, acquiesce, consent, or struggle against them).

In our view, when analyzing the relation between the diverse social processes through which material (re-)production is organized, and the modalities and nature of socio-political interactions accompanying it, two main risks should be avoided at all costs. On the one hand, a reductionist and/or economicist approach to politics needs to be discarded. In other words, political interaction among social agents should under no circumstances be derived in a straightforward fashion from the position the latter occupy in the social organization of material (re-)production. On the other hand, a voluntarist approach to politics, that is, one that understands that individuals have the capacity to re-shape the existing social order according to their respective wills, needs to be equally rejected. In contemporary social theory, these Scylla and Charybdis of social theory may be associated to orthodox Marxism and postmodern social theory, respectively. Instead, the strength and stubbornness of the various social processes delimiting the scope for political action, as well as the latter's contingent instantiation within a given spatio-temporal location, must be acknowledged. Neither are co-existing social domains ultimately immune to capitalism's internal dynamics, nor the latter constitute a sort of all-embracing logic determining, in a mirror-like fashion, the historical evolution of the former.

Before proceeding, some basic methodological precepts that are to inform our theoretical investigation should be laid bare. Only by reference to them can our theoretical goals and motivations be situated, and the more or less successful character of our enterprise be ultimately ascertained.

- Firstly, our societies are not abstract, internally coherent entities, nor mere aggregations of discrete elements. On the contrary, they are societies where capitalism is the dominant mode of production. By mode of production it is understood an ensemble of social relations regulating how, in a given social setting, economic surplus is produced, appropriated, and distributed among the various participants involved. Capitalism is an inherently unstable and crisis-prone social system, where intervals of socio-institutional stability always precede periods of more intense social turmoil and radical transformation. These latter periods are referred to as systemic crises, where profound social change is not only advisable but even necessary from the perspective of systemic preservation, thus considerably widening the existing scope for political intervention. The dominance of capitalism in these social formations means that the internal evolution of the former molds and shapes to a greater extent the historical evolution of the remaining social processes partaking in the latter.
- Secondly, a dimension of conflict and antagonism underlies the social ensembles we are referring to. Social conflicts and antagonisms are not deemed to be a social malfunction nor a historical anomaly but, on the contrary, they are understood to be ontologically primary and constitutive themselves of social objectivity. It thus follows that the social analyst's task is not to discern how conflicts might emerge from an otherwise harmonious social environment but, on the contrary, to appraise how such an antagonistic dimension is perennially channeled and negotiated through and through, so that a social order can be satisfactorily self-reproduced over time. Therefore, societies are not themselves constitutive (meaning that some internal and essential features would hold the key to decipher its outer phenomenological appearance) but constituted through a thoroughgoing and incessant process of pacification of contingent struggles. Moreover, such an antagonistic dimension is also constitutively ubiquitous, insofar as no specific location within the social structure enjoys any sort of ontological privilege regarding the manifestation of social conflicts. As a corollary, it follows, firstly, that no specific social subject can be granted any *a priori* privilege regarding its capacity to initiate anti-systemic struggles and, secondly, that no political agent's identity is derived, in a direct and straightforward manner, from the inner functioning of the underlying social structure but, on the contrary, its emergence is always strictly dependent upon a constitutive and non-determinist process of political mediation.
- Thirdly, the phenomenal diversity these societies show in its outer appearance is utterly irreducible to any common denominator that would

account, in the last instance, for their observed differences. On the contrary, such social heterogeneity is ontologically primary. It is not meant by this that social subjects' self-perceived differences do not share some common determinants related to how society's material (re-)production is organized, but that any observed social unity is always the end result of some process of political production of commonality. In sum, while difference is ontologically primary, social identity is the outcome of political processes aimed at achieving it.

- Fourthly, we argue in favor of an anti-essentialist conception of social sciences. By this we mean that social interaction cannot be reduced to the interplay among essences underlying the social, whose search would thus constitute the *raison d'etre* of social scientists. Instead of splitting social processes into two separate fields (e.g. necessity versus contingency; essences versus appearances), we conceive theoretical processes as co-existing with other social processes within the social totality, with no pre-constituted relations among them. However, rejecting the existence of essences underlying the social does not lead us to praise the utter impenetrability of the social in a nihilistic and postmodern fashion and thus to confine ourselves to merely register the multifarious phenomenological appearance of the world. We do affirm, instead, the necessity of introducing some internal hierarchy among co-existing social processes regarding their differential causal effectivity for, otherwise, we would be abandoning the terrain of social sciences altogether. Nevertheless, these 'knowledges' are not expected to reflect in any sense any essential characteristics of the social processes implicated but are themselves just partial and contingent truths, i.e. truths are deemed to be strictly intra-theoretical. As a corollary, social sciences are not concerned with unveiling 'hidden truths' waiting to be discovered out there but, rather, they represent a radically partisan enterprise (independently, of course, of its practitioners' degree of self-consciousness in that respect).

In sum, we aim at developing a theoretical framework that acknowledges the existence of social structures underlying every social interaction (however incomplete and unstable) without deriving the latter from the nature of the former. We aim at giving due recognition to social agents' capacity of agency without that presuming they operate in an institutional vacuum. We aim at acknowledging that capitalism's internal dynamics are relevant but not all-embracing; that capitalism is a contingent element in human history but in no way a precarious one; crisis-prone but not teleologically driven towards its own dissolution; complex but not inapprehensible; simple but in no way textbook-like. In the same vein, political action is not economically determined nor completely unconstrained; the constitution of political identities is a relatively autonomous process but in no case a fully independent one; political action is neither omnipotent nor tragically doomed to fail.

We are well aware that the twin dangers of falling into either determinist or voluntarist schemes of social explanation stand as an ever-present threat to our theoretical enterprise. However, we are equally committed to the possibility of finding some 'middle ground' among the two, however unstable and slippery, where we would like to situate ourselves.[1] Let's proceed.

The Marxist tradition and the 'middle ground'

This tension between two different explanatory schemes of social transformation, one leaning towards the primacy of human agency and self-consciousness, the other towards the primacy of structural explanation, has permeated the whole Marxist tradition since its very inception. Indeed, both lines of reasoning can already be identified in the works of Marx himself. On the one hand, we find at the beginning of the *Communist Manifesto* perhaps the most eloquent expression to date of the first pole: 'The history of all hitherto existing society in the history of class struggles' (Marx and Engels 2010 [1848]). On the other, the not less famous Preface to *A Contribution to the Critique of Political Economy* holds the opposite view, in what would become the flagship of Marxist orthodoxy in the decades to come. A lengthy quote is due:

> In the social production of their existence, men inevitably enter into definite relations, which are independent of their will, namely, relations of production appropriate to a given stage in the development of their material forces of production. The totality of these relations of production constitutes the economic structure of society, the real foundation, on which arises a legal and political superstructure and to which correspond definite forms of social consciousness. The mode of production of material life conditions the general process of social, political and intellectual life. It is not the consciousness of men that determines their existence, but their social existence that determines their consciousness. At a certain stage of development, the material productive forces of society come into conflict with the existing relations of production or – this merely expresses the same thing in legal terms – with the property relations within the framework of which they have operated hitherto. From forms of development of the productive forces these relations turn into their fetters. Then begins an era of social revolution. The changes in the economic foundation lead sooner or later to the transformation of the whole immense superstructure.
>
> (Marx 1977 [1859])

Between these two extreme poles, Marx's view was definitely more nuanced and complex than has been suggested by the dogmatic, economicist, and fatalist versions to be later instituted as Marxist orthodoxy. While, in Marx's view, certain structural conditions were needed for social upheaval to be successful in reshaping the social order, the key to actual (and progressive) social transformation within capitalism was 'the development of the working class into a self-conscious political subject capable of taking control of society' (Callinicos 2007: 94). Beyond strictly theoretical considerations, it seems that contingent political imperatives were key to determine which facet of Marx's dual scheme was emphasized. While a fatalistic interpretation of history became entrenched within Marxist orthodoxy, singularly in the writings of the leaders of the Second International (e.g. Kautsky, Bernstein), a revindication of human agency's capacity of social transformation was emphasized by certain currents of Western Marxism (e.g. Lukács, Korsch, Sartre), themselves a response to the political immobilism advocated by the former.[2] Commenting upon this duality, Elliot (2006: 201) writes: 'For some Marxists it is a question of either/or. For others, the problem is to integrate the two axioms in such a way that the inverse perils of economistic and voluntarist reductionism are avoided.' Of course, we are ourselves committed to this second option.

In the end, the debate revolved around what the relation was between the economic and non-economic aspects of the social totality, as well as what their relative relevance was in promoting fully-fledged social change. Regarding political subjectivity, the key question was whether the latter was to spring naturally and straightforwardly out of the configuration of the relations of production, or whether, on the contrary, non-economic aspects themselves played a constitutive role regarding political self-consciousness. We follow Resnick and Wolff (1987: 40) in situating Engels as the initiator of the 'middle ground' position, in the sense of acknowledging 'that the debate touched something of great importance, yet also [accepting] it in its unresolved form'. Despite Engels being mostly responsible for the simplified versions of Marxism later to be constituted as orthodoxy (see Engels 1978), a partial theoretical restatement took place in some private correspondence at the end of his life. Some singularly relevant fragments are quoted below:

> According to the materialistic conception of history, the production and reproduction of real life constitutes *in the last instance* the determining factor of history. Neither Marx nor I ever maintained more. Now when someone comes along and distorts this to mean that the economic factor is the *sole* determining factor, he is converting the former proposition into a meaningless, abstract and absurd phrase. The economic situation is the basis but the various factors of the superstructure [...] all these exercise an influence upon the course of historical struggles, and in many cases determine for the most part their form. [...] [H]istory is made in such a way that the final result always arises from conflicts between many individual wills, of which each in turn has been made what it is by a host of particular conditions of life. Thus, there are innumerable intersecting forces, an infinite series of parallelograms of forces which give rise to one resultant – the historical event. [...] Marx and I are ourselves partly to blame for the fact that the younger people sometimes lay more stress on the economic side than is due to it. We had to emphasize the main principle *vis-à-vis* our adversaries, who denied it, and we had not always the time, the place or

> the opportunity to give their due to the other elements involved in the interaction.
>
> (Engels 1890b)

> Political, juridical, philosophical, religious, literary, artistic, etc., development is based on economic development. But all these react upon one another and also upon the economic base. It is not that the economic position is the *cause and alone active,* while everything else only has a passive effect. There is, rather, interaction on the basis of the economic necessity, which *ultimately* always asserts itself.
>
> (Engels 1894)

> If therefore Barth supposes that we deny any and every reaction of the political, etc., reflexes of the economic movement upon the movement itself, he is simply tilting at windmills. [...] What these gentlemen all lack is dialectic. They never see anything but here cause and there effect. That this is a hollow abstraction, that such metaphysical polar opposites only exist in the real world during crises, while the whole vast process proceeds in the form of interaction (though of very unequal forces, the economic movement being by far the strongest, most elemental and most decisive) and that here everything is relative and nothing is absolute – this they never begin to see. Hegel has never existed for them.
>
> (Engels 1890a)

Engels's comments on the debate between economic determinism and social pluralism are relevant for he acknowledged the relevance of the debate itself while refusing to lean towards any of the sides. Moreover, most of the issues that are to articulate successive positions and reformulations of the debate later on are already present in these fragments, namely, the ultimate meaning of the assertion that the economic is determinant 'in the last instance'; the nature of the relative influence of superstructural elements upon the social whole; the political/partisan nature of all knowledge, and hence the extent to which extra-theoretical circumstances came to determine which side of the debate was to be emphasized; the nature of causality in the social world (e.g. whether the effects reverted back upon the causes, how multi-causality was to be understood); how to delimit a domain of necessity as separated from that of contingency; the specific theoretical status of the dialectic, and hence the nature of Marx's relation to Hegel; or the existence of dichotomizing tendencies within the social and whether those become exacerbated in times of systemic crises. Taking Engels's inconclusive commentaries as a starting point, the debate between economic determinism and social pluralism reached a culmination in the work of French Marxist philosopher Louis Althusser, who took the 'middle ground' position to its ultimate, most refined (and, to some, untenable) consequences.

The Althusserian landmark

The debate over the relation existing between economic and non-economic elements of the social totality reached a culmination, we contend, in the works of Althusser. Besides the numerous criticisms he received, the various intra-theoretical problems present in his works, and the utter oblivion into which his figure has unfortunately fallen, some aspects he dealt with nonetheless remain of utmost relevance to contemporary social theory.[3]

Althusser's intervention, simultaneously theoretical and political, emerged as a response to the two most significant variants of Marxism within the intellectual landscape of the early 1960s, namely, 'economism' and 'humanism'. On the one hand, under the banner of 'economism', Althusser referred to the ossified doctrine that, first in the hands of the II International's leading theorists, then through its Stalinist reformulation, was converted into a Marxist catechism during the early Cold War years. This doctrine emphasized a sort of technological determinism where the development of the productive forces, and their intermittent clashes with existing relations of production, stood as the latent driving force of any and every historical course of development. As summarized by Elliot (2006: 129): 'Abstract, reductionist and teleological, economism is a schema in which the economy (and its contradictions) is the pantheistic demiurge of history and individual societies are only variations ("backward" or "advanced") on a universal model'. This evolutionary and determinist scheme of historical transformation had as its inexorable corollary the inevitable supersession of capitalism by communism as a result of the self-unfolding of the former's own internal dynamics. The key consequence of this fatalist scheme was a complete disregard of political action and the active promotion of working-class self-consciousness. That is, the debate about the relation between base and superstructure, between the economic and non-economic elements of the social totality, was not resolved nor reformulated but, rather, neglected.

On the other hand, several thinkers (e.g. Lukacs, Korsch) from the 1920s onwards turned to both Hegel and Marx's Early Works in search of a potential antidote to the political immobilism derived from the II International's, first, and Stalinist, later on, deviations. Based upon Marx's early writings, while clearly inscribing themselves within a Hegelian-Feuerbachian problematic, the themes of human essence, alienation, and human consciousness were brought to the forefront. In France, this current was mainly represented by Sartre and Merleau-Ponty's 'existential' and 'phenomenological' versions of Marxism, respectively. In 'humanist Marxist' schemes, the central role in historical transformation no longer corresponded to the productive forces but to the self-realization of the 'human essence', for it was a 'teleological philosophical anthropology wherein the ineluctable travails of the human essence in alienation presaged its reappropriation and realization under communism' (Elliot 1993: 22). By situating Man or the Working Class center stage in lieu of the development of the productive forces, the articulation between economic and non-economic elements within the social totality (i.e. the existing scope for genuine political action) did not fare any better, for the 'radically non-determinist conception of human freedom which is employed means that theory loses the capacity to illuminate and guide practice at the level of concrete strategies and tactics' (Benton 1984: 8).

Althusser claimed that, while the 'humanist' stance was indeed a denunciation of the inhumanity of Stalinism, it did not suffice to overcome the latter's deviation within Marxism because it fell prey to the very same theoretical misconception: 'The scandal of Althusser's assault upon these doctrines was his identification of them as mirror-images, resembling each other in their underlying theoretical structure [...] and historical messianism' (Elliot 1993: 22). While the 'humanist' version represents historical processes as a 'journey of the human subject through self-alienation to final self-consciousness and self-emancipation' (Benton 1984: 18), its 'economicist' counterpart shared the same teleological structure but with the self-development of the productive forces now occupying center stage. The latter's political fatalism carried out the same difficulties as the former's absolute voluntarism – namely, a lack of a 'concrete analysis of the concrete situation', to express it with Lenin's words, without which the very possibility of politics is unthinkable. The roots of the problem, Althusser argued, were to be found in their shared understanding of both the nature of the social totality, on the one hand, and that of the inner contradiction acting as the latter's driving force, on the other. Marx's accounts of both were wholly distinct, and radically irreducible, to the Hegelian versions grounding both 'economicist' and 'humanist' Marxist accounts.[4] This was the utmost Althusserian wager.

Althusser developed his account of what, in his view, the notions of contradiction of social totality actually meant for Marx in the essays 'Contradiction and Overdetermination' and 'On the Materialist Dialectic', contained in *For Marx* (Althusser 1969), and in his contribution to *Reading Capital* (Althusser and Balibar 2009). Althusser begins his purported demolition of Hegelian dialectics through a critical examination of the metaphor of 'inverting Hegel' in Marx's famous excerpt from *Capital*'s afterword: 'With [Hegel, the dialectic] is standing on its head. It must be turned right side up again, if you would discover the rational kernel within the mystical shell.' Such statement had been commonly interpreted as meaning that, while Hegel's method was the correct one (the dialectic), its object needed to be discarded (idealist philosophy). However, Althusser contends, in Marx's reformulation not only the terms had changed, but also the relation between them: The Marxist dialectic is radically different from the Hegelian dialectic. Wherein lies the difference?

Let's start with Hegel. The Hegelian totality is an *expressive* totality, where each part of the whole can ultimately be reduced to the expression of an inner essence animating it.[5] Its apparent complexity is ultimately not so, as the essence of the totality is immediately present and graspable in each and every one of its single moments, the latter being thus mere manifestations of an inner simple unity: '[The Hegelian dialectic] is completely dependent on the radical presupposition of a simple original unity which develops within itself by virtue of its negativity, and throughout its development only ever restores the original simplicity and unity in an ever more "concrete" totality' (Althusser 1969: 197). Therefore, the *simplicity* of its contradiction is precisely that which grants the totality its unity, thus becoming a 'circle of circles', a totality that is 'reflected in a unique internal principle, which is the truth of all those concrete determinations' (Althusser 1969: 102). Whenever this notion of totality is imported into the Marxist tradition, the question of the effectiveness of the superstructures upon the economic base is ultimately devoid of any meaning, for the former remains implicitly reduced to a mere epiphenomenon of the latter.

Althusser concedes that Marx had never provided an explicit theoretical account of his understanding of dialectics. However, such an account can be found, implicitly, in *Capital* as well as in Marxist (revolutionary) political practice – especially in the works of Lenin and Mao. Marxism 'rejects the theoretical presupposition of the Hegelian model [...] which accepts this original simple unity [...] which will produce the whole complexity of the process later in its auto-development, but without ever getting lost in this complexity itself'. Instead, for Marxism, 'there is no longer any original simple unity [...] but instead, *the ever-pre-givenness of a structured complex unity*' (Althusser 1969: 198–9, original emphasis). Contrary to Hegel's, the Marxian totality, Althusser contends, consists in a number of interrelated instances none of which are reducible to the economic. Each instance of the social totality thus enjoys its own degree of effectiveness and relative autonomy, so that each becomes a determinant, while also being determined in turn, of every other instance of the whole. The possibility of *a priori* splitting the social totality between core and superfluous elements is ruled out from the outset, for the Marxian totality's complexity is both ontologically primary and irreducible: 'simplicity is not original; on the contrary, it is the structured whole which gives its meaning to the simple category' (Althusser 1969: 196).

If the social totality is constitutively complex, then, within the Marxist dialectic, the contradiction at play ought to be constitutively complex as well. The Marxist notion of contradiction differs from the Hegelian one in that its various social determinations appear invariably blended with the contradiction itself, so that every contradiction remains indissociable from its conditions of existence, i.e. every contradiction is *overdetermined*:

> [T]he 'differences' that constitute each of the instances in play [...] '*merge*' into a real unity, they are not '*dissipated*' as pure *phenomena* in the internal unity of a *simple* contradiction. [...] the 'contradiction' is inseparable from the total structure of the social body in which it is found, inseparable from its formal *conditions* of existence, and even from the *instances* it governs; it is radically *affected by them*, determining, but also determined in one and the same movement, and determined by the various *levels* and *instances* of the social formation it animates, it might be called *over-determined in principle*.
>
> (Althusser 1969: 100–1, original emphasis)

Althusser borrows the term overdetermination from Freud's (1976) analysis of the dream-work. In the latter's usage, it referred to the processes of condensation and displacement of elements of the dream-content when appearing into the dream-thought. It was not an arbitrary process of distortion of an initial content suitable to be ultimately recovered intact, but a process constitutive of the dream-thought itself. Althusser is interested in the concept, as it allows him to delineate the manner in which the social totality manifests itself through its effects. By making use of it, scientific knowledge could discern, in Althusser's view, how the various social contradictions at play may contribute either to the inhibition or to the exacerbation of another social contradiction, thus throwing some light upon the internal dynamics of the social structure under consideration.[6]

It should be clear by now that the problem of the particular effectivity of the superstructures is here cast in a completely new light. If every social contradiction is overdetermined, that is, if it is ultimately indissociable from its own conditions of existence, it follows that the intensity of any single contradiction will be strictly dependent upon its position in the social whole and the ultimate configuration of the latter. Therefore, the historical development of the social totality (and, of course, the very possibility and nature of political interventions upon it) requires the apprehension of how multiple contradictions correlate among themselves so that the contradictory character of every other instance is either reinforced or attenuated in turn.

Despite the plurality of irreducible instances constituting the social totality, the resulting ensemble of social domains is, in Althusser's view, not a mere sum of discrete elements but a unified structure. The fact that these various instances cannot be reduced to any common denominator does not mean that we are dealing here with a mere aggregation of discrete determinants. On the contrary, the various instances are hierarchically organized because of the *dominant* role assigned to one of those instances:

> The Marxist whole [...] is constituted by a certain type of complexity, the unity of a structured whole containing what can be called levels or instances which are distinct and 'relatively autonomous', and co-exist within this complex structural unity, articulated with one another according to specific determinations, fixed in the last instance by the level or instance of the economy.
>
> (Althusser and Balibar 2009: 108)

In this sense, the economy is *determinant* 'in the last instance' because, in each mode of production, it assigns the dominant role to one instance of the whole, which in turn organizes the relations of dominance and subordination among the remaining instances. It is characteristic of the capitalist mode of production that in it the economy assigns the dominant role to itself, whereas in other modes of production that attribution might vary. These instances will be relatively autonomous among themselves, each having its own degree of effectivity and hence a peculiar temporality. It follows that the ensuing social totality:

> is a complex structured unity: its complexity lies in the fact that it is a unity of distinct, relatively autonomous instances with different modes of development; its structure lies in the fact that its unity results from the hierarchy the instances possess through the determination by the economy in the final analysis.
>
> (Callinicos 1976: 46)

Therefore, it is precisely the 'determination in the last instance by the economy' which turns a plurality of instances into an integrated unity, thus refuting the charge of pluralism, for 'only [it] makes it possible to escape the arbitrary relativism of observable displacements by giving these displacements the necessity of a function' (Althusser and Balibar 2009: 110). However, while this might be a valid move to avoid being charged with pluralism, the truth is that expressions such as 'the necessity of a function' might force some to question whether Althusser's Marxism could successfully rebut the twin charges of 'economism' as well.

Certainly, some have criticized Althusser for having surreptitiously fallen again into the 'economicist' problematic through his insistence upon the 'determination in the last instance by the economy' (chiefly Laclau and Mouffe 2001; Resnick and Wolff 1987). However, this 'last instance' is neither to be understood as a starting point of historical processes nor as a predetermined telos, for the contradiction within the economic instance between relations and forces of production does not suppress the remaining instances' relative autonomy and social effectivity, but merely organizes the relations of domination and subordination existing among them in a given conjuncture. '[I]n History, these instances, the superstructure, etc. – are never seen to step respectfully aside when their work is done or, when the Time comes, as his pure phenomena, to scatter before His Majesty the Economy as he strides along the royal road of the Dialectic. From the first moment to the last, *the lonely hour of the "last instance" never comes*' (Althusser 1969: 113, emphasis added). Therefore, 'determination in the last instance by the economy' and 'the last instance never comes' are not antithetical propositions. On the contrary, it is their joint consideration, however paradoxical it may be, which opens up the theoretical space through which Althusser attempted to avoid the twin dangers of economism and voluntarism. Both terms are mutually dependent, indicating that no inner essence of the social will ever be retrieved, as the uneven development of the various instances can never achieve any sort of happy resolution: *Overdetermination is universal.* Following Montag (2018: 175), 'Althusser's paradoxes mark the space constituted by two impossibilities: the impossibility of accepting the old conceptions of determination and causality and the impossibility (neither logical nor eternal, but conjunctural and historical) at this moment of producing a genuinely new conception'. Nevertheless, whether Althusser has succeeded in reformulating Marxist theory along anti-essentialist lines while remaining firmly within the Marxist tradition is still an open-ended question. The following section will deal with two paramount criticisms in that respect.

The Althusserian twilight: Some internal problems

Regarding the almost complete disappearance of Althusserian Marxism from the contemporary intellectual landscape, personal, political, and intra-theoretical circumstances are to be held accountable. However, not only has his influence spanned across many different theoretical *milieux*, but, we contend, his early works remain an indisputable reference when posing, at a strictly theoretically level, the questions we are dealing with here. Given that our goal is to offer a theorization of social interaction under capitalism that simultaneously avoids the perils of economism, on the one hand, and pluralism, on the other, we will focus upon two among the main criticisms directed against Althusser's Marxism, namely, the latent functionalism of his theory of ideology and the internal (im)possibility of conceiving social transformation. While these criticisms certainly remain valid to date, the truth is that the various ways in which a resolution has been attempted served not only to discredit it but also to open up new fruitful lines of theoretical scrutiny.[7]

Althusser's reformulation of the Marxian notion of mode of production along anti-historicist and anti-humanist lines did not come without problems. Certainly, conceiving modes of production as specific 'combinations' (*Verbindung*) of invariant elements was a fruitful movement in debunking historicist accounts of social transformation (Althusser and Balibar 2009: 254). Nonetheless, when asserting that a mode of production had to generate its own conditions of existence, thus denying its necessary self-transcendence, they might be implicitly denying the very possibility of fully-fledged social transformation altogether. In his contribution to *Reading Capital*, Balibar attempted to theorize historical transitions through the concept of 'transitional modes of production', which would be characterized by the non-correspondence between forces and relations of production. However, the nature of the transition from a mode of production to a transitional one remains equally enigmatic. Moreover, inscribing its self-dissolution within the mode of production's very conceptual definition cannot but imply a surreptitious return to the very teleological modes of reasoning Althusserian Marxism ultimately set up to combat. The question remains, therefore, how to conceive a social order's self-reproduction without falling prey to functionalist schemes of social explanation; how to conceive the necessity of social change without implicitly embracing teleological logics; how to conceive historical transitions without obliterating structural constraints; how to account for political action without resorting to voluntarist explanations.

Another related problem emerged with regard to Althusser's theory of ideology. If the superstructures were to have any degree of real effectivity upon other social instances (including the economic realm), ideology could not be conceived as simply a reflection/inversion of 'real' material processes. Instead, ideology is conceived by Althusser as the various social representations needed for people to conform to the positions allotted to each in a given social order: 'Ideology, then, is the set of representations of people's imaginary relations to their real conditions of existence required in order for them to function as social agents under any conceivable set of relations of production' (Elliot 1993: 30). People are provided both self-identity and an illusion of autonomy through the (mis)recognition of themselves, so that each can function according to the existing social order's needs: 'There are no subjects except by and for their subjection [to the ruling ideology]' (Althusser 1994: 136). Therefore, ideology responds to a transhistorical need for social cohesion and consent which, in class societies, also needs to provide 'justifications for the existing state of affairs to the exploited and rationalizations of it to the exploiters (if ideologies are opiates, the rulers are equally addicted)' (Elliot 2006: 155). Crucially, this function of ensuring social compliance applies as well to classless societies (i.e. communism): 'In a classless society, as in a class society, ideology has the function of assuring the *bond* among people in the totality of the forms of their existence, the relation of the individuals to their tasks assigned by the social structure' (Althusser 1990: 28). Even in the absence of exploitation, society's structural determinations can never become transparent, as the logic of overdetermination is universal. If ideology involves a 'deforming and mystifying representation' of reality, which in turn is 'indistinguishable from their "lived experience"' (Althusser 1990: 29, 25), then it follows that such deformation is itself constitutive of (what we perceive as) social objectivity, for both rulers and ruled alike.

In this respect, Althusser's main theoretical advance resides in conceiving ideological distortions as constitutive themselves of social objectivity by asserting the radical impenetrability of the various social logics ultimately determining individuals' lives. While the referent, to be sure, is not gone forever, its unmediated apprehension definitely is. No longer conceived as an appendix to reality, and even less as a veil of illusion disguising an otherwise transparent social objectivity, ideological forms are now liable to be studied in their own right. However, by asserting that ideology produces subjects according to the structural requirements for self-reproduction implied by the existing social order, avoiding the charges of 'functionalism' was definitely not an easy task. On the one hand, if ideology shows no internal gaps in its mode of operation, it is difficult, not to say impossible, to conceive how, within this cohesive and self-reproducing social whole, internal subversion and transformation might take place. Instead, it is strictly necessary to conceive these sites of ideological inculcation (schools, religion, the press, etc.) as sites of perennial sociocultural struggle. On the other hand, it is equally difficult to conceive how oppositional ideologies might emerge and encroach on themselves within the social. While in 'Marxism and Humanism' [1964] it is asserted that the 'ruling ideology is the ideology of the ruling class' (Althusser 1969: 234), without an explicit account of how the subordinate groups might make their aspirations heard within the former, this is partially corrected in 'Theory, Theoretical Practice and Theoretical Formation' [1967] when conceding that, '[the ruling ideology] can also give rise, in certain circumstances, to the expression of the protest of the exploited classes against their own exploitation' (Althusser 1990: 30). In a retrospective essay on (his and) Althusser's structural Marxism, Balibar seems to have finally reached the opposite conclusion to that of Althusser: 'The dominant ideology in a given society is a specific universalization of the imaginary of the dominated, [which draws its] potential universal meaning from their belonging to the imaginary of the individuals who live the masses' or the people's conditions. [...] The mystification lies only in the denegation of a structural antagonism between the dominated and the dominant' (Balibar 1993: 12–13). It may be argued that, at least regarding its conception of ideology, Althusserian Marxism might have come full circle. Whereas at the beginning, despite the indisputable insistence upon their relative autonomy, ideological constructions seemed somehow subordinated to structural requirements imposed by the need to keep on securing domination, in Balibar's later view it appears now implicitly submitted to the subjective yearnings of the dominated.

It is our contention that, while accepting several of the criticisms that have been voiced over the last decades regarding Althusserian Marxism, certain intuitions informing its theoretical novelty remain as valid and pertinent today as they were half a century ago. While Marxism remains an indisputable point of reference when delineating a social theory capable of apprehending the historical specificity of capitalism, some of its basic categories need to be further reconceptualized for them to constitute a valid starting point for contemporary reflections. That was the Althusserian wager *par excellence*. While a new and well-defined way forward was indeed initiated by Althusser and his colleagues back in the mid-1960s, the theoretical path initiated by Althusser and colleagues encountered many intra-theoretical problems and dilemmas that it had to deal with along the way. While some of the criticisms it sparked might have been satisfactorily addressed, at least when considered in isolation, the truth is that many of the issues raised by Althusser remain open to date.

Nowadays, we are still concerned with how to conceive ideological expressions/mechanisms in such a manner that they are neither immune to the co-evolution of social processes governing a society's material reproduction, nor ultimately subservient to the structural needs imposed by the latter. Similarly, we aim at conceptualizing the economy neither as an autonomous sphere self-governed by its inner laws of motion, nor as a disaggregate set of interactions free from structural conditioning, but, rather, as an ensemble which, despite not being a fully closed entity, nonetheless remains a coherent whole susceptible to undergoing dissolution as well as recomposition. While these issues, we believe, have not yet been satisfactorily addressed in its entirety, we remain equally skeptical regarding our own capacity to do so. Simultaneously acknowledging the open-ended nature of the debate as well as the utmost relevance it nevertheless still carries, represents the position that we, following Resnick and Wolff (1987), have termed the 'middle ground'. In order to ground our own theoretical stance, we will follow two distinct 'post-Althusserian' avenues which we believe can provide several fruitful insights in the specific direction we are strenuously heading to, namely, Social Structures of Accumulation theory and post-Marxist discourse theory. While the former remains firmly anchored within the political economy tradition, the latter represents a clear and self-conscious departure from it. Nevertheless, before analyzing both in detail, we will attempt in the next chapter to justify the reasons underlying their joint consideration, on the one hand, as well as the various benefits that are to be expected were this enterprise successfully accomplished, on the other.

Notes

1 To my knowledge, the term 'middle ground' originates in Resnick and Wolff (1987).
2 Hamza (2017: 165) offers a similar interpretation of what we are referring to as the 'middle ground' position: 'There are Marxists who read Capital especially in the light of the famous line from the Manifesto: "capitalism produces its own gravediggers" – for them, a crisis in capitalism is a crisis of capitalism, in the sense that it produces the tools for overcoming it. For others, Capital is read in light of another statement from the Manifesto, the one about the permanent social revolution brought about with the bourgeoisie – for them, a crisis is a moment of internal revolution to capitalism, part of capitalism's own form of self-reproduction. Which option is correct? Perhaps neither: The much more frightening realization we have come to grasp is that capitalism does reproduce its own logic indefinitely *and* it does meet an immanent limit point.'
3 Reasons of space prevent us from offering a more detailed treatment of Althusser's Marxism. Instead, we refer the interested reader to Callinicos (1976), Benton (1984), and, especially, Elliot (2006) and Montag (2013).
4 'It is this common structure of the problematic which is made visible when, rather than analyzing the theoretical or political *intentions* of mechanism-economism on the one hand and humanism-historicism on the other, we examine the internal logic of their conceptual mechanisms.' (Althusser and Balibar 2009: 154)
5 By 'expressive totality', Althusser understands 'a totality all of whose parts are so many "*total parts*", each expressing the others, and each expressing the social totality that contains them, because each in itself contains in the immediate form of its expression the essence of the totality itself' (Althusser and Balibar 2009: 105).
6 Althusser acknowledges nevertheless that he imports the term in the absence of any better concept available. 'I am not particularly taken by this term overdetermination [...] but I shall use it in the absence of anything better, both as an index and as a problem' (Althusser 1969: 101). Moreover, 'it is borrowed from two existing disciplines: specifically, from linguistics and psychoanalysis. In these disciplines it has an objective dialectical "connotation" [...] sufficiently related formally to the content it designates here for the loan not to be an arbitrary one' (Althusser 1969: 206).
7 The list of social thinkers who, in some way or another, have remained heavily indebted to Althusser's work is enormous: Michel Aglietta, Alain Badiou, Etienne Balibar, Judith Butler, Stuart Hall, Paul Hirst, Bob Jessop, Ernesto Laclau, Alain Lipietz, Chantal Mouffe, Nicos Poulantzas, Jacques Rancière, Slavoj Žižek...

2 Setting the terrain

Radical Political Economy and post-Marxism

This chapter sets up a dialogue between two arguably 'post-Althusserian' strands of social theory whose common integration might yield, we believe, worthy insights relative to the social theory we intend to bring forward. On the one hand, we have 'Social Structures of Accumulation' (SSA) theory, arguably the most interesting element within the whole Radical Political Economy tradition, which was first developed by David Gordon, Richard Edwards, and Michael Reich in their seminal book *Segmented Work, Divided Workers* (1982). On the other, we have the 'Post-Marxist' discourse-theoretical approach first laid down by Ernesto Laclau and Chantal Mouffe in their co-authored book *Hegemony and Socialist Strategy* (2001 [1985]). In a nutshell, it is our argument that the explanatory power of the post-Marxist approach pioneered by Laclau and Mouffe might be seriously flawed by not paying due attention to capitalism's internal dynamics, while SSA theory's attention to the institutional requirements imposed by capitalist accumulation processes might be equally demeaned by the over-simplistic approach to politics adopted more often than not in the literature. This chapter will be organized as follows. The following section will outline the main features of the social theory we are striving for. The second section will deal with several points of convergence between the above-mentioned approaches which, in our view, favor their joint consideration. Finally, the last section will outline those theoretical aspects identified in each where a sustained dialogue among the two strands of theory might prove most fruitful.

In search of a model

We live in capitalist societies, or, rather, in social formations where capitalism is the dominant mode of production.[1] Any comprehensive social theory must, in one way or another, account for this. For such societies to function correctly, a certain degree of submission to capitalism's inner logics is needed, as well as a generalized acceptance of the various worldviews the former helps to generate. Ubiquitous as it may be, the inherently conflictive substratum of its outer appearance needs to be controlled, pacified, ordered, and organized, inasmuch as the smooth functioning of capitalism crucially depends on its capacity to generate (or, at least, not to do away entirely with) various social consensuses fostering generalized acquiescence regarding the unequal share of rights and duties allotted to each. Every social order is, to some extent, caught up in this duality: It must safeguard capital accumulation requirements while also fostering its widespread acceptance. Crucially, while both objectives might go hand in hand during certain periods, their utter incompatibility will be made manifest at others. Historical becoming under capitalism is thus marked by this perennial alternation between the two, neither an upward march through a linear continuum, nor a purely chaotic succession of disparate events. A nuanced treatment of both its diachronic evolution and its synchronic interplay therefore remains one of our most desired goals.

Our choice of theoretical frameworks responds, precisely, to this duality between accumulation and consent which every capitalist society continually confronts. On the one hand, the recognition of the various structural constraints operating upon co-evolving social processes, derived in the last instance from the dominance of the capitalist mode of production within the social formation under scrutiny, arguably represents the foremost theoretical terrain of SSA theory. On the other hand, the study of how social consensuses may be developed from the heterogeneous magma of expectations, identities, and struggles the social ultimately consists of is the chief concern of Laclau and Mouffe's post-Marxism. Whether a 'middle ground' position exists among them, one that succumbs neither to a purported unitary force of capitalism nor to the phenomenal diversity of the social, is something we expect to discover throughout these pages. Meanwhile, let us assume it does.

Some common threads

Several commonalities between SSA theory and Post-Marxism can be identified which, we contend, may constitute the basis upon which a dialogue between the two can be initiated, namely, a common social context underlying their emergence, marked by the widespread emergence of historically novel social struggles; a shared commitment to develop a new emancipatory political program for the Left; a similar concern with the need to challenge teleological and uni-linear understandings of historical becoming; and, lastly, the presence of more or less implicit Althusserian roots in both their theoretical approaches. We will analyze each in turn.

Overcoming fragmentation: A common social context

Both approaches emerged during the early 1980s, within an intellectual landscape marked by the gradual remittance of the revolutionary impetus that had characterized the previous decade in several Western countries. Perhaps inadvertently at the time, the respective elections of both Ronald Reagan in the USA and Margaret Thatcher in the UK in the immediately preceding years were already signaling a receding tide regarding existing possibilities of radical and progressive social transformation. In this scenario, both strands of social theory emerged as a response to what they perceived as a context of twofold 'fragmentation'. On the one hand, the labor movement appeared increasingly internally divided at the time, with trade unions being under attack almost everywhere in the West, while a diversity of labor arrangements was gradually coming to the fore. On the other, not only did the working class appear increasingly heterogeneous, but a wide variety of struggles, from feminism and environmentalism, to sexual minorities' rights, and struggles against racial oppression, were increasingly challenging the socio-political centrality of the capital–labor conflict. Therefore, the centrality of the working class in the opposition to the capitalist system needed to be deeply questioned: Orthodox Marxism's thesis regarding the gradual polarization and simplification of the social structure could no longer be maintained.

Both interventions were indissociably theoretical and political. In Gordon et al.'s (1982: 2) words:

> Workers and the labor movement in the United States have not yet been able to articulate and advance a program for the resolution of the crisis that defends and furthers not only their interests but also the general welfare, [because] the American working class is internally divided along many economic, political and cultural dimensions.

Laclau and Mouffe (2001: 2) express themselves along similar lines when they assert that '[w]hat is now in crisis is a whole conception of socialism which rests upon the ontological centrality of the working class, [...] and upon the illusory prospect of a perfectly unitary and homogeneous collective that will render pointless the moment of politics'. While their political motivations definitely converged, and the politico-intellectual climate where they emerged was virtually the same, it must be noted that their common motivation, that is, a critique of essentialist, economicist, and determinist versions of Marxism, was conducted at different levels.

The SSA approach did share with more orthodox accounts of Marxism a primary concern with the various processes co-governing socio-material reproduction, in turn grounding their analyses of the working-class's growing political disunity upon earlier studies on the segmentation of the production process itself (e.g. Doeringer and Piore 1971; Edwards et al. 1975; Edwards 1979): '[W]e argue that one cannot understand current divisions in the U.S. working class without tracing the character and effects of labor segmentation, of structural and qualitative differences in the jobs and labor markets through which workers secure their livelihood' (Gordon et al. 1982: 2). Laclau and Mouffe, on their part, shifted the focus of their analysis to the 'discursive' level, by asserting that the political unity of the working class is always, and of necessity, a result of a constitutive process of political mediation and articulation so that, it follows, what remains in need of explanation are not the reasons underlying heterogeneity but unity instead:[2] 'The divisions within the working class are therefore more deeply rooted than many wish to allow, and they are, to a certain extent, the result of the workers' own practices. They are political, and not merely economic divisions' (Laclau and Mouffe 2001: 82). In sum, while the SSA theorists tried to ground the divisions affecting labor at the superstructural level upon the existing segmentation of the production process itself, Laclau and Mouffe started instead by considering the former as the constitutive one.

Democracy: Reconceptualizing emancipation

Intimately linked to their stark opposition to determinist versions of Marxism, as well as to the 'polarization' thesis that stands as the former's implicit corollary, is the need to come up with a new emancipatory political program capable of responding to the plural motivations underlying social contestation at the time. If the heterogeneity of the social world is deemed to be neither a historical anomaly nor a merely transitory historical stage, a novel horizon for political struggle is needed that, while recognizing the irreducible plurality of hopes and motivations animating them, remains nonetheless capable of advancing them all. The name this political program will take will be that of 'democracy'. As Diskin (1992) has correctly pointed out, democracy is a 'name for a political project that takes the relationship among economic life, political action and human consciousness as its object of study', that is, precisely the unity that classical Marxism had taken for granted, a unity that both theoretical projects show to be ultimately spurious.

Regarding the SSA school, despite their original contributions being grounded in the assumption that a further stage of capitalism would necessarily involve a greater statist control of the economy, thus implicitly dismissing the existing transformative potential within capitalism itself, their subsequent works do show an increasing awareness that this might eventually prove not to be true, thus asserting their commitment to a radically democratic project (e.g. Bowles et al. 1983; 1990). In Reich's (1993) words:

> We offered to these distinct movements [i.e. civil rights, feminism, environmentalism, and Third-World national liberation], and to workers, an analysis that contained a strategic political perspective: their separate oppressions had common roots. Instead of seeing their interests as in conflict, we argued that a coalition among them that emphasized economic democracy would advance them all.

Their democratic program was anchored around both a re-embedding of the economy into the political process and a higher degree of workers' control of the labor process. A more democratic economy would have been not only a good feature *per se*, but would have increased economic efficiency as well, as it would have avoided incurring several expenditures derived from the need to reinforce authority and compliance in the workplace and beyond (Bowles et al. 1990).

Laclau's conception of democracy operates at a more ontological level and further from the actual conditions of the labor process in a capitalist economy. In their program, which they term 'Radical democracy', Laclau and Mouffe try to do away with the old-fashioned dichotomy between capitalism and socialism by asserting the irreducible plurality and heterogeneity of struggles and identities in contemporary societies, which are to be articulated through a process of political construction under which no particular struggle is to be privileged in respect of its emancipatory potential. It follows that the so-called 'new social movements' are irreducible to class struggle, so that any further transformative movement will only emerge out of fully recognizing its ultimate heterogeneity.

In sum, both strands of theory propose a new democratic coalition encompassing a wide variety of struggles as a *sine qua non* condition for progressive social transformation within capitalism. At first sight, it would appear that whereas Laclau and Mouffe offer a more philosophically grounded analysis, SSA theorists deliver a more practical and concrete application of these ideas. There is, however, a deeper distinction to be made regarding their understanding of the ultimate heterogeneity of social struggles. Whereas the SSA theorists would contend that their 'separate oppressions had common roots', so that their apparent heterogeneity would emanate from the common principle of them being *positively* integrated within the capitalist mode of production, an anti-capitalist stance therefore being a logical moment of their common project, Laclau and Mouffe would posit their radical heterogeneity as being irreducible to any common ground. The post-Marxist project would then assert that the unity of these struggles cannot be grounded in any commonality but has instead to be produced through a process of articulation, whose commonalities would be *negatively* constituted as a result of their common opposition to the *statu quo*.

Moreover, another similarity among their respective understandings of 'radical democracy', we contend, may be found in the common grounds upon which they reject Marxism *tout court* when elaborating their (purportedly novel) political logics. Laclau and Mouffe (2001) and Bowles and Gintis (1986) reduce Marxism to its most essentialist-mechanicist in order to ground their own defenses of 'radical democracy'. According to the former: '[Marxism's] starting-point and constant leitmotiv is clear: the subjects are social classes, whose unity is constituted around interests determined by their position in the relations of production' (2001: 118). The latter express themselves along strikingly similar lines when they assert: 'Marx did not simply overlook the problem of choice, of course. He believed that interests are related to social structure in a relatively straightforward manner: the structure of exploitation gives rise to a corresponding structure of objective interests' (1986: 21–2).[3] It seems that, by conflating Marxism with Stalinism, their respective theories might prevent an accurate apprehension of capitalism as a comprehensive system of domination, thus delivering an understanding of freedom deeply dissociated from the socio-economic matrices of power co-governing people's choices (Brown 1995).

Temporal dynamics under capitalism

As part of their critiques of determinist versions of Marxism, both strands rejected eschatological conceptions of history that postulate the inevitable implosion of capitalism out of the self-unfolding of its own internal contradictions. Rather, what needed to be accounted for was the co-existence, within capitalism itself, of periods characterized by relative institutional stability, on the one hand, and others marked by intense social change and systemic transformation, on the other. In that respect, while Laclau and Mouffe's (2001) theoretical apparatus enables a very complex apprehension of synchronic political interactions, it nonetheless suffers from a lack of conceptual means to properly theorize the latter's diachronic transformation. In short, *Hegemony and Socialist Strategy* lacks a concept of 'History'.

Post-Marxism's most comprehensive account of historical processes is found instead in Laclau (1990a). Every social order is there understood to be a temporary and contingent articulation of elements whose precarious nature will only be revealed in exceptional moments. Thus, history would consist of a succession of periods of institutional stability, marked by the 'naturalization' of its composing institutions and the relatively pacific co-existence of different groups under such social arrangements, followed up by others where the ultimately contingent nature of the former is revealed, and social struggles to redefine the main contours of the next 'sedimented' stage become more acute.

In *Segmented Work, Divided Workers* (1982), in a similar manner, Gordon et al. provide a periodization of US capitalism by positing a succession of periods characterized by widespread institutional stability, which in turn satisfy the necessary requirements of predictability and low uncertainty that foster rapid capital accumulation, followed up by periods of institutional disintegration due to the exacerbation of the internal contradictions developed during the former period, where accumulation and growth become sluggish, thus opening up a period of political struggle among contending groups to define what the main institutional features characterizing the next period of economic expansion will be like. Gordon et al. (1982) refer to the former periods as 'consolidation', akin to what Laclau (1990a: 34) understands by 'sedimentation', and to the latter as periods of 'exploration/decay', consisting in the temporal co-existence of a decaying SSA and the search for a new one, which would correspond to Laclau's 'reactivation', where the political and contingent nature of any social order comes openly to the fore while agents enter into a dispute to redefine the contour of the new era.[4] Both accounts can readily be referred back to Gramsci's (2013: 281) well-known motto: 'The crisis consists precisely in the fact that the old is dying and the new cannot be born; in this interregnum a great variety of morbid symptoms appear'.

In these periods of institutional redefinition, contending actors struggle to delimit the characteristics defining the next phase of socio-institutional stability. In Laclau's framework, the decomposition of a given institutional structure is prompted by the proliferation of heterogeneous struggles, arising from various separate groups, which bring to the fore the contingent nature of the institutional order they inhabit. These struggles may become 'equivalent' (Laclau and Mouffe 2001: 127–34; Laclau 2005a: 77–83) on the grounds of their shared opposition to the existing socio-institutional order, thus potentially coalescing into a new hegemonic bloc capable of challenging the very definition of the social. For its part, SSA theory also acknowledges, albeit with a different vocabulary, the necessity of bringing forward a political coalition among heterogeneous agents in order to set up the conditions defining the next period of stability. In their seminal work, Gordon et al. (1982: 28, 32) remark that:

> The manner in which the ensuing crisis is resolved is not fully endogenous, for the crisis exacerbates conflict over the structural reforms that are necessary for a recovery, and the resolution of this conflict involves unpredictable political elements. [Moreover,] structural conflicts arising from relations among races, genders, and nations, for example, are also likely to have their own relatively independent logic and dynamics. Such forces are not unimportant or even necessarily less important than those we address in our analysis.

An analogous formulation is offered by Weisskopf (1981) in an earlier article: 'A new SSA depends to a large extent upon the political actions of different classes confronting each other'. The resolution of the struggle can result in either a coalition compromise or a one-side victory (Kotz 1994a; Lippit 2010). Therefore, while the institution of a new SSA is greatly affected by the political actions adopted by the capitalist class, it is also to a large extent the unintended result of the balance of forces in struggle.

In sum, both theoretical endeavors aim at breaking with one-sided narratives of economic development by recognizing the primacy of politics in times of organic crisis. However, whereas SSA theory acknowledges the accumulation process's lack of self-sufficiency to sustain itself indefinitely, thus grounding their political analyses upon the various restrictions imposed by the functioning of capitalist processes on the existing possibilities of institutional transformation, Laclau ultimately does away with any notion of a co-evolving economic structure, thus placing his analyses into a sort of institutional vacuum unable to properly apprehend the structural restrictions imposed by the operation of capitalist processes. Moreover, while the domain of contingency is often not acknowledged in its full right in SSA theory's schemes of diachronic social transformation, Laclau situates the former center stage, in turn risking losing track of how capitalism's evolution is ultimately temporally patterned, however loosely and imperfectly. While SSA theory's pitfalls in that respect will be explored in greater detail in Chapter 4, Laclau's uneasiness with political economy will be critically scrutinized in Chapter 3. Again, it is expected that some sort of 'middle ground' can be found by placing them both into the same theoretical arena.

Post-Althusserian avenues

The last point of convergence between SSA theory and Laclau's work we would like to point out concerns their shared Althusserian influences. While Laclau's early writings were clearly and self-consciously inscribed within an Althusserian problematic, the inclusion of the SSA literature within the post-Althusserian family might be more controversial. Laclau's criticism and reformulation of some Althusserian concepts will be examined in much greater detail in the next chapter, but at this stage only a brief outline will be provided, without critically exploring them in depth.

Laclau (and Mouffe)'s (2001) 'anti-essentialist' revision of the Marxist canon finds in Althusser's work his last stop. While Althusser, they argued, paved the way for a reconstruction of Marxist theory along strictly non-essentialist and non-determinist lines, he eventually ended up surreptitiously embracing Marxist essentialism through the back door. Two theoretical concepts are said to indicate, respectively, Althusser's advancement and retreat, namely, 'overdetermination' and 'determination in the last instance by the economy'. This is, in its most condensed form possible, Laclau and Mouffe's appraisal of Althusser. Laclau and Mouffe's (2001: 97) wager was that 'by radicalizing some of its themes in a way that will explode its basic concepts', a more fertile ground might emerge that would render possible the reconstruction of Marxism along Laclau and Mouffe's desired lines. They praise the import into Marxism of the category of 'overdetermination' because, insofar as it (arguably) refers to the metaphoric/metonymic displacements of meaning within the socio-symbolic space, it helps conceptualize the social as constituted like a language (i.e. a symbolic order). However, this potentially productive movement is counteracted by Althusser's insistence upon the 'determination in the last instance by the economy', which, in Laclau and Mouffe's view, implies reintroducing through the back door the essence–appearance dichotomy, despite Althusser's strenuous insistence on transcending it. Whether or not this is a correct reading of Althusser's theoretical stance is something that will be explored in detail in the pages that follow.

At this point, it suffices to indicate two aspects of Althusser's social theory which have remained utterly relevant in Laclau's later works. Firstly, the understanding of ideology deformations as themselves constitutive of social objectivity is maintained. The trans-historical character of ideology, in Althusser's terms, is maintained by Laclau in order to assert the impossibility of tracing back any social fact/expression to any ultimate literality. However, *contra* Althusser's insistence upon a structure that only manifests itself through its effects, but which remains a structure nonetheless, Laclau denies the very possibility of finding any sort of underlying referent that would account, in the last instance, for the observed phenomenological appearance of the world. In Althusser's view, ideology functions by providing subjects with the *necessary misrecognition* of its actual conditions of existence, in line with the functional requirements emanating from systemic reproduction: '[according to Althusser,] what is misrecognized is the principle of social structuration as such, the closure operated by any symbolic system' (Laclau 1996b: 204). Althusser contends that, from the vantage point of scientific practices, the inner workings of ideology can be ultimately unveiled, so that an unmediated access to the real thus being a possibility to whoever finds herself equipped with the appropriate conceptual means. While Laclau will also maintain an understanding of ideology as a constitutive distortion, he will nevertheless emphatically deny the very possibility of an extra-ideological locus: In this sense, all critique of ideology will be necessarily intra-ideological.

What, therefore, does ideology consist of, according to Laclau? The ideological effect *par excellence*, Laclau argues, is precisely the belief that such an extra-ideological vantage point ultimately exists, that is, the presumption that such an unmediated and objective access to the actual mechanisms co-governing social life might be attainable:

> It is precisely the assumption of this 'zero level' of the ideological of a pure extra-discursive reality, which constitutes the ideological misconception *par excellence*. [...] This is the ideological effect *strictu senso*: the belief that there is a particular social arrangement that can bring about the closure and transparency of the community.
>
> (Laclau 1996b: 202, 206)

In sum, it seems that Althusser's self-purportedly extra-ideological position, in Laclau's view, would be the quintessential ideological stance.

The second line along which Althusserian concepts are 'radicalized' by Laclau refers to Althusser's understanding of modes of production as 'combinations' (*Verbindung*) of historically invariant elements. Laclau's criticism proceeds here along two separate levels. On the one hand, the very notion of a closed, self-sufficient, and self-reproducing structure is deemed to be an ideological notion at its purest. Instead, Laclau postulates the existence of contingent and precarious 'totalizing' effects aiming at providing a provisional closure to the free-play of differences, so that signification is made possible but, simultaneously, continually thriving towards its own self-subversion. While an entity's conditions of existence are nothing but *logical* conditions of existence, its satisfaction ought not be included into such entity's own definition, for 'a relation between concepts does not imply a relation between the objects specified in those concepts' (Laclau and Mouffe 2001: 102).

Therefore, Laclau rejects the notion of self-reproducing totalities in favor of 'totalizing' effects derived from hegemonic attempts to provide some sort of contingent form of closure. The nature of the ensuing (necessarily transient and incomplete) totality would thus be dependent upon the particular hegemonic relation that creates an exterior in relation to which a signifying interiority may emerge. *Contra* Althusser, such precarious totality cannot be endlessly self-reproduced as it constitutively depends upon an exterior, the borders of which will forever remain subject to contention and dispute:

> The problem, however, is that the very possibility of signification is the system, and the very possibility of the system is the possibility of its limits. [...] Thus, we are left with the paradoxical that what constitutes the condition of possibility of a signifying system – its limits – is also what constitutes its condition of impossibility.
>
> (Laclau 1996a: 37)

Moreover, Laclau's criticisms are directed not only to the nature of the relations existing among historically invariant elements but also to the self-identity of the elements themselves, for deconstructing the former without questioning the identity of the latter would mean, in Laclau and Mouffe's (2001: 102) happy expression, merely '[moving] from an essentialism of the totality to an essentialism of the elements, [just replacing] Spinoza with Leibniz'. Not only are the relations among objects contingent, but contingency also affects the very identity of the objects themselves. Their own identity is affected from the relations they enter into, so that, in the end, both the relations existing among the various elements and the very constitution of the elements themselves ought to be conceptualized at the same ontological level. The name this relation will take will be 'articulation': 'We will call *articulation* any practice establishing a relation among elements such that their identity is modified as a result of the articulatory practice. The structured totality resulting from the articulatory practice, we will call *discourse*' (Laclau and Mouffe 2001: 105, original emphasis). In sum, it is precisely this 'affirmation of the incomplete, open and politically negotiable character of every identity', what, in Laclau and Mouffe's (2001: 104) view, Althusser's logic of overdetermination was ultimately intended to signal. Before examining whether this is a correct reading of Althusser's work, let us first turn to the potential 'post-Althusserian' nature of SSA theory.

To date, no theoretical intervention has yet explored the nature and extent of SSA theory's Althusserian heritage. When accounting for its origins, and the theoretical currents underlying it, emphasis is generally placed on Baran and Sweezy's (1966) Marxism, Doeringer and Piore's (1971) early studies on Labor Market Segmentation, Braverman's (1974) thesis regarding the gradual de-skilling of labor under capitalism, or the long-cycles' tradition associated to, among others, Kondratiev (1935) or Mandel (1995) (e.g. Barceló 1998; Coutrot 2008). It is our contention that, while perhaps not explicitly acknowledged, a certain Althusserian imprint may also be identified within SSA theory's theoretical corpus.[5]

Firstly, there should be an emphasis on a holistic vision of social reality that, notwithstanding a more acute concern with the vagaries of the capitalist production process, nevertheless understands the latter to be inextricably linked to the remaining elements of the social formation under consideration (i.e. in Althusserian terms, its 'conditions of existence'). Secondly, there should be an understanding of capitalist activity as dependent upon an ensemble of social relations, ultimately irreducible to merely passive reflections of the production process. In the last instance, that which provides coherence to the resulting whole are but the relations of complementarity and mutual co-determination emerging among its various components at a given time and place. Moreover, these various relations constituting the social totality are also potential sites of social contradictions, whose successful containment proves equally relevant for the aforementioned totality's self-reproduction as those internal to the capitalist economic process itself, insofar as no pre-arranged hierarchical relation is presumed to exist among the aforementioned social contradictions.

Nevertheless, there are several other dimensions along which SSA theory that can be said to have gone beyond Althusser (in this regard, the French Regulation School has also proceeded in a similar manner). Firstly, SSA theory shares with Althusserian Marxism an emphasis on synchronic configurations of elements as a means to construct a diachronic periodization of history. The following passage, from Balibar's contribution to *Reading Capital* (2009: 228, original emphasis), is instructive in that respect:

> [T]wo principles on which is based the transformation of history into a science: the principle of *periodization* and the principle of the *articulation of the different practices* in the social structure. One diachronic principle, it seems, and one synchronic principle. The principle of the articulation of practices refers to the [...] mechanism of 'correspondence' in which the social formation is presented as constituted out of different levels. [...] As for periodization, it distributes history according to *epochs* of its economic structure.

SSA theory reformulates, albeit implicitly, Althusser and Balibar's theoretical program along two interrelated lines. On the one hand, the emphasis is shifted from a purported periodization of history in terms of successive modes of production to an attempt to offer a periodization internal to the capitalist mode of production itself (e.g. McDonough 1994a; 2011). Instead of conceptualizing modes of production as historically invariant combinations of discrete elements, the focus is shifted towards the identification of the various *stages* succeeding each other *within* 'capitalist' history. On the other hand, Althusser's rigid scheme of practices is abandoned in favor of institutions as the elements now to be articulated into tendentially coherent wholes. Each stage within capitalism would thus be associated with the operation of successive institutional assemblages which provide support to ongoing capitalist activity by securing its historically specific conditions of existence. In sum, the identification of successive SSAs is the element through which historical periodization will be attempted. However, *contra* Balibar, the elements will no longer be historically invariant (i.e. economic base, legal and political forms, and ideological forms), but historically contingent instead:

> Capitalism does not always function in the same way; there are several solutions, several possible forms of reorganization at the time of its great crises and the choice very much depends on the forms of institutionalized

> compromise which the dominating classes are capable of proposing or imposing.
>
> (Lipietz 1993: 114)

Moreover, Althusser and Balibar's rigid schemes of 'combination' would now be replaced with a certain theoretical agnosticism regarding both the elements and the nature of the ensuing relation among them (see Kotz 1994a). Therefore, the door is open to study the different instantiations of capitalism in different temporal and geographical contexts. In sum, no longer capitalism in the singular, but plural capitalisms instead (McDonough 2015).

Secondly, the above-mentioned bias towards functionalist schemes of social reproduction was to be forcefully opposed. While Althusser's emphasis upon the structure's self-reproduction might have been an appropriate antidote against mechanicist-teleological versions of Marxism dominant at the time, a hypostasis of reproduction stood as an ever-present risk. While the latter might have appeared historically congruent in the mid-1960s, the turbulent social climate of the next two decades could not but turn it into a theoretical-historical aberration. Lipietz's (1993: 101) words, though referring to the Regulation School, seem equally pertinent in relation to the SSA approach:

> It is precisely in a return to the contradictory character of social relations, which inhibits their reproduction, and in taking into consideration the conscious element, the active role of "representation" in reproducing itself, that the approaches based on "regulation" found their origin.

Whereas in Althusser and Balibar's account fully-fledged historical transformation was implicitly deemed to be the exception rather than the norm, SSA theory shifted its focus from the necessary reproduction of capitalism's conditions of existence to its intrinsically crisis-prone nature. Therefore, recurrent capitalist crises were now to occupy center stage. Now, it was self-reproduction, rather than crises, that stood in need of theoretical explanation and scrutiny.

Two lines of inquiry were thus opened up, in strict relation with Lipietz's words quoted immediately above. On the one hand, the contradictory character of social relations is stressed, now including commodity circulation as a potential site of capitalist crises. It is implicit in the Althusserian understanding of the workings of capitalism that market relations are of secondary importance in order to apprehend the diachronic evolution of the structure, so that the only potential source of economic crises would be found in the production process itself (Lipietz 1979; Bustelo 1994). It was thus implicitly assumed that the surplus value generated in the production process was always unproblematically validated by the market. However, this need not be the case (Wigger 2017). A self-conscious study of the contradictory relations embodied in the commodity form; the structure of markets, and hence the nature of competition among individual capital units; the nature and modality of state involvement in the economy; and, crucially, the very possibility of crises of surplus value realization, are thus crucial elements of capitalist economic activity which, in the hands of SSA theorists (and 'regulationists' alike), were to gain analytical prominence.

On the other hand, political subjectivity was to be radically recast under SSA schemes. Agents were no longer mere passive bearers of social relations whose ultimate meaning was to remain forever foreclosed to them. Ideological interpellation was no longer totally successful. Indeed, the emphasis now fell upon the means through which the capitalist class managed to obtain consent and compliance, not only from workers, but also from the various groups present in society at a given time and place. The former, crucial to their analysis of the historical evolution of labor market segmentation dynamics, occupied center stage in Gordon et al.'s (1982) seminal work. The latter, in turn, were further explored in the power-theoretic version of SSA theory championed by Bowles et al. (1983; 1990). In sum, non-compliance with capitalist arrangements was deemed to be analytically primary, so that what needed to be accounted for were, instead, the various strategies employed to contain and channel social conflicts while simultaneously satisfying capitalist requirements.

In sum, both Laclau and the SSA theorists aimed at counteracting Althusserian Marxism's functionalist traits by giving much greater scope to the domains of historical contingency and human subjectivity in their analyses. They did also try to retain Althusser and Balibar's emphasis upon 'combinatory' logics to apprehend systemic reproduction and change. However, they differed sharply in their respective attempts to transcend Althusser's perhaps too monolithic understanding of capitalism. While SSA theorists aimed at providing a more nuanced treatment of 'actually existing' capitalism by exploring the different modalities in which it could manifest itself, Laclau opted instead for dismissing the notion of capitalism altogether as a valid object of analysis, subsuming its historical specificity into an almost undifferentiated magma of intertextuality. While the former replaced Capitalism with capitalisms, the latter rejected the notion of mode of production altogether.

A necessary dialogue: Towards a fruitful synthesis

Considering the similarities between the work of Laclau and SSA theory pointed out above, there are a number of dimensions where, in our view, a dialogue between the two might not only correct certain shortfalls identified in each but, also, contribute to ground the social theory we are here striving for. In the previous section, the importance of Laclau's intervention to overcome some of the difficulties emerging, on the one side, from the historical situation of the Left in post-1968 Western capitalist societies and, on the other, from the interiority of essentialist and economicist versions of Marxism, has been underlined. However, due to his emphasis on the category of 'discourse', from which the constitutive dimension of hegemony regarding the social structure is derived, many criticized the little relevance that processes of material reproduction seem to have in his theoretical framework (e.g. Geras 1987; Diskin 1992; Veltmeyer 2000; Lewis 2005).[6] Neglecting the internal dynamics of capitalism's material reproduction runs the risk of not subverting, but merely inverting, the very terrain upon which classical Marxism was built, for, as Rustin (1988) has rightly pointed out, it would mean to 'substitute an equally one-dimensional theory of ideological determination for the monistic theory of economic determinism', thus coming too near to a one-dimensional idealism too reminiscent of the hard-lined materialism Laclau wanted to do away with. Hence, while it helps to conceptualize the importance of non-class struggles, Laclau's position remains vulnerable to criticisms, such as Žižek's (2000: 98):

> Postmodern politics definitely has the great merit that it 're-politicizes' a series of domains previously considered 'apolitical' or 'private': the fact remains, however, that it does not in fact re-politicize capitalism, because the very notion and form of the political within which it operates is grounded in the 'de-politicization' of the economy.

In this respect, referring the multiplicity of the social back to the institutional requirements necessary for ongoing capitalist activity, thus introducing an element of materially grounded commonality into Laclau's heterogeneous struggles, turns out to be a promising route in order to situate the specificities of the capitalist mode of production at the very center of the analysis. By focusing on how a given institutional structure divides and structures the working population (either paid and/or unpaid), one can have a better grasp of the elements of sameness in their various modalities of oppression, without this leading to a straightforward reduction of every social difference being the expression of one single essence.

In this respect, SSA theory's analytical concern with the institutional requirements imposed by a well-functioning accumulation process, on the one hand, and the inherently conflictual nature of capitalist relations of production, on the other, might help introduce a certain degree of hierarchy within the multiplicity of institutions and practices making up the social whole, i.e. an immanent criterion organizing, at least for heuristic purposes, the otherwise uncontrolled free play of differences and identities. Nevertheless, clear agreement has yet to be reached within the SSA literature regarding what the exact criteria should be in order to introduce such a hierarchy. The initial formulations of SSA theory emphasized, in Keynesian fashion, the necessary requirements of stability and predictability that capitalists *qua* class require in order to provide a high rate of accumulation (Gordon et al. 1982: 42). Subsequent formulations have criticized the emphasis placed on the quantitative aspects of the accumulation process, arguing in favor of paying deeper attention to its qualitative aspects instead. Thus, others have pointed out the crucial role institutions play in maintaining and/or enhancing the power of the corporate class (e.g. Bowles et al. 1983; 1986; 1990); the role the former play in regulating conflicts inherent to capitalist production (e.g. Kotz 1994a; Wolfson 2003), or the interrelations existing among the key components of the ensuing institutional environment (e.g. Gordon 1980; Lippit 2010), as possible entry points through which to introduce some conceptual hierarchy upon which capitalism's institutional diversity can be analyzed. Therefore, the emphasis placed by SSA theory either upon the requirements imposed by capitalists in order to foster a vigorous rate of accumulation, or upon the necessary containment of social conflict so that an effective appropriation of surplus value can be safeguarded, permits grounding the analysis of institutional diversity upon the specificities of the capitalist mode of production while, at the same time, not falling prey to a reductionist vision of its functioning, insofar as the necessarily plural interconnections between the processes of accumulation and surplus value extraction and the institutional environment surrounding it are duly acknowledged.

In sum, Laclau is right in denying the existence of any necessary connection between the social dynamics and the constitution of political subjectivity. Nonetheless, while it is certainly true that the social conditions leading to the emergence of social antagonisms cannot be directly apprehended from an isolated analysis of social processes, it should neither be implicitly derived from the former that the notion of class for itself remains the only one worthy of theoretical scrutiny. While Laclau is definitely right in questioning the attribution of any sort of ontological priority to the social relations of production when appraising multifarious political expressions, he might be falling prey to an inverse monistic essentialism by doing away with the domain of material relations altogether.

However, despite SSA theory recognizing the primacy of political struggle and social indeterminacy during the periods of SSA's simultaneous demise and construction, the very process through which this struggle is conducted remains, in our view, relatively under-theorized, most positions ultimately ranging from stark theoretical agnosticism to blunter economic determinism. The early SSA literature had already acknowledged the unpredictability of further institutional construction in times of systemic crisis, a process which would be dependent, in the last instance, upon the relative balance of class forces. For instance, Weisskopf (1981: 13) asserts that 'compared to the endogenous nature of the crisis, the subsequent recovery is usually more autonomous. [...] What kind of new structure eventually gets established depends to a large extent upon the political actions of different classes confronting each other.' Later contributions, such as Lippit (2010: 66), have expressed themselves in a similar manner when asserting that 'in understanding the processes of SSA formation and collapse, it is helpful to recognize that non-class as well as class struggles play a role, and to recognize the manner in which both processes are over-determined'. However, there is a lack of theoretical development within the SSA literature regarding how non-economic demands and expectations are to be related to the successful appropriation of surplus value on the side of capital. Intimately connected to this last point, albeit perhaps even more important to our declared purposes, there is also an under-theorization of how political actors are constituted in periods of heightened struggle among contending actors derived from an SSA's decomposition.

Most of the literature emphasizing the relevance of the balance of class forces when the need for institutional redefinition becomes insurmountable seems to assume a straightforward translation between the position agents occupy in the production process and their participation as political actors. As argued before, recent decades have witnessed the emergence of a multiplicity of struggles in Western Capitalist societies, irreducible to class struggle, on whose articulation the viability of any wide-ranging political project ultimately depends. As long as an SSA is understood to comprehend a wide variety of institutions, irreducible to those directly implicated in structuring the capitalist production process, the heterogeneity of struggles has to be acknowledged if any prediction about the direction of further institutional transformation is to be made.

It is at this point, we contend, that a dialogue with the work of Laclau becomes the most pertinent for SSA theory. Laclau and Mouffe's (2001: 126) conception of *antagonism* as the 'limit' of the social, or the limit of all objectivity, is intended to challenge the centrality of the capital–labor relation as the main engine of social transformation in capitalist societies. In that respect, Laclau (1990a: 9) writes:

> the conflict [between capital and labor] is not internal to capitalist relations of production (in which the worker counts merely as a seller of labor power), but takes place between the relations of production and the worker's identity outside of them, [...] this constitutive outside is inherent to any antagonistic relationship.

That is, the wage-labor relation is not antagonistic in itself but can become so only on condition that it affects negatively whichever identity the agent involved might cling to outside the domain of work. However, despite the relations between capital and labor not being essentially antagonistic in nature, it needs to be acknowledged that they do contain the seeds to become so. For instance, the individual capitalist has a permanent interest in both enlarging and intensifying working time as a strategy for maximizing profits which, in turn, would affect negatively the worker's ability to rest and, say, spend time with her family. Whereas the emergence of an antagonism around capital–labor relations does require a process of subjectification through which a relation of exploitation (i.e. one involving surplus value extraction) is elevated into a relation of oppression, the material conditions that would render it possible are nonetheless an ever-present feature of capital–labor relations themselves. Therefore, in order to appraise the antagonistic nature of social relations under capitalism, close attention should be paid to how the various struggles pertaining to the productive sphere are overdetermined by the multiplicity of identities outside them. The lines of fracture and struggle in the social field are multiple. While some of them are directly related to the production process, others might only touch it tangentially, so that, when it comes to understand the rationality behind agents' political alignments, emphasizing the question of class struggle should obliterate no other struggle. In Laclau's (2005a: 150) words: 'A globalized capitalism creates myriad points of rupture and antagonism – ecological crises, imbalances between different sectors of the economy, massive unemployment and so on – and only an over-determination of this antagonistic plurality can create global anti-capitalist subjects capable of carrying out a struggle worth the name'.

Within the SSA literature, the recent work of Lippit (2005; 2010; 2014) certainly points in this direction when forcefully arguing in favor of making overdetermination the central concept through which to apprehend the existing interrelation between the different institutional spheres partaking of the social totality. Rather than positing a single institution or event that would account for the structural integrity of an SSA, it is argued that what yields coherence and unity to a given ensemble of institutions are nothing but the existing interrelations among its constituent components:

> In considering the forces that may ultimately undermine each institution and ultimately the entire structure of which it is a part, the interaction of these same factors [other institutions, the full array of social processes and exogenous events] must be recognized as playing a role, together with the internal contradictions that tend to arise in all institutions.
>
> (Lippit 2010: 83)

This line of inquiry, which refuses to grant any ontological privilege to any single locus or institution within the social regarding the possibility of forcing an institutional breakdown, and which underlines the necessity of considering economic together with non-economic factors, is better suited to understand the potential lines of both rupture and re-composition in a given institutional structure. In sum, while refusing to presume that subjects are already pre-given when they enter the political struggle, so that there is no direct translation of the relations taking place within the economic realm into the political arena, one should neither succumb to the postmodern tendency to dissolve all meaning of political action into an infinitely malleable web of intertextuality, but instead to investigate how capitalism does affect workers *qua* workers, women *qua* women, students *qua* students, etc.

In sum, while SSA theory's emphasis on the dynamics and institutional requirements of the co-evolving processes of capital accumulation and surplus value extraction constitutes a useful counterweight to Laclau's elusive appraisal of capitalism's social dynamics, the latter's emphasis on the irreducibility of heterogeneous struggles to that of class and, thus, on the importance of articulatory practices when apprehending political dynamics, serves to counteract some too reductionist and economicist versions of the SSA approach. Considered simultaneously, each theory clarifies the other, countervailing some pervasive uses or interpretations. On the one hand, a voluntarist approach to politics – one that understands that the primacy of politics over economic processes is an ever-present feature, thus obliterating the constraints imposed on political action by capitalism's internal dynamics – is avoided. On the other, determinist approaches to capitalism's evolution over time are discarded, as it is recognized that those constraints imposed by the economic process periodically come to a halt, so that its resolution is occasionally dependent upon contingent events and political action. Before attempting to offer a synthesis of the various theoretical insights outlined in the present chapter, we will first consider certain theoretical inconsistencies in Laclau's work derived from his uneasy relationship with the political economy tradition.

Notes

1 This text is plagued by expressions such as 'capitalism' or 'capitalist societies'. We kindly beg the reader to replace them in their mind, whenever they encounter them, by the more acute but also more cumbersome expression, 'social formations where capitalism is the dominant mode of production'.

2 It must be noted that Laclau and Mouffe (2001: 81–2) praised *Segmented Work, Divided Workers* for having challenged Harry Braverman's (1974) homogenization thesis by incorporating non-economic variables into their analysis of the labor process. Gordon et al. (1982: 21) do credit as well Laclau's (1979) previous work for having challenged mechanical-determinist accounts of historical change.

3 Astonishingly, they draw the conclusion that 'Classical Marxism is theoretically anti-democratic in the same sense that any political philosophy that fails to conceptualize the threat of state authoritarianism, and the centrality of privacy and individual liberty to human emancipation, provides a haven for despots and fanatics' (Bowles and Gintis 1986: 20).

4 Laclau takes the concepts of 'sedimentation' and 'reactivation' from the work of Edmund Husserl. While the former refers to 'routinization and forgetting of origins' of social practices/institutions, the latter refers to the moments where the former's ultimate contingency is made apparent, thus forcing (and being forced by) a process of social contention for its redefinition.

5 We draw extensively upon Lipietz's (1987; 1993) account of Althusser's influence upon the French Regulation School. The existing parallelisms between SSA theory and the Regulation School have been well documented elsewhere (e.g. Kotz 1994b; Mavroudeas 2006; McDonough and Nardone 2006).

6 I am well aware that the Laclauian category of 'discourse' is not equivalent to 'speech' or 'ideas', so that I am certainly not arguing that his is an idealist position. However, by dissolving every and any (meaningful) human practice under the category of 'discourse', he might me lacking the appropriate conceptual means to properly appraise the nature of socio-material reproduction as distinct from other social practices. These issues will be further developed in chapter 3.

3 Ernesto Laclau's post-Marxism

Some internal problems

Ernesto Laclau's post-Marxist political theory has been at the center of various debates within contemporary political philosophy in recent decades. While it has offered, in our opinion, a very complex cartography of socio-political interactions in contemporary societies, it is our contention that the ultimate political value of Laclau's formulations are seriously vitiated by its difficulties to theoretically apprehend the fact that those societies Laclau has in mind are, at the end of the day and with virtually no exceptions, societies where capitalism is the dominant mode of production. In our view, the roots of Laclau's departure from Marxism are to be found, on the one hand, in the misrepresentation of the Marxist tradition he consistently puts forward in order to ground his own theoretical stance and, on the other, in his reading of Althusser's work. Nonetheless, far from demanding an abandonment of post-Marxism's core ontological postulates, we argue that further theoretical development is needed if a satisfactory account of the institutional realm wherein hegemonic logics are immersed and, crucially, of the specifically capitalist dimension of those institutional ensembles, is to be provided.

This chapter will be organized as follows. The first section will offer a brief review of Laclau's theoretical evolution, starting from his early Althusserian works up until his late reflections on populism. Then, Laclau's reconstruction of the Marxist tradition and, in more detail, his reading of Althusser, will be critically examined. The third section will examine the impoverished conceptualization of socio-economic interactions resulting from Laclau's discourse-theoretical account. Finally, the fourth section will provide a symptomatic reading of Laclau's undeclared omission of political economy insights from his political theory, focusing on four crucial dimensions of the latter, namely, the process of 'individuation' of political demands; the unilateral treatment of 'class' as a mode of political identification; the unsatisfactory treatment it provides of the temporal dynamics under capitalism; and certain antinomies arising from his theorization of populism.

Laclau's theoretical evolution

Laclau's Althusserian origins

Laclau's first major work to appear in English was *Politics and Ideology in Marxist Theory* (1979). Although his theory was, from the very beginning, strongly influenced by his prior experience as a militant of the Argentinian Peronist Left, whose imprint can be observed in all of his later works (see Acha 2019), at this stage Laclau was definitely an unorthodox Marxist, but a Marxist nonetheless. Clearly inscribed within the Althusserian tradition, this book deploys great effort to further open and develop the latter's constitutive conceptual elements (e.g. 'articulation', 'determination in the last instance by the economic', 'interpellation') while retaining its basic conceptual architecture. Laclau's most relevant theoretical advances appear in those chapters devoted to analyzing two types of political ideologies where class reductionist schemes of explanation appeared significantly ill-suited to explain them, namely, fascism and populism.

Laclau's main concern at this stage was, prominently, to broaden the scope of the political, that is, in Althusserian terms, to explore and sustain the relative autonomy of the political and ideological superstructures. Laclau asserts, *contra* Poulantzas (1974), that not all elements susceptible to being articulated into ideological discourses have a necessary and pre-determined class-nature. The capitalist mode of production would be but a regional area of any social formation in which it finds itself inscribed, whose constituent relations of production invariably generate two antagonistic poles, capital and labor. However, capitalist class relations are not all-embracing because, on the one hand, there might be other modes of production operating within the same social formation and, on the other, some people might not even partake of relations of production of whichever type. Such heterogeneity of structural positions will be manifested not through class interpellations, but through popular interpellations instead.

> The 'people' form an objective determination of the system which is different from the class determination: the people are one of the poles of the dominant contradiction in a social formation, that is, a contradiction whose intelligibility depends on the ensemble of political and ideological relations of domination and not just the relations of production. If class contradiction is the dominant contradiction at the abstract level of the mode of production, the people/'power bloc' contradiction is dominant at the level of the social formation.
>
> (Laclau 1979: 108)

Therefore, Laclau broadens the disjunction between class realities (abstractly determined by the mode of production's operation, though lacking any straightforward political expression), and the politico-ideological struggle (conducted at the level of the social formation, where non-capitalist elements play a crucial role), without downplaying one pole in favor of the other as, while 'the "people" do not, obviously, exist at the level of production relations' (1979: 118), 'classes as the poles of antagonistic production relations [have] no necessary form of existence at the ideological and political levels, [where they exist] in a process of articulation and not of reduction' (1979: 159–61).

While, in Laclau's account, social classes and actual/empirical social groups will no longer be superimposed, both levels of analysis are nonetheless still retained insofar as the Althusserian tenet regarding the 'determination in the last instance by the economic' is maintained. Social classes configured at the level of relations of production will remain fundamental in appraising the social formation's historical becoming, but their struggle will take place within a politico-ideological field it will no longer totalize. Class struggle, therefore, will revolve around, precisely, articulating non-class elements and antagonisms into their respective ideological discourses.

> Class struggle at the ideological level consists, to a great extent, in the attempt to articulate popular-democratic interpellations in the ideological discourses of antagonistic classes. *The popular-democratic interpellation not only has no precise class content, but is the domain of ideological class struggle par excellence.* Every class struggles at the ideological level *simultaneously* as class and as the people, or rather, tries to give coherence to its ideological discourse by presenting its class objectives as the consummation of popular objectives.
>
> (Laclau 1979: 108–9, original emphasis)

As a corollary, classes do not succeed in the ideological struggle when they manage to impose their explicit class discourses upon the rest of the population but when they manage to transform of their respective class objectives into popular-democratic ones (Laclau 1979: 174).

While Laclau's future works will evolve from a heterodox Althusserianism to a markedly post-Althusserian theoretical stance, several points of continuity can nonetheless be identified between the two. Firstly, a constant leitmotiv in Laclau's work is an explicit contention that the category of class 'in itself' will never suffice to explain actual political developments, nor to advance strictly class-related goals themselves. Secondly, an emphasis upon articulatory practices as the *raison d'etre* of political action is already present at this early stage, as the ambivalent nature of most ideological elements means that the political struggle will always remain constitutively open, incessantly calling for their articulation through strategic alliances with other social groups. Lastly, there is a continuous insistence that social antagonisms are not pre-given but, on the contrary, they ought to be actively produced. It thus follows that the key political question for those aiming at radical social transformation should not be how to properly represent underlying antagonisms but, instead, how to construct them in a manner that enables the advancement of one's own socio-political objectives.

However, at this stage, classes configured at the level of capitalist relations of production still retain an ontological primacy over remaining social partitions regarding politico-ideological articulations, despite the former no longer being expressed straightforwardly through the latter. As explored below, dissolving such an ontological privilege will be, precisely, the cornerstone of Laclau's future 'post'-Marxist approach.

The post-Marxist turn

The publication of *Hegemony and Socialist Strategy*, jointly with Chantal Mouffe (1985 [2001]), signals Laclau's abandonment not only of the Althusserian tradition but of Marxism *tout court*. This very dense book of political ontology set as its primary antagonistic 'Other' what they considered to be the most essentialist and economicist versions of the Marxist paradigm. In Laclau and Mouffe's view, the whole Marxist tradition was marked by an irresoluble tension since its inception: On the one hand, a closed paradigm which expects the social world to fit into very rigid schemes of socio-historical transformation; on the other, an irreducibly complex and plural world which stubbornly refuses to be encapsulated into those same reductionist schemes. This tension, they argue, has been made manifest in the growing use of the category of 'hegemony' within the Marxist tradition in order to account for the domain of social contingency within historical processes. From its early uses by Russian Social-Democracy to its consolidation in the work of Gramsci, it signaled, at least implicitly, the unaccounted-for in the general Laws of History that, again and again, actual historical processes refused to comply with.

This increasing use of the category of hegemony within Marxist theory, reflecting a growing awareness of the domain of contingency when accounting for socio-historical transformation, reached a culmination, Laclau and Mouffe argue, in the work of Gramsci. Political subjects would no longer be social classes but, rather, 'collective wills' formed by the articulation of various politico-ideological elements with no necessary class belonging (Laclau and Mouffe 2001: 67). However, a complete break with Marxist 'essentialism' was not attained, they claimed, because of Gramsci's insistence on placing some fundamental social class at the very core of the resulting social articulations. The only step that remained to be taken was, therefore, merely to let go of these last redoubts of essentialism, and thus to conclude that no specific location within the social structure should be granted ontological primacy regarding the initiation of sociopolitical transformation. The following section will explore, in much greater depth, the extent to which their insistence in combating orthodox Marxism's essentialism led them to dissolve any notion of an overarching social structure into an infinity of social differences, apparently disconnected from the various social processes implicated in society's material reproduction.

This dissolution of any notion of overarching social structure led Laclau and Mouffe to discard the notion of *mode of production* in favor of that of *discourse*. While the former arguably referred to a closed system whose actual shape was ultimately regulated by the operation of internal logics, thus restricting politics to a mere epiphenomenal activity, the category of discourse was intended to comprise instead the totality of meaningful social practices. In this regard, two precisions ought to be mentioned. On the one hand, it must be noted that Laclau and Mouffe's use of the category of discourse does not lead them to embrace an idealist social ontology, for the very distinction between discursive and non-discursive practices is dissolved within the notion of discourse itself. No object or practice in the world has an intrinsic meaning previous to its involvement in human interaction. On the contrary, its meaning/identity will be contingent and differentially constituted through the relations it enters with other objects: 'The creation of an identity implies the establishment of a difference, difference which is often constructed on the basis of a hierarchy, for example between form and matter, black and white, man and woman' (Mouffe 2005). A long quote from Laclau and Mouffe (2001: 108) might help to clarify this notion:

> An earthquake or the falling of a brick is an event that certainly exists, in the sense that it occurs here and now, independently of my will. But whether their specificity as objects is constructed in terms of 'natural phenomena' or 'expressions of the wrath of God', depends upon the structuring of a discursive field. What is denied is not that such objects exist externally to thought, but the rather different assertion that they could constitute themselves as objects outside any discursive condition of emergence.

On the other hand, the category of discourse has a double inscription in Laclau and Mouffe's theory (see Retamozo 2017). It figures as an ontological category, referring to the above-mentioned totality of meaningful practices, but it also appears as an ontic category, referring to particular discourses competing among themselves (i.e. in the sense of 'populist discourses' or 'fascist discourses'). This undecidability between the ontic and the ontological will permeate most of Laclau's later writings as well.

Once the category of discourse has been introduced, the key theoretical category to conceive of socio-political interactions will no longer be that of *social class* but *hegemony* instead, by which they refer to articulatory practices among discursive elements so that a dimension of commonality is produced among them.[1] While the social world is constituted by ontologically fragmented and isolated elements, for signification to take place some sort of relation among them ought to emerge so that those differences can be intelligible among themselves. Crucially, it must be noted that hegemonic relations do not establish relations among pre-existing objects and/or identities but, rather, constitute the latter through their very operation. Therefore, social objectivity would appear as constituted by competing hegemonic attempts to integrate social elements within themselves, i.e. to transiently transform them into internal moments. Hegemonic articulations would thus introduce some partial fixation of meaning into an otherwise chaotic and disordered field of differences through the operation of *nodal points*, the 'privileged discursive points of this partial fixation' (Laclau and Mouffe 2001: 112).

Again, an example might help in clarifying this difficult notion. In contemporary Western societies, almost every political force claims to be defending 'liberty'. However, the meaning attached to the word liberty cannot be derived from the concept's intrinsic properties but depends, on the contrary, on the relations it enters into with other notions. Whether liberty is understood as absence of immigrants in surrounding neighborhoods, or as the necessity to enjoy minimum levels of material welfare, or merely as the capacity to vote periodically, will be precisely a major locus of political contention. That is, the very meaning of 'liberty' is determined relationally, and the political battle will revolve around partially fixing it: Liberty functions as a nodal point. Once a partial fixation of its meaning is finally attained, the meaning attached to other terms such as immigrants, welfare, and elections, will be partially affected in turn by the understanding of liberty that becomes, for a time, hegemonic. Of course, hegemonic struggles to partially fix meanings will affect other co-existing terms, affecting in turn the very meaning attached to 'liberty' itself. It follows, therefore, that the hegemonic struggle is not only never-ending but also constitutively ubiquitous. No social domain will ever be immune from hegemonic contention.

The ontological impossibility of a final and complete fixation of meaning, i.e. the contingent nature of every social identity, leads Laclau and Mouffe to discard the notion of *contradiction* in favor of that of *antagonism*. In their theoretical scheme, the former appears linked to an understanding of an underlying social structure governed by internal laws of motion, whose historical development would appear dictated by the periodical clash between its internal components. However, in their crusade against orthodox Marxism's belief that political action can be straightforwardly derived from the position agents occupy in such an underlying structure, Laclau and Mouffe forcefully argue that orthodox Marxism's notion of contradiction does not involve any antagonistic dimension. Antagonisms, instead, would be the result of the differential constitution of every system of signification, 'the "experience" of the limit of all objectivity. [...] Strictly speaking, antagonisms are not *internal* but *external* to society; or rather, they constitute the limits of society, the latter's impossibility of fully constituting itself'. (Laclau and Mouffe 2001: 123, 125). At a more general level, the concept of antagonism serves Laclau to ground his rejection of dialectical logics. At a lower level of generality, it enables Laclau to justify his assertion that no antagonism between capital and labor can be straightforwardly read off from capitalist relations of production when taken in isolation: 'Antagonism is established between the relations of production and something external to them, not within the relations of production themselves' (Laclau 1990a: 11). That is, for an antagonism to emerge capitalist relations of production ought to interfere with (read: 'deny') whatever social identity the worker holds outside the domain of work.

The road to populism: new reflections and emancipation(s)

Among the various early criticisms the publication of *Hegemony and Socialist Strategy* sparked, the one causing the greatest effect upon Laclau's theoretical reformulation of the post-Marxist project during the following years was the one provided by Žižek (1990). According to him, Laclau and Mouffe's account of antagonism runs the risk of reifying into a positive entity a dimension of negativity that pervades and haunts every single identity, which cannot be subsumed under the antagonistic relation present among actually-existing social positions.

> It is not the external enemy who is preventing me from achieving identity with myself, but every identity is already in itself blocked, marked by an impossibility, and the external enemy is simply the small piece, the rest of reality upon which we 'project' or 'externalize' this intrinsic, immanent impossibility. [...] We must then distinguish the experience of antagonism in its radical form, as a limit of the social, as the impossibility around which the social field is structured, from antagonism as the relation between antagonistic social-positions: in Lacanian terms, we must distinguish antagonism as real from the social reality of the antagonistic fight.
>
> (Žižek 1990: 252–3)

Laclau's next major work (1990a) will acknowledge the pertinence of Žižek's criticisms by effecting some major theoretical changes with respect to his (and Mouffe's) previous work. On the one hand, Laclau responded to Laclau and Mouffe's (2001) lack of any notion of structural crisis, that is, any intra-theoretical justification of why and how a hegemonic ensemble might be internally subverted, by introducing the notion of *dislocation* (Harrison 2014). Not only every political identity, but also the single elements it articulates, are constitutively open to contention and redefinition. Insofar as every identity is relational (i.e. it is what others are not), it is perennially dependent upon a 'constitutive outside' which, while continually threatening it, simultaneously represents its very condition of possibility: 'Every identity is dislocated insofar as it depends on an outside which both denies that identity and provides its condition of possibility at the same time' (Laclau 1990a: 39).

Hence, dislocations are an effect of the differential and contingent nature of every symbolic structure, that is, an effect of its ontological impossibility to constitute itself as a fully closed system. Dislocations manifest themselves through the occurrence of events that cannot be domesticated by the existing structure, in turn bringing to the fore incomplete nature (Torfing 1999). Now, antagonisms will be symbolic responses to a dislocated structure, a way to master it, to domesticate it, by providing dislocations with some sort of symbolic inscription. In Lacanian terms, whereas the early formulation of antagonism is conceptualized in terms of the 'imaginary', now the emphasis is laid upon a radical disjunction between the 'real' and the 'symbolic' (Biglieri and

Perello 2011). The Marxist notion of contradiction is thus radically reformulated. It no longer corresponds to an internal feature of a given structure but, instead, stands as an effect of its internal impossibility.

The concept of dislocation enables Laclau to abandon the Foucauldian-inspired notion of 'subject-positions' in favor of a category of *subject*, of markedly Derridean inspiration, constituted by the lack within the structure: 'Apart from the subject, in this radical sense, there are only *subject positions* in the general field of objectivity. But the subject, as understood in this text, cannot be objective: it is only constituted on the structure's uneven edges' (Laclau 1990a: 61). This subject will be a mythical subject, insofar as it does not partake of the general field of objectivity but, rather, subverts it by emerging as a response to the latter's failure. Moreover, the subject will also be constitutively metaphorical, insofar as its particular content will attempt to symbolize an impossible plenitude the current dislocated structure cannot offer: 'It is not the "structurality" of the dominant structure to which the mythical space is opposed, but its *de*-structuring effects. The mythical space is constituted as a critique of the lack of structuration accompanying the dominant order' (Laclau 1990a: 62). Finally, if the subject is successful in responding to a dislocated structure, it will gradually dissolve itself into a new objectivity, that is, it will be converted into another 'subject-position'.

Some years later Laclau (1996b) published another collection of essays mainly concerned with the issues of multiculturalism and identity politics. He purported to deconstruct the theoretical premises grounding the main emancipatory 'grand narratives' of European modernity (e.g. Enlightenment, Marxism), which, Laclau argued, were ultimately based upon the secularization of the Christian logic of the incarnation of the Universal into the particular. However, contrary to the typically postmodern celebration of the free play of differences, the very notion of the Universal had to be reformulated in order to remove from it its teleological and/or totalizing implications but, and this is Laclau's strongest claim, the notion of the Universal did not have to be rejected.

As already noted, Laclau conceives all identity to be differentially constituted: 'the problem, however, is that the very possibility of signification is the system, and the very possibility of the system is the possibility of its limits' (Laclau 1996b: 37). Therefore, it is strictly necessary that an element within the system of signification stands for the totality itself, symbolizing its limits as well as what lies beyond it. These elements, gradually devoid of particular content, for they ultimately stand for the totality as such, will be termed *empty signifiers*. According to Laclau, the hegemonic struggle will consist precisely in determining which particularity will be elevated to the place of the universal: 'All positive content of the Universal is the contingent result of a hegemonic struggle – in itself, the Universal is absolutely empty' (Laclau 2000b: 79). The hegemonic struggle is now recast as a contention between particularities to determine which one is to transitorily occupy the empty place of the Universal.

Identifying the particularity that occupies the place of the Universal is relevant because all the differences internal to the system will have it as a context, being constituted with reference to it. In order to change the relations of power internally articulating a given society, it is not enough to alter the differential positions the various particularities occupy within the system, as this would leave the hegemonic closure of the social untouched. Instead, what is needed is, precisely, to contest the Universal itself, framing the differences internal to the system. It is then the hegemonic articulation between the particular and the Universal which will determine which social claims will be intelligible, that is, which ones will be constituted as differences internal to the system, and which others will be relegated to the ostracism of radical negativity.

In sum, the subject emerging from a dislocated structure will advance some particular claims as a response to the latter. In case it is found to successfully respond to the existing structure's perceived social needs, its strictly particular content will become gradually blurred through its own universalization, thus functioning in turn as a surface of inscription for the remaining particularities. In the words of Laclau (1990a: 64): 'The condition for the emergence of an imaginary is the metaphorization of the literal content of a particular social demand'.

On Populist Reason

Laclau's latest major work, *On Populist Reason*, deals explicitly with the issue of populism. Nevertheless, his lifelong theoretical preoccupations are still present (e. g. the production and subversion of a social order, the nature of political identities, the essence of the political), and the basic theoretical coordinates of the post-Marxist project are maintained. Contrary to the all-too-common understanding of populism as a vague, imprecise and self-consciously deceitful ideology, Laclau (2005a; 2005b) aims at rehabilitating the concept within political philosophy. Populism is not only deemed worthy of serious theoretical inquiry but, crucially, it is presented as 'the royal road to understanding something about the ontological constitution of the political as such' (Laclau 2005a: 67).

One of Laclau's key theoretical displacements is to conceive populism in strictly formal terms, as a logic regulating the constitution of political identities in times of intense institutional disintegration, thus avoiding making any reference to the specific content actually articulated: 'A movement is not populist because in its politics or ideology it presents actual *contents* identifiable as populistic, but because it shows a particular *logic of articulation* of those contents – whatever those contents are' (Laclau 2005b: 33, original emphasis). Hence, by focusing on strictly formal logics, Laclau avoids introducing normative judgments regarding populist articulations while, simultaneously, doing away with any understanding of language *qua* mere appendix to material reality. Indeed, that understanding of language as reflection of the material world could not be more at odds with Laclau's social ontology: 'Synonymy, metonymy, metaphor are not forms of thought that add a second sense to a primary, constitutive literality of social relations; instead, they are part of the primary terrain itself in which the social is constituted' (Laclau and Mouffe 2001: 110).

In a context in which a number of heterogeneous demands cannot be satisfied by the existing institutional order, despite them *a priori* not sharing anything in common, a 'relation of equivalence' among them may be drawn out of their common rejection of/by the *statu quo*, thus potentially coalescing into a new 'popular' identity capable of challenging the institutional order as such. That is, those demands may become 'equivalent' among themselves not out of some essential commonality they might ultimately share but, on the contrary, because of something they are *not*. In the words of Laclau (2006: 655, original emphasis):

> Once we move beyond a certain point, what were requests *within* institutions became claims addressed *to* institutions, and at some stage they became claims *against* the institutional order. When this process has overflown the institutional apparatuses beyond a certain limit, we start having the people of populism.[2]

The resulting popular subject will be constitutively split: On the one hand, it will comprise various social demands whose particular content will never be completely eradicated; on the other, it will present itself as the embodiment of the interests of the whole community: 'It is in this contamination of the universality of the *populus* by the partiality of the *plebs* that the peculiarity of the "people" as a historical actor lies' (Laclau 2005a: 224). This co-implication between the universal and the particular in order to conceive of political subjects is fully consistent with Laclau's previous works, as already noted. A more nuanced treatment of his understanding of populism will be offered in the pages that follow.

So far, a brief review of Laclau's theoretical evolution has been provided. As indicated at the beginning of this chapter, in what follows the attention will fall primordially upon Laclau's relation with the political economy tradition and the theoretical consequences that ensue. The next section will examine the nature and motives that justify Laclau's rupture with Marxism and, concretely, the reinterpretation of some Althusserian concepts he puts forward in order to ground his own.

Misrepresentation of Marxism, misreading of Althusser

As indicated, the publication of *Hegemony and Socialist Strategy* (Laclau and Mouffe 2001) signaled a radical break in Laclau's intellectual trajectory, thus giving birth to the so-called post-Marxist paradigm. In order to ground their own theoretical position, Laclau and Mouffe provided a theoretical reconstruction of the Marxist tradition in which the latter is depicted as being constituted by an unending struggle between, on the one hand, a necessarily closed theoretical paradigm and, on the other, an open-ended heterogeneous world that resists itself to be encapsulated into those same schemes. This journey, where various attempts succeeded each other in granting an ever-increasing role to the domain of contingency when explaining social phenomena, culminates in the work of Althusser. According to Laclau and Mouffe, an inexorable diagnostic thus follows: The whole tradition is inevitably flawed by an essentialist and economicist understanding of social relations which make it utterly incapable of coming to terms with the irreducible heterogeneity of the social world. In our view, whereas the representation of the Marxist tradition they put forward is an over-simplistic one, to say the least, their argument ultimately rests upon a contestable interpretation of Althusser's Marxism.

Laclau and Mouffe accuse the Marxist tradition of being constitutively essentialist, that is, of positing a single factor as the ultimate explanation of every conceivable social phenomena, so that every attempt to grant due recognition to the heterogeneity of the social world is deemed to be exterior to the very fundamentals of Marxist theory. While this line of argumentation is reminiscent of Althusser's strategy to purge Marxism of its (allegedly foreign) rationalist and empiricist influences, in Laclau and Mouffe's hands this line of argumentation is not used to discriminate between 'good' and 'bad' versions of it but, on the contrary, to indict Marxism *tout court*. In a nutshell, the argument is that, because Marxism is irremediably monist/essentialist while the social world is irreducibly complex, all authors in that tradition were forced, in one way or another, to have recourse to a dualist scheme of social explanation, whereby the necessary laws of motion of a closed paradigm were to be supplemented by some external element in order to account for the irreducible complexity of the social world. Ironically, however, while accusing every preceding Marxist theorist of 'dualism', they put forward an equally rigid dichotomy when judging competing social explanations: Either one social principle is able to explain everything, or else no causal explanations can be provided. As noted by Wood (1986: 78), in Laclau and Mouffe's explanatory schemes, 'where there is no simple, absolute, mechanical, unilinear, and non-contradictory determination, there is no determinacy, no relationship, no causality at all'. It seems that, beyond pointing out some illegitimate schemes of social explanation, Laclau and Mouffe are close to censoring every possible scientifically grounded account of social phenomena, as 'a social theory which does not attend to the relative causal weight of different practices, institutions, and agents is strategically worthless and conceptually empty' (Callinicos 1993: 44).

While, according to Laclau and Mouffe, Althusser was the Marxist theorist who came the closest to finally giving due recognition to both social heterogeneity and the domain of contingency, he could not get rid of the essentialist remainders that had vitiated Marxism's explanatory power since its inception. The argument goes as follows. The import of the category of 'overdetermination' from psychoanalysis apparently signaled a move in the right direction, as it asserts that 'the social constitutes itself as a symbolic order' (Laclau and Mouffe 2001: 97–8).[3] That is, contrary to the essentialist/reductionist explanatory trends proper to Marxism, which insist on reducing the phenomenal diversity of the social to mere epiphenomena of a single essence, overdetermination would indicate that '[t]here are not two planes, one of essences and the other of appearances, since there is no possibility of fixing an ultimate literal sense for which the symbolic would be a second and derived plane of signification' (Laclau and Mouffe 2001: 98). However, this potentially productive movement was radically counteracted by Althusser's falling back into old-fashioned Marxist essentialism, signaled by his insistence on the 'determination in the last instance by the economy', for, 'if society has a last instance which determines its laws of motion, then the relations between the overdetermined instances and the last instance must be conceived in terms of simple, one-directional determination by the latter' (Laclau and Mouffe 2001: 99). Therefore, the conclusion adopted by Laclau and Mouffe is that, in order to fully embrace the open-ended contingent character of the social world, the only step that remains to be taken is that which Althusser did not dare to take, namely, to forget about every reference to 'determination in the last instance' to conceive the social as being constituted by competing hegemonic attempts to suture the open-ended field of socio-symbolic differences and thus to provide a provisional and precarious form of closure.

Is this a correct reading of Althusser's theoretical stance? Are those two terms ('overdetermination' and 'determination-in-the-last-instance-by-the-economy') actually irreconcilable and hence contradictory? For Laclau and Mouffe's reading to be consistent, it must be accepted that Althusser borrowed the category of overdetermination from psychoanalysis merely to indicate that the world functions like a language, that is, to refer to the mechanisms of condensation and displacement of struggles and identities within the socio-symbolic field. However, overdetermination means something significantly different for Althusser and is utterly indissociable from his notion of totality. It refers to the manifestation of the whole in each and every one of its contradictions in an irreducibly complex manner, i.e. to the impossibility of fully dissociating a social contradiction from its conditions of existence. In a nutshell, overdetermination refers to '[t]his reflection of the conditions of existence of the contradiction within itself' (Althusser 1969: 206) – therefore, not to a plurality of meanings unable to be traced back to an ultimate literality, as maintained by Laclau and Mouffe, but, rather, to the mode of interrelation of the various spheres constituting the social totality, to the manifestation of the whole in each of its contradictions in an irreducibly complex manner.

It follows that 'overdetermination' and 'determination-in-the-last-instance' are but two complementary ways of referring to the mechanisms through which the totality exerts relations of causality among its components, that is, a totality that only shows itself through its effects, but a totality nonetheless. However, 'determination-in-the-last-instance' cannot be assimilated to unidirectional determination by the economic because it is simultaneously asserted that 'the lonely hour of the "last instance" never comes' (Althusser 1969: 113). Such paradoxical formulation signaled a refusal to downplay one pole in favor of the other, a commitment to develop a novel account of social causality at the intersection of two impossibilities: 'the impossibility of accepting the old conceptions of determination and causality and the impossibility (neither logical or eternal, but conjunctural and historical) at this moment of producing a genuinely new conception' (Montag 2018: 175). Far from reverting to essentialist accounts of social causality, Althusser is implicitly contending that the logic of overdetermination is universal, i.e. that every single contradiction contains within itself its own position in the structure in dominance, so that the 'conditions of existence' of any social process will be but the 'existing conditions'. Therefore, overdetermination is nothing but the hierarchical, contingent and historically unique mode of presentation of the complex whole in each and every one of its components, that 'model of organization and articulation of the complexity [which] is precisely what constitutes its unity' (Althusser 1969: 202). In sum, 'whereas Althusser develops overdetermination as an index which is essentially determined by a material real and which reveals that real, Laclau and Mouffe offer a definition of overdetermination as a symbolic order with no essential ties to any determining objects or practices' (Lewis 2005). Althusser's emphasis on the constitutive role of the conjuncture discredits Laclau and Mouffe's indictment of economism. Althusser's self-awareness of this danger is made paramount in a fragment of *On the Materialist Dialectic* worthy to be quoted at length:

> It is economism (mechanism) and not the true Marxist tradition that sets up the hierarchy of instances once and for all, assigns each its essence and role and defines the universal meaning of their relations; it is economism that identifies roles and actors eternally, [...] It is economism that identifies eternally in advance the determinant-contradiction-in-the-last-instance with the role of the dominant contradiction.
>
> (Althusser 1969: 213)

Hence, Laclau and Mouffe's rejection of Althusser's notion of 'determination in the last instance' while (nominally) retaining the concept of overdetermination to refer to the metaphoric/metonymic constitution of struggles, identities and demands in the socio-symbolic field underlies their different conceptualizations of the social totality. While Althusser posits a totality that is ultimately decentered, constituted by the overdetermined interrelations among its constituting instances, Laclau and Mouffe reject the notion of totality altogether in favor of a plurality of 'totalizing' effects derived from different hegemonic attempts to provide a provisional form of closure to the field of heterogeneous, free-floating differences. Althusser's assertion that the internal movement of the totality cannot be predicted does not lead him to deny it as an object suitable to scientific scrutiny (an index of which is provided by the category of overdetermination), thus standing in stark contrast to Laclau and Mouffe's theoretical agnosticism regarding the structural conditionings of political action. Althusser's overdetermined totality, 'in that it recognizes and takes into account a plurality of diverse factors and determinants (including the economic), [rests] on a firmer basis and is more complete than those epistemologies that insist on the ideological nature of all knowledge' (Lewis 2005), so that, by doing away with the materialist dimension of Althusser's notion of overdetermination, Laclau and Mouffe end up '[substituting] the ideological mechanisms of subject-formation for the materialist principles of social production as rules for the composition of the social field' (Boucher 2009: 92).

In sum, by asserting the impenetrability of the social in conjunction with an understanding of social relations as infinitely malleable and contingent, Laclau and Mouffe are led to dismiss Marxism as merely a political discourse generative of political identities, rather than as a scientific paradigm capable of throwing some light upon the internal dynamics of the capitalist mode of production. It follows that the formal complexity and richness of Laclau's discursive theory of hegemony remains unable to apprehend the specifically capitalist nature of the societies it is supposed to be referring to. In order to lay bare their theoretical position, Laclau and Mouffe misrepresent Marxism to the extent of producing a caricature of it, in opposition to which their own theoretical position can be laid bare. The following fragment of their argument with Geras (1987) is illustrative of it: 'In a sense, Marx clearly remains within the idealist field – that is to say, within the ultimate affirmation of the rationality of the real. The well-known *inversion of dialectics* cannot but reproduce the latter's structure' (Laclau and Mouffe 1987: 88, emphasis added). On the one hand, even if that judgment were appropriate when referred to *Marx* himself, it can hardly stand as an indictment of *Marxism* as a whole. On the other, if actually referred to Marxism, is the 'inversion' metaphor still a valid line of attack against the whole Marxist tradition once Althusser's criticism of it has already been provided? Given that Althusser himself is included in that tradition, having resort to a pre-Althusserian social ontology can hardly be admitted as a valid argument against the Marxist tradition as a whole.

However, before outlining Laclau's reconceptualization of the 'economy', it is necessary to stress the argument we do not favor. We do not argue in favor of granting any sort of epistemological privilege to the subjective involvement in capitalist production processes when devising anti-capitalist political alternatives, nor do we argue in favor of there being any essential relation between the conflictive nature of capitalist institutions and the political expressions liable to emerge from the latter. Nor do we argue that anti-systemic struggles must of necessity be articulated around class-related identities, nor under explicitly 'anti-capitalist' banners. Much less do we argue for a subsumption of non-class-related struggles or identities under narrowly defined class struggle, or for any attempt to trace back the heterogeneity of struggles permeating the social to an essential commonality derived from their common partaking of capitalist-related social processes. What we explicitly advocate is not the incompatibility of Laclau's theory of hegemony with the tradition of political economy but, on the contrary, the necessity of retaining theoretical insights from the latter if the former is to have any strategic value in political terms, that is, an explicit recognition of the specifically capitalist nature of the societies in which hegemonic logics are operating, an oblivion of which seriously vitiates the epistemological and political/strategic value of post-Marxist discourse theory.

Whither political economy?

Laclau's critique and reformulation of the Marxist tradition leads him to expel the tradition of political economy among the vast array of his theoretical influences. Indeed, a related and symptomatic omission grounds both Laclau's theoretical framework and the sort of postmodern politics that, more often than not, finds in the former one of its most sophisticated theoretical justifications. The import of various insights from linguistics, psychoanalysis, or deconstruction into the post-Marxist tradition obliterated the extirpation of political economy insights from the latter for, as Miklitsch (1995: 170) has noted, '[Laclau's] political-theoretical project derives, if only by way of inversion, from its discursive-methodological Other: political economy'. As a result, contrary to the profound and novel elaboration of political concepts that characterizes discourse theory, their use of economic concepts has not undergone the same process of theoretical re-elaboration: 'There are economic concepts in *Hegemony and Socialist Strategy*, but no concept of the economy' (Diskin and Sandler 1993: 30). This failure to integrate the analysis of economic realities into the theoretical coordinates of discourse theory grounds an understanding of capitalism as a homogenous and unitary force (Diskin and Sandler 1993; Gibson-Graham 1996), ultimately conflated with the continuous expansion of the logic of the commodity throughout the social field (Laclau and Mouffe 2001: 161).

However, it is our view that Marxian political economy, on the one hand, and Laclau's critique of it on the grounds of it being ultimately essentialist, on the other, operate at qualitatively different levels of abstraction. Whereas Laclau's approach is concerned with the ontological grounding of any and every institutional structure that manages imperfectly to reproduce itself, Marxian political economy is concerned with analyzing the internal dynamics of one specific and (however imperfectly) sedimented structure – the capitalist mode of production. In the words of Best (2014: 276), '[i]f the object of discourse theory is the logical (im)possibility of the social – the (in)capacity of its sedimentation – the object of political economy is one ongoing instance of sedimentation/reactivation in action'. Discourse theory, by conflating these two different levels of abstraction, runs the risk of drawing a critique of all theories where institutional sedimentation is not ontologically explained but simply assumed. In this sense, Mouzelis (1988: 16) rightly notes that 'Laclau and Mouffe, because of their excessive fear of reifying institutional structures, go to the other extreme and analyze practices in an institutional vacuum'. Laclau (1990b: 223, original emphasis), in turn, vehemently denies the existence of an 'institutional deficit' in his own theoretical framework: 'institutions are fully present in our approach: they are what we have called *systems of differences*. [...] In opposition to the postulation of two *separate* metaphysical entities – agents and structures – we suggest [...] that there are merely relative *degrees* of institutionalization of the social'. While asserting that institutions are, in the end, 'systems of differences' may be indisputable at a high level of abstraction, the truth is that it does complicate more than it enables an in-depth analysis of institutional environments from a discourse-theoretical perspective. Insofar as populism is understood to constitute 'the royal road to understanding something about the ontological constitution of the political as such' (Laclau 2005a: 67), and populism is intimately associated to the social prevalence of equivalential logics and de-institutionalization dynamics, a self-conscious study of the interplay between political action and the institutional environment seems to be precluded (Miró 2019). As noted by Panizza and Miorelli (2013) 'if politics is populism and populism is anti-institutional by definition, then politics cannot be about institutions'.

Nevertheless, starting from Laclau's (1990a: 34) distinction between the social and the political, a much more fruitful line of inquiry might be opened. While the former refers to the domain of sedimented social practices, that is, routinized, largely repetitive patterns of social interaction, whose ultimately contingent character is in turn obliterated, so that they become 'objectified', the political refers to those moments where the ultimately contingent, and thus contestable, character of the former is brought to the fore through social quarrels over their very constitution. Given that 'social relations are constituted by the very distinction between the social and the political' (Laclau 1990a: 35), it thus follows that one should speak of different 'degrees of institutionalization' constituting the social, rather than of self-contained institutional blocks (Hansen 2008; Jacobs 2019), as indicated by Laclau himself in the quote above.

In sum, no strict incompatibility should be assumed between the ontological postulates of post-Marxist discourse theory, on the one hand, and those required by an institutionally grounded analysis of capitalist dynamics, on the other. Whereas the sedimentation/reactivation conceptual couple is certainly a productive one when considering a general social ontology, further theoretical work is nonetheless required to develop a conceptual apparatus which, while respecting post-Marxism's core ontological postulates, nonetheless enables apprehending the differential constraints and opportunities derived from the institutional environment in which hegemonic logics operate, as well as the differential degree of resilience of its core building blocks. Such a lack of theoretical development has been certainly enhanced by an illegitimate conceptual leap from contingency to precariousness when describing the social. From the fact that any and every sedimented institutional structure is contingent, no judgment can be made *a priori* regarding their higher or lesser temporal durability. However, Laclau and Mouffe (2001: 96, 98, emphasis added) consider 'the diverse social orders' not only as ultimately contingent, and hence always-already susceptible of being altered, but 'as *precarious* and ultimately failed attempts to domesticate the field of differences'. Similarly, because 'society and social agents lack any essence', it is concluded that 'their regularities merely consist of the relative and *precarious* forms of fixation which accompany the establishment of a certain order'. Therefore, a more nuanced treatment of the varying degrees of resistance and/or proclivity to change of the various institutional components of a social order is needed, one that cannot be provided by simply collapsing every single institution under the common banner of 'systems of differences'. Moreover, not only can individual components show a higher or lesser resistance to change when considered in isolation, but it is also strictly necessary that conceptual tools are provided that permit apprehending how the various blocks of an institutional ensemble may coalesce into a relatively coherent whole for a certain time through the emergence of relations of complementarity and/or dissonance among them, in turn either supporting or complicating their joint reproduction over time.

As noted above, no strict incompatibility should be assumed between the ontological postulates of discourse theory and political economy, respectively. They simply operate at different levels of abstraction (Best 2014). Therefore, starting from discourse-theoretical postulates, further theoretical development is required in order to be able to apprehend, firstly, the different degrees of resilience corresponding to a given social order's main components; secondly, how relations of complementarity and/or dissonance may emerge among themselves so that, through their joint occurrence, the internal dynamics harbored by each may be either enhanced or attenuated in turn, and; thirdly, how such an unevenly sedimented terrain either favors or constrains particular forms of social action. In this sense, while respecting an anti-essentialist social ontology, one should start from considering how diverse social practices or processes, despite there being no *ex ante* relations drawn among them, will nonetheless become contingently interlocked with other processes, with different degrees of intensity and duration, giving way in turn to stabilized 'logics' informing their iterative repetition (Glynos and Howarth 2007), so that, once their modality of interaction favors the reproduction of the interaction itself, they become sedimented, i.e. they are turned into institutions. This way, a topography of the social would be produced, in turn enabling an empirically grounded analysis of the contingent rugosity of the social relative to the specific social conjuncture under scrutiny. Laclau and Mouffe, however, by conflating structural functions with institutional apparatuses (Boucher 2019), are led to dismiss any systematic study of the internal dynamics of the capitalist mode of production as an intrinsically reductionist/essentialist operation. As a result, '[they are] therefore unable to theorize the hierarchy of effective causes within an overdetermined phenomenon and must necessarily reduce to a descriptive list, progressively renouncing explanation for interpretation' (Boucher 2009: 11).

The question remains, however, of how to approach the study of capitalist dynamics once such an institutional environment has been constructed from anti-essentialist ontological premises. While the bulk of post-Marxist studies has been generally oblivious to the relevance of capitalism in both constraining social action and conditioning the social structure's diachronic evolution, some attempts have been made to study capitalism in its own right without renouncing to discourse theory's ontological commitments. In this regard, both Daly (2004) and Dahlberg (2014) tentatively advocate for a '*Radical* Political Economy' which, by being grounded in discourse-theoretical postulates, would acknowledge the inherently discursive constitution of the economy, on the one hand, and the ultimate lack and negativity haunting every positivized system, on the other. Analyzing capitalism from these ontological postulates would bring to light, according to Daly (2004: 14), the contingent but ever-present possibility of politicization of every domain of social life, as well as the dependence of every system's positivization upon underlying dynamics of inclusion/exclusion, whereas, according to Dahlberg (2014: 261), it would prominently 'involve exploring and explaining capitalism's discursive systematization and ideological stabilization'. However, the question remains of how to go beyond the mere description of its phenomenal appearance when analyzing capitalist dynamics, that is, how to theorize the different causal weight carried by the various social processes and institutions present in a given conjuncture such that a hierarchy among their respective degrees of social effectivity can be obtained. It is our contention that the most promising way forward in this regard would be to relate discourse theory to some middle-range, non-teleological and holistic framework for analyzing capitalism.

In that respect, Howarth (2013) and Torfing (1998) argue in favor of reinterpreting French Regulation Theory's categories (e.g. Aglietta 1979) along post-structuralist lines. Howarth (2013: 215), for instance, argues that:

> regulation is best conceptualized as a particular type of hegemonic practice [insofar as it involves] linking together contingent elements, which exist and operate in a particular discursive field, so as to construct particular institutional complexes that enable, without ensuring, the ongoing reproduction of social relations.

Both sides are expected to benefit from such an enterprise for, 'while regulation theory enables accounting for the contradictory logics of capitalist and non-capitalist social formations', discourse theory enables '[considering] the various logics of difference that function to breakdown and reabsorb potential challenges to a regime of accumulation' (Howarth 2013: 220–1). Torfing (1998: 132) expresses himself along similar lines when he states that 'we should begin to rethink the concept of regulation in terms of a hegemonic practice'. Understanding regulation as a hegemonic articulatory practice among dissimilar elements would respect post-Marxism's primacy of the political over the social while simultaneously acknowledging differential degrees of resilience within the latter, as regulation would be recast as 'the ensemble of institutionally mediated processes which provide conditions for the reproduction of the social system of capitalism, in spite of its conflictual and crisis-ridden character' (Torfing 1998: 107).

The option we favor is to relate post-Marxism's insightful account of socio-political interactions to SSA theory, on the grounds already exposed in chapter 2. While such enterprise, we contend, would illuminate the contingent, relational, and contestable character of any institutional order, it would also provide conceptual means to analyze the socio-symbolic matrix regulating capitalist social relations, throwing light upon the common-sense frameworks and legitimation strategies through which agents both rationalize and contest their partaking of the latter. This way, we believe, the 'institutional deficit' currently haunting post-Marxist discourse theory could be tackled by appraising the specifically capitalist dimension of the discursive formations it seeks to investigate.

Symptoms of an undeclared omission

The rest of this chapter will examine the implications, both epistemological and political, derived from the repression of political economy insights from Laclau's theoretical *corpus*. Borrowing the term from Althusser, a symptomatic reading of the Laclauian problematic is provided, throwing into light the internal assumptions upon which it is grounded by paying attention not only to what it explicitly says but also to its silences and omissions. The core thesis defended here is that the omission of political economy from the list of post-Marxism's main theoretical sources is not just one omission among many but, on the contrary, one ultimately constitutive of the resulting politico-theoretical stance. In order to substantiate this claim, four main areas will be scrutinized in detail, namely, the implications of considering social demands as the primary unit of analysis; the effects of recasting class as merely one type of identity politics; its understanding of temporal dynamics under capitalism; and, lastly, certain aporias resulting from his understanding of populism. While the upcoming discussion will be focused upon Laclau's work, some references will be made to other authors in the post-Marxist tradition.

Social demands qua *primary unit of analysis*

Laclau's (2005a; 2005b) later work has been mostly devoted, though not exclusively, to the study of populism. In order to avoid any sort of determinism, economic or otherwise, in analyzing socio-political interactions, Laclau (2005a: 72) postulates the category of 'social demand' as the 'minimal unit of analysis' in his analysis of the constitution of political subjects. Although this notion was not explicitly advanced at the early stages of the post-Marxist project, it remains fully consistent with the 'post-foundational' theoretical coordinates of the latter (Marchart 2007). Postulating social demands as the minimal unit of analysis, rather than presuming a pre-existing political subject whose proffered political demands could have been pre-determined *a priori* on the basis of the position it occupies in the social structure, allows Laclau to posit a subject of politics who is not constitutive but, on the contrary, constituted by 'relations of equivalence' among those demands. Laclau's consideration of the socio-symbolic level not only as constitutive of social objectivity but, also, as the only one worthy of in-depth theoretical scrutiny definitely avoids any sort of economic determinism in appraising the process of constitution of political identities. However, several other problems emerge.

Firstly, by taking social demands as the most elementary unit of analysis, post-Marxist discourse theory is unable to apprehend how the conflict-ridden nature of contemporary societies is 'individuated' into a set of individually isolated social demands – that is, in the terms employed by Laclau and Mouffe (2001: 105), how 'elements' are transformed (i.e. discursively articulated) into 'moments'. Among the multiple conflicts and tensions arising from the interaction among the various social processes comprising the social totality, not all of them have the same chances of being 'individuated' into social demands able to acquire intelligibility within the sphere of political representation. In order to apprehend the degree to which certain grievances are more likely to enter the political arena than others, it is necessary to consider the uneven institutional environment from which those social demands will always spring.

The category of 'social heterogeneity' (Laclau 2005a: 140), which some have argued in favor of constituting as the central category of discourse theory (e.g. Thomassen 2005), refers precisely to that excessive remainder excluded from the sphere of representation which, nevertheless, continually haunts and threatens the latter. Thus, not only every positivized system, but also every socio-symbolic domain, is ultimately dependent upon a 'constitutive outside'. However, it follows from Laclau's account that those unsatisfied demands susceptible of being incorporated into competing relations of equivalence must be, of necessity, always-already constituted as demands (Barros 2006). Nevertheless, apprehending the existing constrains operating upon their constitution as socially intelligible demands requires, precisely, being able to appreciate the differential institutional depth of the various blocks composing a given social order, a task which, in turn, is precluded by the dissolution of any and every overarching social totality into an undifferentiated magma of symbolic differences.

Advancing a social demand in response to a situation of social dislocation requires enjoying the appropriate symbolic and material resources, together with certain organizational capacities, whose apprehension requires a more nuanced treatment of institutions than that provided by collapsing every existing institution under the common banner of 'systems of differences'. Moreover, because of the differential inclusion enjoyed by social agents within the social complex, the very means needed to advance a demand into the political arena will always be unevenly distributed. Therefore, restricting the analysis to already-constituted demands misses the constraints and opportunities imposed upon political intervention by a social structure which, however contingent, nonetheless remains real in its effects.

Secondly, and perhaps more importantly, no hierarchical ordering of the various possible social demands can be provided in terms of their higher or lesser anti-systemic potential. Either if the hegemonic struggle is conceptualized as an unending struggle among particularities to occupy the empty place of the Universal (e.g. Laclau 1996c; 2000a) or, in more recent terms, as competing attempts by individual demands to empty themselves of their own particular content so that they can function as surfaces of inscription of other unsatisfied demands (e.g. Laclau 2005a), there is a (self-conscious) theoretical agnosticism regarding the specific ontic content those demands/particulars might take.

It seems that, in combating class reductionism, the argument slides from stressing that partaking in capitalist relations of production does not grant any privileged access to anti-systemic consciousness, so that 'there is no reason why struggles taking place *within* relations of production should be the privileged points of a global anti-capitalist struggle' (Laclau 2005a: 150, emphasis added), to asserting that the politicization of any social domain can be equally threatening to the reproduction of the existing order: 'The crucial point is that there is no special location within a system which enjoys an a priori privilege in an anti-systemic struggle' (Laclau 2000c: 203). We agree with Laclau in asserting that no specific area within the social can be ascribed, *a priori* and for any and every conceivable social formation, higher anti-systemic potential than others. However, these demands will always be framed and advanced in a given institutional environment, featuring different degrees of proclivity and/or reticence to change, where systemic reproduction (however imperfect) will be more dependent upon the particular evolution of certain institutional blocks as compared to others. In order to ascertain the context-specific anti-systemic potential of a given social demand it is required, precisely, a conjunctural analysis capable of illuminating the differential degrees of robustness existing among the main blocks of a given institutional environment, a type of analysis which, we claim, current post-Marxist discourse theory can only provide through vague and theoretically unelaborated terms (Boucher 2019).

As explored in detail in the next chapter, the capitalist mode of production never exists in a purely empty space but, on the contrary, appears always incarnated in historically specific institutional settings where, regarding the continuation of ongoing capitalist activity at a macro level, certain institutional domains will be more relevant than others. In this respect, anti-systemic demands will be those which manage to bridge contemporary common sense with the (context-specific) structural requirements of a well-functioning capitalist environment. Take, for instance, a social formation where private housing provision is the norm, where national capital had managed to secure dominant positions in the real estate sector, and where wealth effects derived from housing prices' revalorization are crucial to sustaining an ascending aggregate demand. Within such an environment, a demand such as 'public housing for all' would show much higher anti-systemic potential than it would in other institutional settings where the opposite was the case. By doing away with any notion of an overarching social structure, post-Marxist discourse theory, in its currently dominant form, is thus constitutively blind to the structural limitations imposed by the fact that our societies are, at the end of the day, societies whose own reproduction is heavily affected by capitalism's ability to reproduce itself.

Class qua *identity politics*

One of the main deficiencies of Marxism, according to Laclau's narrative, is the former's 'class reductionism' when considering revolutionary subjectivity.

Laclau vehemently denies, on the one hand, the existence of *any* link between the structural position occupied by agents and the political expression ensuing and, on the other, that revolutionary subjectivity must of necessity be anchored around the category of 'class'. Actually, the very notion of structural position is dissolved in Laclau's schemes for, as noted in previous sections, any notion of social structure is replaced by infinitely malleable hegemonic articulations aimed at (re-)constituting that failed object that society ultimately is. It follows that the very distinction between 'class-in-itself' and 'class-for-itself' collapses as the latter, because of the disappearance of any trace of institutionality in Laclau's social ontology, is deemed to be the only conceptual category worth serious theoretical scrutiny. However, it is one thing to complicate their relationship while exploring the relative autonomy existing between the two levels, and another one entirely to do away with the very notion of 'class-in-itself' because any attempt to study structural positions is deemed to be inherently reductionist. Hence, as noted by Rustin (1988: 154), by rejecting any reference to objective material processes in constituting classes, '[Laclau and Mouffe] substitute an equally one-dimensional theory of ideological determination for the monistic theory of economic determinism'.

Therefore, the way is paved for an understanding of class and capitalism as 'largely fetishes dispossessed of any precise meaning', and class struggle as 'just one species of identity politics, and one which is becoming less and less important in the world in which we live' (Laclau 2000c: 201–3). For those statements to have any sense, the reduction of the category of class to one specific type of socio-symbolic collective identification must first have been accomplished, so that the lower political salience enjoyed nowadays by the symbolic universe constructed around the 'Fordist' industrial working class can be taken for evidence of the decreasing relevance of the category of class to understand contemporary anti-systemic struggles. However, the unilateral treatment of class *qua* one type of collective identification obscures the contemporary relevance of class *qua* social process, one that provides a politico-epistemological structuring of the socio-economic space without this necessarily implying falling back into an essentialist social ontology (e.g. Diskin and Sandler 1993; Resnick and Wolff 1987).

Indeed, the various phenomena that Laclau (2000a: 299–300) mentions to account for the lower relevance today of the category of class cannot be considered entirely foreign to the category of 'class' insofar as they can be correctly apprehended only through the very structuration of the social space that the category of 'class' enables (Boucher 2009). Firstly, the 'decline of the working class [...] in absolute numbers' that Laclau cites must be considered an unambiguously wrong proposition, insofar as the amount of people securing their livelihood through selling their labor power has risen during the last decades both in core and peripheral countries alike. What has indeed declined is the number of male workers employed in manufacturing in Western countries. However, taking the latter to exhaustively represent the working class *tout court* serves only to obscure ongoing transformations in the domain of labor relations during the last decades. Secondly, the decline of the working class's 'structural organization', as indicated, for instance, by decreasing trade union density rates, appears in turn intimately related to the relocation of manufacturing activity (where work homogeneity and the large scale of plants did favor trade union membership) away from Western countries; the proliferation of 'atypical' labor arrangements in the now expanding service sector; or the widespread implementation of neoliberal policies explicitly aimed at curtailing trade unions' structural power (Pontusson 2013). Thirdly, increasing involvement in a 'generalized mass culture [which] has seriously eroded the separate working-class identity' appears related, on the one hand, to the exhaustion of the Fordist paradigm in the 1970s, articulated around the mass production of homogenous consumer goods, and its substitution by more diversified production patterns and the consolidation of a 'flexible specialization' paradigm in the Western world (Piore and Sabel 1984), and, on the other, to the higher casualization and heterogeneity of labor contracts during the neoliberal era, which in turn complicates the consolidation of social identities articulated around work experiences (Kalleberg 2009; Standing 2011). Fourthly, Laclau cites the 'levels of unemployment, which are putting into question the very notion of "class"' on which Marxism has rested. While it is bizarre enough to take a historical transformation of labor relations as evidence of the decreasing relevance of class realities nowadays, Laclau seems to forget that the functionality of the 'industrial reserve army' to capital accumulation, as well as capital's compulsion to purge labor out of the production process, are acknowledged by Marxist theory insofar as they are constitutive elements of its own understanding of class. Lastly, 'the divisions of the workers in terms of nationality' and 'the incorporation of women into the labor market', far from signaling the declining relevance of class realities, reveal the inherently racialized and gendered character of class realities nowadays (Bakker and Gill 2003). These transformations within the internal composition of 'core' capitalist countries' working class, in turn, are but the obverse of the numerical decline of the white male industrial working class in Western countries which Laclau erroneously takes as synonymous with the working class as a whole (Creighton 1999; Overbeek 2002). In sum, the lower hegemonic depth nowadays enjoyed by 'class' *qua* political identity finds some explanation, precisely, in the historical evolution of 'class' *qua* social process. Following Wood (1986: 97), '[t]he absence of explicit class "discourses" does not betoken the absence of class realities and their effects in shaping the life-conditions and consciousness of the people who come within their "field of force"'.

Any society in which capitalism is the dominant mode of production has a structural necessity of (re-)producing the wage-labor relation irrespective of the self-awareness shown by its participants, so that 'every discursive construction of wage-labor is also always overdetermined by the structural necessity of wage-labor for the continued functioning of the capitalist machine' (Best 2014: 278). The category of class, while invariably overdetermined by its conditions of existence (such as, prominently, race and gender relations), points precisely to this structural and contradictory feature of capitalism, where capital requires wage-labor while simultaneously finding itself compelled by the relations of intra-capitalist competition to purge it from the production process, a feature which, in turn, constitutes a structural invariant of all social formations where capitalism is the dominant mode of production. In this sense, Daly (2004: 18, original emphasis), working under discourse-theoretical ontological presumptions, crucially acknowledges that, '[w]hile capital works ceaselessly to transform and commodify all existing social relations, what it refuses to bargain with (in fact, *cannot* bargain with) is precisely its exploitative conditions of possibility'. In sum, by ignoring the sort of epistemological structuration of the social space that the category of class enables, one runs the risk of taking changing class realities for evidence of the growing irrelevance of the category of class *tout court*, instead of realizing that, precisely, it is the category of class that can make those phenomena intelligible in a coherent and structured manner.

Temporal dynamics under capitalism

Another of Laclau's main lines of attack against Marxism concerns the latter's alleged presumption of an inevitable defeat of capitalism out of the self-unfolding of its internal contradictions, socialism being a necessary consequence of the immanent laws of history. Again, reducing Marxism to its most reductionist-economistic-teleological versions enables Laclau to lay out his own alternative, namely, 'a vision of history that is different from economic stagism: a succession of dislocatory junctures' (Laclau 1990a: 46).

However, there was already a long intellectual tradition within Marxism which, arguing precisely against teleological visions of history, tried to offer a periodization internal to capitalism by identifying existing 'long-waves' regarding capital accumulation, from the initial works of Lenin (1917), Bukharin (1973), and Hilferding (1980), through those of Mandel (1995) and Sweezy (1968), up until its culmination in, on the one hand, French Regulation theory (Aglietta 1979) and, on the other, SSA theory (Gordon et al. 1982). The main idea behind these theories is that the capitalist mode of production does not take place in an institutional vacuum but, on the contrary, is always necessarily embedded in (relatively) coherent and long-lasting institutional ensembles susceptible to undergoing fully-fledged disintegration (McDonough 1994a). While these institutional ensembles must, for a time, guarantee sustained capital accumulation and surplus value extraction by the capitalist class, sooner or later, however, a point may be reached at which those institutions stop promoting further growth and start functioning as barriers to it. Whenever several among the main social contradictions can no longer be successfully contained by the existing institutional architecture, the decomposition of the latter carries with it a generalized breakdown of associated social consensuses. That is, systemic crises eventually turn into organic crises. Despite the various social processes forming the social totality enjoying different temporalities, not amenable to be subsumed under a great master line of historical development, they are nonetheless ultimately threaded up together, however loosely. It follows that capitalist history is marked by a succession of periods of relative institutional stability followed up by others of intense social turmoil where profound institutional transformation is not the exception but the norm.

Laclau's (1990a: 39, 67) claims about 'the uncontrolled rhythm of capitalism', about its 'accelerated tempo of social transformation and the continual rearticulatory interventions the latter demands', or about 'the proliferation of dislocations peculiar to advanced capitalism' seem hardly a good substitute for Marxist long-wave theory which, whatever its shortcomings, is better positioned to provide a valid periodization internal to capitalism by paying explicit attention to actually-existing institutional arrangements. Post-Marxist discourse theory self-consciously ignores the evolution, as well as the internal contradictions, of the capitalist accumulation process under the presumption that, if it did not, that would imply positing an (illegitimate) essential ground to which all other social processes would be ultimately referred. It thus comes as no surprise that, having done away with any notion of an overarching institutional structure, Laclau is led to reinterpret Gramsci's notion of organic crisis as 'a general breakdown of hegemony, conceived as a unifying symbolic order' (Rustin 1988: 159) with no ties to underlying material processes (including economic, but also gender, race, and nature itself among others). In the words of Laclau (1990a: 28):

> The 'necessity' and 'objectivity' of the social would depend on the establishment of a stable hegemony, with the periods of "organic crisis" characterized as those in which the basic hegemonic articulations weaken and an increasing number of social elements assume the character of floating signifiers.

Responding to the lack of conceptual means in Laclau and Mouffe (2001) with which to appraise structural crises, Laclau (1990a) introduced the category of 'dislocation' (Harrison 2014). Dislocations, being an effect of the differential and contingent character of every articulation, are manifested in an event, or a set of events, which 'cannot be domesticated by the structure' (Torfing 1999: 149), that is, an occurrence which dominant hegemonic articulations of social meaning cannot successfully integrate within themselves, in turn bringing to the fore the ontological impossibility of every structural articulation to fully self-reproduce itself. Therefore, far from being self-sufficient, every socio-symbolic configuration will have to react to a prediscursive reality in the guise of dislocatory events. However, in the post-Marxist literature, dislocations' conditions of existence are seldom interrogated in detail, more often than not being simply assumed or registered, but rarely explained or accounted for.

Glynos and Howarth's (2007) 'logics approach' is representative of such a theoretical lacuna. Their approach takes social practices as its starting point, and then examines how these coalesce in different logics informing social action, institutions, and discursive regimes. In their theoretical scheme, dislocations refer to events whose occurrence reveals the ontological incompleteness of every structure, in turn giving way to practices of various kinds through which subjects reshape their social environment. However, it is symptomatic that, while their approach certainly excels in exploring how the social field is reshaped in response to structural dislocations, the very occurrence of such dislocations remains nonetheless unexplained. Take, for instance, their example about the effects of a 'major economic depression' (Glynos and Howarth 2007: 104). While the conceptual structure certainly enables a fine-grained analysis of the potential responses to such an economic crisis, the latter's very occurrence remains nonetheless merely registered rather than interrogated in discourse-theory's own terms. Similarly, Stavrakakis's (2000) analysis of Green ideology suffers from an analogous shortcoming. While stressing that 'dislocation [...] can be found at the root of all paradigm, discursive, or ideological shifts', being in turn 'a necessary precondition for the emergence of Green politics' (Stavrakakis 2000: 110–2), dislocations remain nonetheless unexplained (Townshend 2003). Somehow paradoxically, insofar as Stavrakakis's (2000: 100) self- purported aims are to develop a 'theory of dislocation', dislocation itself is conceptualized as a sort of *deus ex machina* which continually sets in motion ideological reconfigurations, instead of as an event whose conditions of emergence deserve close theoretical scrutiny. A social theory capable of engaging with current socio-political developments cannot limit itself to stress the ontological undecidability of every structure but needs to be able to shed some light upon the timing, nature, and social location of those dislocations. However, that would require being able to provide first a regional topography of the social within the specific conjuncture under scrutiny, one which would acknowledge the differential thickness of its core building blocks, as well as the context-specific relations existing among them.

In our view, for the category of dislocation to be of any use for social theory, it would be necessary to differentiate between, on the one hand, dislocation *qua* effect of the differential constitution of every social system, manifested in the ontological undecidability affecting every positivized system/identity and, on the other, dislocation *qua* profound and wide-ranging decomposition of a given social order, i.e. the institutional mechanisms grounding and organizing social co-existence. Recognizing the ultimate relevance of the latter, however, would require acknowledging the existence of an overarching structure, however transient and incomplete, whose internal tempo modulates the various patterns of social transformation undergone by co-existing social processes. Denying its existence altogether implies that, for instance, the different opportunities and constraints imposed upon political intervention by the onset of the Great Recession cannot be properly conceptualized with conceptual means internal to discourse theory, nor can it be the ultimate reason why several political demands currently remain 'unsatisfied', thus opening the way for those populist interventions that discourse theory takes as one of its central theoretical preoccupations.

In sum, by doing away with any notion of a social structure susceptible of undergoing disintegration, discourse theory is ill-fated to appraise the relations of mutual co-implication existing among the various social processes constituting the social totality. Positing a rigid alternative between, on the one hand, a unilinear and teleological conception of historical processes and, on the other, a multiplicity of social processes with no discernible common trajectories, discourse theory, in its current form, remains unable to apprehend the 'intertwining of the different times [...] i.e. the type of "dislocation" and torsion of the different temporalities produced by the different levels of the structure, the complex combination of which constitutes the peculiar time of the process's development' (Althusser and Balibar 2009, 116). In sum, by denying any systemic study of the capitalist machine due to its allegedly essentialist implications, Laclau ends up not 'radicalizing' the Althusserian project, as he purportedly attempted to, but, on the contrary, compromising the very possibility of social sciences altogether.

The aporias of populism

The last point we would like to call attention to are certain ambiguities arising from Laclau's conception of populism. As previously noted in the first section of the current chapter, Laclau understands populism as a formal logic regulating the constitution of political identities in times of sharp institutional disintegration. To recap, populism is argued to be a prominent modality of constitution of novel political identities in times marked by the simultaneous emergence of a wide variety of initially heterogeneous demands the existing institutional order cannot satisfy, so that a possibility emerges that those demands be articulated into a new political identity grounded in their common rejection by the existing order. However, by not grounding their emergence in its underlying socio-economic conditions of existence, certain theoretical ambiguities arise.

Firstly, it follows from Laclau's (2005b; 2005a) theoretical account of populist phenomena that the more or less simultaneous and widespread emergence of unsatisfied demands is a necessary precondition of populist articulations. Otherwise, there would be no room for their transitory 'equivalence', produced by virtue of their common dissatisfaction, to coalesce into a newly emerging popular identity. However, one wonders, why does the existing institutional order suddenly stop being able to satisfy those demands in the first instance, so that populist equivalential logics can operate? Is it an ever-present threat in whichever political community? Is it instead an ever-present possibility only within societies where capitalism regulates social reproduction? Or, perhaps, does this situation reflect the political stakes in those moments under capitalism where the latter's self-reproduction is compromised to the extreme (i.e. systemic crises)? By grounding Laclau's understanding of populism upon the political economy tradition, we argue, these apparent aporias might be led to a fruitful resolution. Later on, we will explore in much greater detail the existing connections between populism and systemic crises under capitalism.

Moreover, a second problematic issue concerns the capacity of populist logics to initiate a process of institutional decomposition. On the one hand, Laclau has consistently entertained the idea that the political is ultimately constitutive of social relations, either by acknowledging that it has a 'primary structuring role' (Laclau 2006: 664), or by defining it as the 'instituting moment of society' (Laclau 1996a: 47). On the other hand, Laclau's recent work has virtually equated the political with populism when asserting that 'populist reason [...] amounts [...] to political reason *tout court*' (Laclau 2005a: 225). Therefore, if the political is constitutive of social relations and populism represents the quintessence of the political, it should follow that the operation of populist logics should be sufficient to trigger the deinstitutionalization of a given social order or, at least, to effect significant changes upon its most general coordinates.

However, several other passages from *On Populist Reason* seem quite conducive to an opposite conclusion, for the supposed primacy of politics would seem not be so as it is indicated that 'some degree of crisis in the old structure is a necessary precondition of populism' (2005a: 177). Furthermore, Laclau (2005a: 191) asserts that 'when we have a highly institutionalized society, equivalential logics have less terrain on which to operate; as a result, populist rhetoric becomes a commodity lacking any sort of hegemonic depth'. Therefore, as Arditi (2010: 494) has noted, 'if the political has a primary structuring role, then it must also be able to trigger a de-institutionalization of the given system instead of depending of the presence of a crisis to generate its subversive and reconstructive effects'. Again, one wonders what that 'degree of crisis' Laclau speaks of amounts to in the end, as well as what 'old structure' ultimately refers to, as the very possibility of a social structure underlying the play of differences seems to be forbidden by post-Marxism's own theoretical premises. Grounding the latter upon capitalism's constitutive features and institutional requirements might help not only to clarify these issues but also to push post-Marxist discourse theory beyond its own self-imposed limits.

Let's recap. It is our contention that Laclau's revision of Marxist theory, while certainly successful in recasting the study of political interactions along markedly non-essentialist lines, appears nonetheless seriously flawed, on the one hand, by an over-simplistic account of the actual diversity of social institutions and, on the other, by an insufficient consideration of the extent to which capitalism's internal dynamics affect the diachronic evolution of the societies under scrutiny. The intra-theoretical effects of the omissions just indicated can be observed, we contend, in a number of areas of his work. It is precisely the need to theoretically confront these issues which motivates our having recourse to SSA theory. However, before attempting a sort of synthesis between the two, it is necessary to review in detail what the pitfalls of SSA theory are in our view, and how the latter would profit from incorporating certain Laclauian insights. The next chapter is devoted to these issues.

Acknowledgments

Parts of this chapter have already been published as 'Ernesto Laclau's oblivion of political economy. Capitalism and institutions in post-Marxist discourse theory' in *Rethinking Marxism*, 32 (2), 2020. The author thanks Taylor & Francis for granting permission for re-printing them here.

Notes

1 'The differential positions, insofar as they appear articulated within a discourse, we will call *moments*. By contrast, we will call *element* any difference that is not discursively articulated' (Laclau and Mouffe 2001: 105).

2 'Let us give the example of a straightforward demand: a group of people living in a certain neighborhood want a bus route introduced to transport them from their places of residence to the area in which most of them work. [...] Let us suppose that the request is rejected. A situation of social frustration will, no doubt, derive from that decision. But if it is only *one* demand that is not satisfied, that will not alter the situation substantially. If, however, for whatever reason, the variety of demands that do not find satisfaction is very large, that multiple frustration will trigger social logics of an entirely different kind. If, for instance, the group of people in that area who have been frustrated in their request for better transportation find that their neighbors are equally unsatisfied *in their* claims at the levels of security, water supply, housing, schooling, and so on, some kind of solidarity will arise between them all: all will share the fact that their demands remain unsatisfied. That is, the demands share a *negative* dimension beyond their positive differential nature.

'A social situation in which demands tend to reaggregate themselves on the negative basis that they all remain unsatisfied is the first precondition – but by no means the only one – of that mode of political articulation that we call populism. [...] [T]he more social demands tend to be differentially absorbed within a successful institutional system, the weaker the equivalential links will be and the more unlikely the constitution of a popular subjectivity; conversely, a situation in which a plurality of unsatisfied demands and an increasing inability of the institutional system to absorb them differentially co-exist, creates the conditions leading to a populist rupture' (Laclau 2005b: 36–7).

3 '[Overdetermination] is a very precise type of fusion entailing a symbolic dimension and a plurality of meanings. [It] is constituted in the field of the symbolic, and has no meaning whatsoever outside it' (Laclau and Mouffe 2001: 97).

4 Social Structures of Accumulation theory

A re-assessment

This chapter will attempt a reformulation of SSA theory along anti-essentialist lines with the help of certain theoretical elements from the work of Ernesto Laclau. Firstly, SSA theory's two initial formulations will be reviewed. While they helped define the initial shape of SSA theory in its early stages, some internal assumptions prevented an accurate appreciation of the historical novelty represented by neoliberalism during the last decades. In relation to the former, secondly, the reformulation introduced by Wolfson and Kotz will be presented, as it managed to overcome such limitations in order to study the historical specificity of neoliberalism in its own right. While their version does represent a clear improvement with respect to previous formulations, there are still some internal problems which, in our view, reduce to a certain extent its explanatory potential. To that extent, thirdly, we will outline two separate criticisms related to some essentialist traits we find in their approach, namely, the risks involved in privileging the capital–labor contradiction regarding the formation of new political subjectivities over other social conflicts and the risk of downplaying the domain of historical contingency in their schemes of long-term historical transformation.

The first two versions

Initial formulations of SSA theory postulated the existence of an interlocking set of institutions, displaying internal relations of complementarity, whose existence signaled the presence of favorable conditions for sustained capitalist economic activity over the long run. The integrated and self-reinforcing character of their articulation granted the resulting institutional configuration the capacity to be jointly reproduced over time. Its eventual dissolution would indicate increasing difficulties for continuing capitalist activity, thus giving rise to identifiable stages within capitalist history. Despite their multiple commonalities, two different strands of SSA theory in its early days can be identified. Their most relevant difference derives from the nature of the ultimate role institutions are supposed to play in fostering systemic reproduction. On the one hand, Gordon et al. (1982) stress the necessary requirements of predictability and institutional stability capitalists demand for productive accumulation to proceed. On the other, Bowles et al. (1983; 1990) lay their emphasis instead on the role institutions play in securing and safeguarding capitalist class's power over other social groups. Each will be analyzed in turn.

Segmented Work, Divided Workers

The publication of *Segmented Work, Divided Workers* (1982) by David Gordon, Richard Edwards, and Michael Reich constituted the first systematic exposition of SSA theory to date. Aimed at providing an explanation for the systematic recurrence, in societies where capitalism is the dominant mode of production, of long periods of (relative) institutional stability followed up by others marked by intense social upheaval and institutional transformation, they drew from various intellectual sources. From Marxist political economy, they derived their understanding of capitalism as an inherently conflictual system, plagued by several internal contradictions manifested in recurrent blockages upon the accumulation process; from Keynesian economics, their view of investment decisions as being inherently unstable, subject to diachronic fluctuations derived from changing expectations and recurrent imbalances between consumption and investment; from institutional economics, they drew the impossibility to fully dissociate economic activity from the overall social environment in which it finds itself embedded; and, lastly, they took from the pre-existing Labor Market Segmentation literature their analyses of the labor process as being grounded in existing capitalist-induced divisions within the working class.

It argued that capital accumulation cannot take place in an institutional vacuum, as neoclassical economics would contend, but, on the contrary, it needs a set of institutions supporting it: 'The accumulation of capital through capitalist production cannot take place either in a vacuum or in a chaos. [...] Without a stable and favorable external environment, capitalist investment in production will not proceed' (Gordon et al. 1982: 23). In a recognizable Keynesian fashion, they argued that individual capitalists' microeconomic investment decisions were necessarily undertaken within an environment plagued by uncertainty, so that institutions were needed in order, on the one hand, to stabilize the various links existing between capital accumulation and other social processes and, on the other, to ensure a minimum degree of predictability about the expected rates of return of the aforementioned investment decisions. An SSA, therefore, referred to 'all the institutions that impinge upon the accumulation process' (Gordon et al. 1982: 23).

These institutions ought to display some degree of internal coherence for their joint reproduction to be secured over time. However, sooner or later, the symbiotic relation between this institutional architecture and capitalist accumulation and/or growth will come to an end, for 'successful capital accumulation ultimately either runs up against limits imposed by the existing institutional structure or begins to destabilize that structure' (Gordon et al. 1982: 29). Once these limits are reached, economic activity will not proceed as it used to, giving rise in turn to a new period marked by widespread social contention to determine the institutional underpinnings characterizing the next period of long-lasting institutional stability. It thus follows that successive SSAs ultimately correspond to distinct and identifiable stages of capitalism:[1]

> A stage of capitalism can be conceived as the ensemble of economic, political and ideological institutions which serve to reproduce capitalist relations of production and accumulation. This is the definition of the SSA. Capitalism proceeds from one stage to the next when the SSA undergoes disintegration, producing crisis. The crisis can only be resolved through the construction of a new SSA, inaugurating a new stage of capitalism. The successive stages of capitalism are thus the successive SSAs in capitalist history.
>
> (McDonough 1994a: 80)

As a theory of capitalist stages, SSA theory represented significant theoretical advancements when compared with previous formulations. On the one hand, the emphasis on cyclical regularity of the first versions (e.g. Kondratieff 1935; Schumpeter 1939) was abandoned in favor of an explicit recognition of historical contingency, thus preventing any ex ante prevision of capitalist stages' temporal duration. On the other, single-factor explanations of long-swing were abandoned by situating the resulting institutional structure, together with the interrelations among its components it contains, at the very center of the analysis. However, several theoretical issues were left unspecified or, at least, unsatisfactorily addressed.

Firstly, no clear indication was provided regarding which institutions ought to be considered as integral parts of an SSA, and which others were to be considered external to the former. Gordon et al. (1982: 23–4) provide a list of 12 different institutions satisfying diverse requirements of a well-functioning accumulation process, ranging from the system of money and credit, through the labor process, to the pattern of state involvement. This 'laundry list approach' (Kotz 1994a: 54) would need to be supplemented by some sort of immanent theoretical criteria specifying the conditions determining whether one institution deserves to be included within the list of constituent institutions. Otherwise, it merely stands as a discretionary list of various elements with no theoretically specified relations among themselves. Secondly, it is not clear what it is that grants the ensuing list of institutional requirements some sort of internal unity. Without specifying the ultimate nature of their interconnection, SSA theory is unable to play the role assigned to it as a theory of capitalist stages for, as McDonough has rightly noted, 'a SSA as a whole can only experience breakdown if it contains some internal unity which is in turn susceptible to disintegration' (McDonough 1994a: 77). These issues will be dealt with in much greater length in the following sections of this chapter.

Capitalist power at the center of the analysis

Soon after the publication of *Segmented Work, Divided Workers*, a distinct, but clearly interrelated, strand of SSA theory emerged in subsequent publications (e.g. Bowles et al. 1983; 1986; 1989; 1990; Gordon et al. 1987; Weisskopf et al. 1985). The conflation of successive SSAs with equally successive capitalist stages is here maintained, as well as the existing link between a well-operating SSA and high rates of growth and/or accumulation. This time, however, the crucial role played by its constituent institutions is not restricted to granting the required levels of predictability and stability for individual capitalists to reinvert their profits in productive activity. Instead, the focus is now shifted to the role institutions play in securing capitalist power against competing social groups. A definition of SSAs thus ensures, as 'the institutional structures which regulate both the conflicting interests in the profitmaking process and the closely associated process of accumulation and growth' (Bowles et al. 1989: 112).

They picture capitalist societies as comprising several distinct social groups with antagonistic interests, of which the capitalist class is deemed to be the most relevant one when appraising societies' historical evolution: 'Capitalism may be insightfully analyzed as a contradictory system of power relationships that evolves in large measure through the continuing but changing forms of class struggle, international conflict and other tensions to which its structure gives rise' (Bowles et al. 1986: 157). The role of SSAs in securing capitalist power affects the level of the profit rate which, in turn, conditions the level of productive investment that is to be obtained from such institutional structure: 'Profitability conditions the pace of accumulation which in turn substantially regulates the rate of economic growth' (Gordon et al. 1987: 47). It thus follows that profits are eminently political in nature, a result of the capacity of the capitalist class to fight back competing claims by subordinate social groups:

> Profits are [...] a deduction from net output made possible by the power of the capitalist class over other economic actors with which it deals. [...] It may be illuminating, then, to consider profits as the spoils of a three-front war fought by capital in its dealings with workers, foreign buyers and sellers, and the state (or indirectly with the citizenry).
>
> (Bowles et al. 1986: 137)

Their analysis of the Postwar SSA in the US is illuminating in this respect. Bowles et al. (1983) argue that it comprised three main institutional pillars, each reflecting the temporary stabilization of the relations between the capitalist class and the remaining social groups with which it necessarily had to interact. Firstly, the 'Capital–Labor Accord' accepted unions as legitimate representatives of workers' interests, sharing with capital the gains derived from rising productivity, in exchange for, on the one hand, the purge of the most militant unions and, on the other, absolute control by capital over the management of the labor process (Bowles et al. 1983: 70–5). Secondly, the 'Capitalist–Citizen

Accord' permitted greater State's involvement directed at alleviating some of the most pervasive side effects of a market economy (e.g. granting a minimum of economic security to the general population, environmental protection, consumer product safety) in exchange for not questioning capital accumulation requirements as the supreme guide of public policy (Bowles et al. 1983: 75–9). Thirdly, the dominion of the US worldwide, which the authors termed '*Pax Americana*', ensured a steady supply of the raw materials needed for expanding US industrial production, while, at the same time, the US's foreign aid served as a primary source of demand for US exports (Bowles et al. 1983: 65–70). Lastly, Gordon et al. (1987: 46) contended that 'capital's ability to fight effectively on these three fronts will further be affected by the intensity of inter-capitalist competition, determining how tightly and cohesively its troops are organized for battle', thus adding a fourth pillar to the postwar institutional architecture, the 'Moderation of Inter-Capitalist Rivalry', where attenuated competition, in the form of eminently oligopolistic markets, together with a considerably stable and rising aggregate demand, granted capital long-term horizons when planning their investment decisions.

One of the most important corollaries to this strand of SSA theory is the postulate that no perfect balance will ever be found, in the long run, regarding the strength of capital relative to other subaltern social groups. Internal contradictions may be managed and/or pacified, but never completely eradicated: Capital can be either 'too strong' or 'too weak' (Weisskopf et al. 1985; Gordon et al. 1987). In the former case, when capital is 'too strong', it can skew the income distribution to its favor, thus compromising its most relevant sources of aggregate demand. In this case it gives rise to 'underconsumption' crisis tendencies, ultimately leading to crises of surplus value realization. On the contrary, when capital is 'too weak', working class action reduces the rate of exploitation, squeezing existing profits and thus compromising further investment, ultimately giving rise to crises in surplus value production. This theoretical intuition will be widely used in subsequent reformulations of SSA theory, including our own.

While the emphasis on the relation existing between the social determination of economic surplus and co-existing political struggles is one we certainly favor, the understanding of power these authors put forwards is remarkably at odds with the post-Althusserian, post-foundationalist approach we are here advocating. For in their framework, power appears as something external to agents, something they can make use of, instead of something that constitutes them as agents in the first place. Moreover, their interest in econometric modeling leads them to impute to agents a type of rationality perhaps too reminiscent of neoclassical rationality (Norton 1988). Although indisputably more nuanced and complex than the orthodox approach, agents' interests appear *a priori* fixed and immutable, thus leaving virtually no room for relatively autonomous political logics to operate. This reductionist understanding of political interaction, which abstractly determines agents' behavior without properly acknowledging the constitutive role of contingent social logics regarding those agent's very identity, as well as their interests, constitutes of our main axes of contention with this version of SSA theory.

The riddle of neoliberalism: Wolfson and Kotz's reformulation

Both versions of SSA theory were elaborated at a time when the decay of the Postwar SSA in the US seemed to be self-evident. The smooth functioning of capitalism that had hitherto characterized the three decades after 1945 in the main Western economies was being interrupted at the time by an accumulation of both internal and external imbalances. Discerning which shape those economies would be taking in the coming years was one of the main aims of the theory.

In this context, emerging as a middle-range theory trying to account for capitalism's diachronic and synchronic variety, SSA theory inevitably took the postwar period as a historical standard against which to measure other historical stages.[2] Both Gordon et al.'s (1982) version, which focused, in sharp Keynesian fashion, on how a well-established SSA reduced the inherent uncertainty and instability affecting the capitalist accumulation process, as well as Bowles et al.'s (1983; 1986) slight reformulation of the former, which emphasized the ability of institutions to secure and enhance capitalists' power, linked the successful operation of an SSA with high rates of both capital accumulation and economic growth in the economy as a whole. Whereas those links certainly seemed to characterize the postwar period in most Western economies, neoliberal capitalism had been showing neither high rates of capital accumulation nor high rates of growth, thus apparently questioning one of the central tenets of the theory.

After a decade of intense institutional restructuring in the 1980s, it seemed clear that a new coherent institutional ensemble had been put in place by the early 1990s, despite its performance in terms of growth appearing considerably poorer in relation to those attained during the previous long expansion. Therefore, the initial interpretation of SSA theory seemed to be in need of reformulation if an accurate account of neoliberal capitalism was to be provided. Lippit (1997) and Reich (1997) argued that a new institutional structure had consolidated from the 1980s onwards, once the negative effects of the 'Great Repression' (Bowles et al. 1983) in terms of growth had been overcome. The apparent success of the 'New Economy' in the United States led others to follow these same conclusions (e.g. Kotz 2003a; McDonough 2003).

Nevertheless, the conclusion that a new SSA had been eventually consolidated during the 1980s was not unanimously adopted. In a series of articles, O'Hara (2006) argued that US neoliberalism had been generating too much systemic instability, as well as recurrent recessions, to be considered a successful SSA. He argued that financial deregulation, one of the main pillars of the new institutional structure, had been generating too much financial instability; labor productivity growth had been sluggish all throughout the period in question; and he found no empirical correlation between growth rates across countries and the implementation of neoliberal policies or with the transnationalization of firms. Contrary to these views, we argue in favor of understanding neoliberalism as a successful SSA due to its duration, its ability in promoting profit making, and, crucially, the high degree of complementarity shown by its constituent institutions.

In order to incorporate O'Hara's criticisms within the SSA framework, Kotz (2003b) and Wolfson (2003) severed the link between institutional stability and rapid growth and/or accumulation that had characterized SSA theory's earlier versions. To that extent, they introduced the concept of Institutional Structure (IS), understood as a:

> coherent set of economic, political, and cultural/ideological institutions that provide a structure for capitalist economic activity. [It] supports the appropriation of surplus value, the pursuit of which drives the circuit of capital. Surplus value has various uses, one of which is the accumulation of capital.
>
> (Kotz 2003b: 264)

Therefore, they displaced the focus of the analysis from the accumulation process to the circuit of capital. Well-functioning SSAs ought to protect the main interest of individual capitalists, that is, to guarantee a sustained appropriation of surplus value over time.

Therefore, it is implicit in their formulation that the *pace* of capital accumulation at the aggregate level is not a 'core' interest of individual capitalists but a by-product of their aggregate individual decisions. Hence, while some institutional ensembles might foster rapid accumulation, others might be equally successful, in the sense of securing surplus value appropriation, despite not yielding a high rate of aggregate growth. Furthermore, the resulting institutions must show a certain degree of internal coherence: 'The economic, political, ideological, and cultural institutions of any SSA are mutually compatible and supportive of each other' (McDonough et al. 2010: 2), so that a unified and internally coherent ensemble results. Wolfson and Kotz (2010: 80) postulate that the ultimate rationale for its internal coherence is given by the role played by institutions in (temporarily) stabilizing the core contradictions of capitalism, that is, that between capital and labor as well as those internal to each class.

When grounding their theoretical reformulation, Wolfson and Kotz (2010) claimed that in Gordon et al.'s (1982) seminal contribution there is an unjustified theoretical leap from a qualitative discussion of the support provided by institutions to the circuit of money-capital, on the one hand, to quantitative remarks on the pace of capital accumulation, on the other. In the circuit of money-capital, usually symbolized as M–C–C′–M′, the last term M′ is not yet money-capital, as Gordon et al. (1982) seem to assume, but money-revenue. Capital accumulation will only take place if money-revenue is put back into the first stage of the circuit of money-capital, that is, if it becomes money-capital again (Kotz 2006). The conditions determining the transformation of money-revenue into money-capital will constitute, precisely, the main criteria to distinguish among different ISs.

Accordingly, they posit the existence of two types of IS, a Liberal IS and a Regulated IS. Whereas the former will be characterized by a clear dominance of capital over labor, cut-throat competition among capital units, limited regulation of market forces by the State, and a 'free-market' and individualist ideology, the latter will exhibit a certain degree of cooperation between capital and labor, active involvement by nonmarket actors in regulating the economy, co-respective behavior among capitalists, and a dominant ideology defending the 'mixed' management of the economy. Under this scheme, the Postwar SSA would qualify as a Regulated IS, whereas the Neoliberal SSA would qualify as a Liberal IS. Despite both institutional frameworks securing the systematic appropriation of surplus value by individual capitalists, only Regulated SSAs will deliver high rates of capital accumulation, as the anarchic, cut-throat inter-capitalist competition that characterizes Liberal SSAs causes a high degree of instability that eventually discourages the reinvestment of surplus value into the circuit of money-capital.[3]

With this distinction in mind, a wide agreement has emerged in the SSA literature regarding the characterization of neoliberalism as a coherent institutional structure that has enabled the capitalist class to secure a growing appropriation of surplus value, despite not having fostered high rates of economic growth and capital accumulation. Nonetheless, there has been a certain degree of variation in identifying the key features of this neoliberal SSA, and, thus, the ultimate source of its historical specificity. Some have pointed out the intimate link between neoliberalism and heightened global economic integration (McDonough 2003; Nardone and McDonough 2010); the growing relevance and power of financial capital (Tabb 2010); the reconfiguration of the labor process due to the continuous threat of spatial relocation facilitated by the global integration of the circuit of capital (Wallace and Brady 2010); a new alliance between managers and financial capital, replacing the old 'Capital–Labor Accord' (Boyer 2010); or the new conditions of international competition being faced by big capital (Kotz 2002). Notwithstanding a certain disagreement in identifying which is the key institutional trait of the neoliberal period, there is a wide agreement over most of its main institutional features. A comprehensive list is provided by Lippit (2014), who singles out seven main features characterizing the neoliberal SSA: Strengthening of capital relative to labor, growing importance of financial innovation and speculation, limited government action, deregulation of market activities, globalization of trade and investment, corporate restructuring through the financial sector, and lastly, capital markets favorable to entrepreneurial companies.

However, the relatively long lifespan of the neoliberal SSA does not mean that it does not contain internal contradictions. Quite the contrary; it is precisely its ability to contain and displace such severe contradictions that forces us to qualify it as a successful SSA. Kotz and McDonough (2010) identify seven such contradictions:

1. A growing imbalance between rising profits and stagnating wages.
2. The speculative nature of the financial sector.
3. A tendency for asset bubbles to emerge due to growing concentration of wealth and limited real investment opportunities.
4. A high degree of global integration that synchronizes the business cycles of the major countries.
5. The dollar as global reserve currency, together with persistent US Balance of Payments deficits.
6. Capital domination over labor, which may prompt radical class rebellion.
7. Depletion of natural resources and risk of climate change.

The severity of these contradictions eventually led to the financial crisis of 2008, which marks the beginning of the systemic crisis of the neoliberal SSA. Its abrupt occurrence is characteristic of Liberal SSAs, where the growing imbalance between stagnating real wages and increasing labor productivity harbors a major contradiction between the necessary conditions for the creation of surplus value and the conditions for its realization. This situation would have led to a major implosion of the neoliberal SSA early on, because it was ultimately counterbalanced by two other main institutional pillars of the neoliberal SSA, and of any Liberal SSA in general, namely, an increasingly autonomous financial sector prone to highly speculative and risky activities, and an inner tendency for asset bubbles to emerge. Hence, the same developments that threatened the occurrence of a crisis of underconsumption, due to the systematic transfer of income and wealth toward the upper layers of the distribution, set the conditions that allowed for both a debt-financed consumption explosion in times of wage repression.

The neoliberal SSA renders clear the degree to which an SSA's very stability is granted by the mutual containment and sustainment of its composing contradictions, that is, it is the degree of complementarity and mutual co-implication among its internal contradictions which grants stability to the whole. The assertion that the current crisis symbolizes the decay of the neoliberal SSA due to the internal implosion of its contradictions finds virtually no objection within the SSA literature (e.g. Kotz 2010b; 2015; Lippit 2010; 2014; Nardone and McDonough 2010). SSA theory firmly concludes that a period of heightened conflict and struggle among different groups is a necessary corollary to any process of SSA decomposition, the final outcome of which cannot be known in advance by looking exclusively at the development of its internal contradictions.

Nevertheless, despite the several merits present in Wolfson and Kotz's (2010) reformulation, it is our view that certain issues related to the length of the crisis period, the structure and form of its internal struggles, and the degree of path-dependency in the process of institutional restructuring, which to a certain extent have permeated SSA literature since its inception, remain in need of further theoretical clarification and reformulation.

Overdetermination: From the heterogeneity of struggles to internal unity

SSA theory contends that profound and wide-ranging institutional restructuring should follow the disintegration of the neoliberal SSA. However, in order to think about radical institutional change within the SSA framework and, thus, the nature and content of such a change, it becomes necessary to analyze the conditions given in the literature to ascertain the unity and internal coherence of a given institutional ensemble. It has already been noted above how Gordon et al.'s (1982: 24) definition of SSAs as 'all the institutions that impinge upon the accumulation process' was intrinsically flawed, insofar as it was not supplemented by any intra-theoretical criteria determining the precise conditions required for any single institution to be included within the list; nor was any indication given about the nature of their interrelation, that is, about what turned an amalgam of discrete elements into a (more or less) coherent whole. Thus, by not integrating them into a unity, they leave the theory ill-suited to account for long swings of capital accumulation:

> Without a theory of the SSA as a whole, the SSA is unable to play the role assigned to it in the explanation of long waves. [...] An SSA as a whole can only experience breakdown if it contains some internal unity which is in turn susceptible to disintegration.
>
> (McDonough 1994a: 74)

It is this theoretical inconsistency that both Kotz (1994a) and McDonough (1994a) aimed at offering an answer to. Kotz (1994a) argued that the institutional integrity of a given SSA is derived from the existence of a set of 'core' institutions, namely, those that manage to stabilize the conflicts inherent to capitalist relations of production (class conflict and intra-class competition). Only these 'core' institutions must necessarily be in place at the beginning of a new long expansion, while the 'peripheral' ones will be added subsequently as the upsurge of capital investment consolidates itself. Therefore, according to Kotz (1994a), stabilizing class conflict and competition is at the core of any SSA formation and durability. It follows that the institutions directly implicated in such 'pacifying' activity ought to be in place at the beginning of the expansion phase, as well as to show a high degree of stability throughout such SSA's time span.

In contrast, McDonough (1994a) offers a qualitatively different answer to the nature of SSA integrity. He asserts that each SSA is always configured around a single institution or event that serves as its 'unifying principle', historically contingent and unique to each SSA. Hence, he parallels Kotz in identifying a limited set of institutions or events that can account for SSA's unity. Nevertheless, these are not related to any structural feature of the capitalist mode of production but, rather, to a contingent event whose ultimate nature is left unspecified. For instance, the Postwar SSA in the US would have been anchored around the 'unifying principle' of World War II which, despite conditioning the nature of the remaining institutional buttresses of that SSA, did not have any direct relation to the circuit of capital or to the accumulation process (McDonough 1994b).

With respect to its seminal formulation by Gordon et al. (1982), these two approaches offer compelling advantages to think of radical institutional change within the SSA framework. On the one hand, Kotz stresses the inherently conflictual nature of social relations under capitalism, which thus conditions and limits the possibilities existing at the purely political level to undertake institutional and social transformation. Only an institutional arrangement that manages to pacify the inherently conflictual relations between capital and labor will be able to consolidate itself in the long term. On the other hand, McDonough's intervention can be read as an invitation to acknowledge the relevance of the external environment in which accumulation takes place, while at the same time escaping from certain teleological Marxist narratives that limit the scope of strictly political action in redefining the contours of social life under capitalism.

In our view, Kotz's understanding might prove to be too narrowly confined to class relations, thus obliterating the ultimately heterogeneous and incommensurable nature of social conflicts in contemporary capitalist societies, while McDonough might be advocating for a too-open approach, as virtually no limits are set to the nature of the events or institutions that can function as a unifying principle for a newly emerging SSA. Furthermore, as Lippit (2010) has pointed out, while Kotz (1994a) can correctly account for the interrelation between different institutional spheres through a partition between 'core' and 'periphery', he cannot properly account for the structural integrity of an SSA, as no indication is provided regarding the mode of interrelation between the two, nor about the constraints operating on the emergence of 'peripheral' institutions once the 'core' ones are already well established. McDonough (1994a), by directing his attention to a single unifying principle, manages to avoid that problem.

Although these two contributions constitute a significant advancement with respect to previous accounts of structural integrity in the SSA literature, they are still grounded in a conception of SSAs that links institutional stability to high aggregate rates of growth and/or accumulation. As it was argued above, this framework needed to be modified to account for the specificities of the neoliberal SSA. The modifications introduced by Wolfson and Kotz (2010) in the SSA framework in order to account for the sluggish rates of both labor productivity and aggregate economic growth that characterize the neoliberal SSA have already been commented on above. The stability and persistence shown by the neoliberal SSA led them to reinterpret an SSA as a 'coherent institutional structure that supports capitalist profit-making and also provides a framework for the accumulation of capital, but it does not necessarily promote a "rapid" rate of capital accumulation' (Wolfson and Kotz 2010: 79).

Thus, on the one hand, Wolfson and Kotz (2010) build upon Kotz's (1994a) previous insight that the 'core' institutions of each SSA are those that manage to stabilize class conflict and competition, while enlarging it to the extent that 'the institutions that constitute an SSA, including those of neoliberalism, reflect the (temporary) stabilization of the contradictions of capitalism' (Wolfson and Kotz 2010: 80), by which they mean contradictions internal to each class and, above all, the one between capital and labor. On the other hand, whereas Kotz (1994a) could not satisfactorily account for SSA's internal unity, Wolfson and Kotz (2010: 80) somehow build upon McDonough's (1994a) 'unifying principle' to assert that 'the stabilization of the contradiction between capital and labor provides the foundation for the institutional restructuring that produces a new SSA'. Therefore, pacifying/stabilizing capitalism's central contradiction between labor and capital becomes the cornerstone of each new institutional structure, whose ultimate goal is to support the process of capitalist profit-making while, in turn, implicitly framing the process of capital accumulation. At this point, two objections ought to be posed to the framework presented by Wolfson and Kotz (2010). The first one is related to their privileging of the capital–labor contradiction, and the second one to a somehow veiled historical determinism.

Privileging the capital–labor contradiction

Wolfson and Kotz (2010: 80) conceive the capital-labor contradiction to be 'the most important contradiction in capitalist society, [whose stabilization] provides the foundation for the institutional restructuring that produces a new SSA', a contention at odds with the anti-essentialist approach advocated here. From the assertion that the stabilization of the capital–labor relation is a central component of any well-established capitalist institutional environment, so that the continuous extraction of surplus value is enabled over time, it is illegitimate to conclude that the stabilizing function of '*all* the stable institutional structures of a capitalist society' (Wolfson 2003: 258, emphasis added) can be referred, in the last instance, to either between- or intra-class conflicts. This would imply introducing again, we contend, an economicist and essentialist account of social relations the initial formulations of SSA theory aimed at doing away with, insofar as one particular social conflict would be posited to constitute the ultimate rationale for the multifarious institutional appearance of a given capitalist society. Despite the conflict between capital and labor being the most important one to understand social dynamics under capitalism, due to its constitutive role in the production process, not all social conflicts can ultimately be referred back to it. Contradictions, including those between capital and labor, never present themselves in isolation, but always appear blended with phenomena pertaining to other institutional spheres, so that there is a process of co-implication and mutual constitution between contradictions pertaining to very different institutional domains, each reflecting the temporary fix of other co-existing ones. Indeed, these different institutional domains are but the reflexive effect of the successful stabilization or sedimentation of these contradictions, which can under no circumstances be ultimately reduced to one single principle. Whereas objectivity itself emerges out of the pacification of social contradictions, as Wolfson and Kotz would maintain, we disagree with positing one of them as the 'hidden truth' of the rest.

While, certainly, the extraction of surplus value, and, thus, the production process, is a central element of any capitalist social totality, referring back to the existing multiplicity of social conflicts and antagonisms to the production process cannot but obscure the potential lines of fracture existing in a given institutional ensemble at a given point in time. Insofar as the social totality is constitutively complex, its inner coherence being derived from contingently drawn relations of mutual constitution among its different institutional domains, no social domain can be presumed to hold the key to decipher its outer appearance. Social complexity is ontologically primary. Take, for instance, struggles having to do with race, gender, or even generational conflicts such as those between pensioners and workers. While they are definitely overdetermined by the institutional fix of the production process, they cannot be subsumed within the latter. Not only are these non-class struggles affected by a wide array of cultural-historical social processes whose relation to the configuration of the production process is indirect at most, thus displaying the latter's own imprint upon their historically specific shape, but, also, they themselves affect the very form of the capital–labor relation itself. It thus follows that the level of social institutionalization that is needed to obtain a sustained extraction of surplus value over time cannot be reduced to the pacification and control of the labor process, for the stability of aspirations and expectations that are needed for a smooth functioning of a capitalist society also concern workers' identities as consumers, or citizens, or family members, and, therefore, needs the temporary pacification of all those domains whose relation to the production process might be merely tangential.

Without a majority of agents assuming a certain degree of 'naturalness' regarding their respective roles in the social whole, the resulting level of social unrest would have utterly compromised the systematic appropriation of surplus value by the capitalist class. While stabilizing the conditions under which the production process is undertaken (most prominently, the capital–labor relation) is, indeed, crucial to attain a high degree of social peace in any capitalist society, it is the latter, we contend, that stands as the ultimate foundation for any long period of institutional stability under capitalism. Thus, while the reach of such social peace exceeds those struggles directly affected by the configuration of the production process, it simultaneously constitutes a *sine qua non* condition for the latter to function properly. In case these other (incommensurable) struggles were not correctly pacified, thus overflowing the existing institutional channels to deal with them, the resulting level of social turmoil would have compromised the sustained surplus value extraction that is found at the very core of any well-functioning SSA.

Within the SSA literature, the voice that has put greater emphasis upon the relevance carried by non-class struggles to apprehend institutional stability is Lippit's (2005; 2010; 2014): 'Society is the site of a multitude of conflicts, and the way in which these play out often bears on creating favorable conditions for accumulation without specifically seeking that objective' (Lippit 2005: 35). Nevertheless, while these conflicts are ultimately irreducible to each other, a certain alignment among their political expression must be produced which, far from eradicating them, ensures that their own respective manifestation does not unsettle the stability of the social whole. Laclau and Mouffe's (2001) understanding of hegemony refers, precisely, to such socio-symbolic framework through which a certain element of commonality among initially plural demands and subjectivities is produced, while, simultaneously, establishing internal relations of hierarchy among those included within the hegemonic articulation itself. A sedimented objectivity thus ensues where the differential and hierarchical integration of certain social groups co-exists with the outright exclusion experienced by others. In terms of the current discussion, the crucial insight here is that the basis for the aggregation of these differential conflicts does not rest in each conflict's own identity, but on an inherently political intervention for, despite 'the centrality of economic processes in capitalist societies, [...] capitalist reproduction [cannot] be reduced to a single, self-defining mechanism' (Laclau 2005a: 237). In sum, whereas the contradiction between capital and labor is the cornerstone around which any capitalist institutional structure is to be anchored, to appraise the conditions for institutional stability, and, thus, for social transformation, attention should not be directed exclusively to the former but, rather, to how initially plural subjectivities and antagonisms are articulated so that something in common among them emerges out of that very act of political articulation.

A veiled historical determinism?

The second objection has to do with the hypothesized tendency of Liberal and Regulated SSAs to alternate periodically with each other (Kotz 2003b; Kotz and Wolfson 2004; Wolfson 2003). Building upon Polanyi's (1957) 'double movement', it is posited that:

> the stabilization of the contradictions of capitalism has a certain coherence, which is represented either by the principle of the free market or the principle of regulation. Moreover, that coherence is shaped in large part by the stabilization of the fundamental contradiction between capital and labor.
>
> (Wolfson 2003: 259)

Therefore, the two varieties of SSA differ on how the capital–labor contradiction is temporarily stabilized.

On the one hand, Regulated SSAs show a tendency to 'profit-squeeze' crises due to the accumulation of demands over existing profits. Thus, crises would emerge due to capital being 'too weak' (Gordon et al. 1987). On the other hand, Liberal SSAs are characterized by capital being 'too strong', which tends to lead to 'over-production' crises, whose source can be found either in underconsumption, overinvestment, or asset-bubble crisis tendencies (Kotz 2009). Theoretically, each ideal type of SSA can counterbalance the other's archetypical crisis tendency. Inasmuch as Regulated SSAs tend to undermine capital's structural power in the production sphere, its internal problems can be countervailed by reinforcing capital's prerogatives in the latter, that is, by building up a Liberal SSA. Conversely, insofar as capital's dominance in several social spheres tends to lead to insufficient aggregate demand in Liberal SSAs, it is argued that a Regulated SSA can fix the latter's internal imbalances by redistributing acquisitive power towards subaltern groups. Hence, as a result of the centrality granted to the stabilization of the capital–labor contradiction in understanding long-term social dynamics under capitalism, 'there seems to be a historical tendency for Liberal SSAs to alternate with Regulated SSAs' (Wolfson and Kotz 2010: 85).

This apparent cyclicality and determinacy between Regulated and Liberal SSAs has received several criticisms. McDonough (2010: fn13) remarks that, despite this formulation having a certain appeal at the theoretical level, Kotz (2003b) is forced to propose a questionable periodization of US capitalism, while Lippit (2010) criticizes this cyclicality for focusing too narrowly on the capital–labor contradiction while not paying due attention to non-class struggles as well as to other social processes external to capitalism's internal dynamics.

In our opinion, despite being defensible at the theoretical level that the inner contradictions and imbalances of each type of SSA can be correctly counterbalanced by the other one, there is a risk of this being just another way of imposing some sort of internal coherence to historical development. This would obliterate the role played in historical transformation by the constitutive role of politics and by historically contingent events whose occurrence cannot be accounted for by merely analyzing capitalism's internal dynamics. Moreover, the necessarily narrow set of historical observations (i.e. the four historical periods comprising capitalist history in the United States) makes theorizing an internal movement of history an inherently troublesome task. For instance, during the crisis phase of the Postwar SSA in the United States, many took for granted a historical tendency towards an increasing role of the State in the economy, which implied that the historical specificity of neoliberalism took until it was already well established to be theoretically grasped (see Reich 1993). There is a risk that by adding a fourth observation to that sample, that is, the neoliberal capitalist stage, one could incur the same sort of difficulties when trying to infer a historical tendency out of a small number of historical observations.

However, it must be noted that certain qualifications have been introduced to the apparent cyclicality of the theory, thus avoiding the potential indictment of having given in to some sort of outright mechanical determinism. Contingent historical conditions would thus play a role regarding the eventual implementation of both Liberal and Regulated SSAs, respectively. For instance, commenting upon the emergence of the neoliberal SSA in the United States, Kotz (2010a) points out that a more corporatist way out of the crisis of the Postwar SSA could have been a possible solution, were it not for concrete historical factors: 'It is not obvious that in the 1970s neoliberal restructuring was the only way, or the best way, to restore capitalist power'. He indicates four such conditions that explain why history followed the path it did, namely, a reference to an imagined perfect past that had certain appeal for big capital, the fact that socialism was no longer a threat to the dominance of big capital, the Great Depression seemed too far away for big capital to fear another system-threatening crisis, and, most important, the erosion of the monopoly power previously held by big capital in each country due to increasing globalization, which made them unable to benefit from the long-term advantages of a more regulated institutional structure. Nevertheless, it is still argued that:

> both theoretical considerations and historical evidence suggest that, within capitalism, the resolution of the long-run crisis of a liberal SSA requires the construction of a new regulated SSA, while the resolution of the long-run crisis of a regulated SSA is found in a new liberal SSA.
>
> (Kotz and Basu 2019: 21)

These issues acquire singular theoretical salience in the face of the current systemic crisis of neoliberalism. Regarding its eventual resolution, Kotz (2017) contends that, besides a potential transition to socialism, the current phase of economic stagnation can only be solved by a more statist version of capitalism, political action thus being capable of merely affecting whether an eminently progressive or regressive version of it ultimately triumphs. However, even though a transition towards a more regulated version of capitalism, capable of restoring aggregate demand growth, might be beneficial to capitalism's own systemic preservation, certain structural traits of the neoliberal stage might prevent such a scenario from eventually taking place.

On the one hand, any transition towards a more regulated version of capitalism would have to radically undo the current balance of forces between industrial and financial capital to the benefit of the former. However, given current worldwide over-accumulation problems in the tradable sectors (Brenner 2006), the average levels of profitability to be expected in the manufacturing sector make it implausible that the capitalist class will undertake such a movement in the absence of external coercion. On the other hand, the current transnational fragmentation of capitalist production processes heavily curtails the potential viability of any transformation towards a regulated version of capitalism that remains restricted to a single geographic area, insofar as the former would block the synergies between expanding productive capacity and rising aggregate demand that are found at the core of every Regulated SSA (Jaffee 2019). Moreover, a sustained downwards redistribution of income, together with widespread debt cancellation would be required if aggregate demand is to grow in line with productive capacity. In the end, these transformations would necessarily demand the emergence of a collective agency capable of curtailing financial capital's current prerogatives. Otherwise, in its absence, a self-perpetuating 'interregnum' where low growth rates, rising inequality, and mounting indebtedness mutually reinforcing each other might ensue (Streeck 2016). In sum, while Kotz and Basu (2019) might be right in asserting that only a more regulated version of capitalism will be able to overcome the current stagnation phase, in the absence of countervailing forces to financial capital's drive for self-preservation, irrespectively of its potentially beneficial consequences to the capitalist system as a whole, there are absolutely no guarantees that the current stagnation will not endlessly perpetuate itself.

Concluding comments

Let us recapitulate the argument so far. It has been contended that, despite the many advantages present in Wolfson and Kotz's reformulation of SSA theory, it carries within two main complications to apprehend the terms of radical institutional change within the SSA framework, namely, the privileges granted to the capital–labor contradiction to think of SSA formation and change, and certain presumptions of historical determinacy that run counter to SSA theory's initial aims. Indeed, the latter can only be maintained insofar as one holds to the former assumption. Refusing to grant such centrality to the stabilization of the capital–labor contradiction would render it impossible to postulate any sort of internal coherence to history by referring its evolution back to the expression of one single principle.

Within the current SSA literature, Lippit (2005; 2010; 2014) has upheld the position most proximate to our own regarding the scope of social processes to be considered when appraising a given SSA's institutional stability and/or change. Contrary to what he considers to be 'essentialist' accounts of SSA structural integrity provided by Kotz (1994a) and McDonough (1994a), he refers to Gordon's (1980) early insight that what gives unity to a given SSA are but the interrelations existing among its different institutional units. However, whereas Gordon seems to consider each institutional sphere as an isolated unit, Lippit argues in favor of the Althusserian concept of overdetermination, as reworked by Resnick and Wolff (1987), to apprehend the sources of SSA structural integrity, suggesting that 'each [institution] is shaped by and incorporates elements of the other institutions and social forces with which it interacts' (Lippit 2010: 55). That is, both the shape and the internal dynamics of each institutional sphere are constitutively affected by the joint interaction of all other spheres, together with other social processes and historical factors.

In order to grasp ongoing social dynamics, one should not look exclusively at how the capital–labor contradiction evolves, nor at how its necessary stabilization might itself foster a process of institutional restructuring but, instead, one has to consider precisely how these processes mutually constitute each other and interact with other social processes whose occurrence cannot be directly traced back to capitalism's own internal dynamics. This way, 'the forces contributing to the eventual collapse of all SSAs become more transparent' (Lippit 2010: 57). It thus follows that no privilege ought to be granted *a priori* to any given contradiction over the rest, as the key to correctly apprehend the internal dynamics of institutional change lies precisely in the interrelations existing between the multiple institutional spheres permeating the social field.

If social domains, on the one hand, are not immune to each other, and thus appear always 'contaminated' by developments occurring in co-existing spheres, and, on the other hand, they are constitutively affected by socio-historical processes idiosyncratic to the social formation under consideration, then it follows that no *a priori* hierarchy of social contradictions will ever be retrieved which remains valid for any and every social formation where capitalism is the dominant mode of production. Nevertheless, far from leading to some sort of epistemological nihilism, a hierarchical ordering of the various social contradictions at play in terms of their different degrees of social effectivity can only be obtained through a concrete analysis of the given conjuncture under consideration. Such an analysis should begin by identifying which among the main social processes and institutional domains play a more important role in ensuring the reproduction over time of the whole institutional assemblage under consideration; secondly, to ascertain the direction and intensity of their respective individual dynamics; thirdly, to identify what are the main internal contradictions these institutional domains harbor within themselves; and then, lastly, to examine how the latter relate among themselves at a given point in time, so that the internal dynamics of each can be either enhanced or attenuated through, precisely, their joint interaction.

Despite not denying the centrality that processes belonging to the sphere of capitalist production have to understand social dynamics under capitalism, we agree with Laclau in that the capital–labor contradiction can never find its expression without political mediation. Refusing to give any *a priori* primacy to any specific institution or struggle over others implies that, in a social field crisscrossed by multiple antagonisms (race, gender, environmental, etc.), a process of political articulation is needed so as to create a political subject susceptible of bringing about actual institutional transformation. Despite the centrality of the production process in accounting for social dynamics under capitalism, the social identities at play in the political struggle implicitly shaping the configuration of the former might bear no relation to those directly springing out of the production process itself.

That is, from the multiple conflicts and tensions that arise from the interaction among the various social processes that comprise the social totality, nothing can be inferred *a priori* regarding the concrete character of their political manifestation. While the existence of social antagonisms is an ineradicable feature of capitalist societies, their relative influence upon the ultimate direction of social change, as well as their very character as political demands, is ultimately determined through the hegemonic struggle itself.

Indeed, Laclau asserts that antagonism is not something that occurs in the interiority of the relations of production, but something that has to be discursively constructed by showing how the integration of agents into the production process denies other identities they have outside of it:

> It is obviously not being denied that conflicts exist between workers and entrepreneurs, but merely that they spring from the logical analysis of the wage-labor/capital relation. [Rather] the conflict is not internal to capitalist relations of production [...] but takes place between the relations of production and the worker's identity outside of them.
>
> (Laclau 1990a: 9)

Therefore, it is from the co-implication between the multiple identities each agent has that an antagonistic frontier in anti-capitalist lines can emerge, and not out of any essential quality of the capital–labor relation. Hence, relations of exploitation (i.e. the extraction of surplus labor) will only become politicized when the agents involved convert them into antagonistic relations. In order to grasp the sources of institutional change in the antagonistic nature of social relations under capitalism, therefore, one has to look for the overdetermination between the struggles pertaining to the production sphere and the multiplicity of identities outside of them. Every hegemonic articulation establishes a hierarchical relation among the subjects and conflicts it articulates, delimiting in turn which ones will enjoy a higher degree of visibility and which others will become peripheral.

Social stability under capitalism depends crucially upon the attainment of a level of social peace high enough for continued economic activity not to be disrupted by conflicts of various kinds. And this is specially so under neoliberalism, as capitalist relations of production have been increasingly extended to domains different to that of work, thus affecting agents not only as workers, but as pensioners, students, or citizens, for instance. In case these various non-class struggles were left unresolved, an oppositional movement that challenged the *statu quo* could emerge that, despite not having been constructed around explicit class-related identities, might as well foster social upheaval that, in an overdetermined manner, would affect the capital–labor relation itself. That is, whereas providing an institutional fix to the capital–labor relation is a *sine qua non* condition for any SSA to be consolidated, it need not figure explicitly in the very terms of the contention, even though the shape of the former will ultimately condition the very terrain upon which the latter will take place.

In sum, if it is acknowledged that social relations under capitalism are inherently conflictual, and that a well-established SSA is synonymous with enjoying a high degree of institutional stability that enables the extraction of surplus value to be sustained over time, then it follows that it is precisely the attainment of high levels of social peace which ultimately reveals the existence of a well-established SSA. Therefore, it is not only the control of the labor process (despite its utmost importance), nor even of all those aspects directly related to the production process, that which ensures the level of social stability necessary for maintaining high levels of economic activity. It is strictly necessary as well that agents show a level of consent sufficiently high regarding their multiple positions in the social fabric so as to satisfy the conditions characterizing a well-established SSA. But this level of consent also pertains to all those spheres of the social that only affect capitalist production tangentially, from which it follows that, for the dynamics of social change to be apprehended correctly, it is necessary to consider non-class identities and antagonisms together with their mode of articulation. In sum, it is our view that the theoretical categories of overdetermination and hegemony should become necessary elements of SSA theory to address its long-time concerns regarding SSA's establishment and decay. With these ideas in mind, the next chapter will attempt to slightly reformulate existing versions of SSA theory in order to offer a more nuanced treatment of political processes and interactions by granting greater scope to non-class struggles and expectations as well as to historical contingency, while simultaneously referring them back to capitalism's internal dynamics.

Acknowledgments

Parts of this chapter have already been published as 'Institutional change in Social Structures of Accumulation theory. An anti-essentialist approach', in *Review of Radical Political Economics*, 50 (2), 2018. The author thanks Sage Publishing for granting permission for re-printing them here.

Notes

1 Although initial formulations of SSA theory were concerned with the existence of 'long swings' regarding capital accumulation, greater recognition of the role played by historical contingency shifted the focus to 'capitalist stages' instead, due to the former's implicit assumption of cyclicality and/or regularity regarding its diachronic evolution.
2 See Mavroudeas (2006) for the difficulties implicit in 'middle-range' theories when trying to account for capitalism's diachronic variation.
3 Although both Wolfson and Kotz initially employed the term 'Institutional Structure', Wolfson and Kotz (2010) already adopt the term 'Social Structure of Accumulation' instead. However, the term now appears as completely devoid of connotations regarding the *rhythm* capital accumulation will display.

5 Social orders and capitalism

Towards an expanded SSA approach

The main objective of this chapter is to develop an understanding of social orders from a political economy perspective. As noted in previous chapters, the SSA literature lacks a comprehensive account of how socio-political alignments and consensuses are both established and subverted in relation to capitalism's internal dynamics, while, conversely, Laclau's discourse-theoretical account of political interactions needs to be supplemented by an equally rich apprehension of capitalist dynamics. In order to grant due recognition to the role played by capitalist dynamics in shaping the environment where socio-political interactions occur while, simultaneously asserting the irreducibility of the latter to any sort of epiphenomenal reflection of the former, we attempt to recast SSA theory along two main lines.

On the one hand, it is necessary to broaden the scope of SSA's lenses over social processes to include nonmarket activities.[1] Singularly, it remains crucial to our purposes to consider the manifold unpaid activities undertaken within households, including those which can be readily assimilated to labor (e.g. cleaning, cooking, etc.) as well as those more emotionally loaded and thus more difficult to commodify (those activities commonly grouped under the category of 'care'). On the other hand, we intend to significantly expand SSA theory's understanding of political agreements/consensuses in order to include the various activities and symbolic representations through which social orders are both instituted and subverted, reflecting the fact that well-functioning SSAs have to secure not only the various stages comprising the circuit of money-capital, but also the various social consensuses through which the various agents implicated in the former will come to terms with their own social condition. Moreover, an interpretation of the nature of the interrelation existing between the aforementioned social consensuses and the internal dynamics of the capitalist mode of production will be offered. Were our enterprise successfully accomplished, the resulting theoretical framework would be better suited, we contend, to illuminate the diachronic vagaries of the social totality under consideration.

Social orders: Between material rewards and symbolic recognition

The form and conditions under which social reproduction occurs in a given spatial setting represents our foremost object of inquiry. Our understanding of social reproduction is not limited to the mere reproduction of capitalist relations of production over time, nor to the biological reproduction of the human species and the ongoing reproduction of labor power (e.g. Bakker and Gill 2003). Rather, we use in the widest possible sense to comprise the reproduction of society as a whole, including those processes and institutional spheres whose relation to capitalist dynamics is, at most, merely tangential (e.g. Bhattacharya 2017a). In this sense, securing social reproduction requires the completion of manifold activities which are widely heterogeneous among themselves in terms of their relative physical hardship, temporal location and duration, degree of routinization, emotional attachment, symbolic recognition, and material rewards. While some of these tasks and activities will be undertaken under wage-labor arrangements, several others will be undertaken outside the scope of capitalist social relations, not being guided by strictly monetary considerations, or, at least, not exclusively by them. In this sense, we follow Bakker and Gill (2003) in reserving the term 'work' to refer to human beings' theoretical-practical activity through which they transform the social environment in which they find themselves immersed, while retaining the term 'labor' to refer to such work activities when undertaken under heteronomous conditions in exchange for a certain amount of monetary compensation. While the former is a category pertaining to the domain of social ontology, the latter is a historically specific one with contingent conditions of existence.

Some mechanism of coordination must always exist among these heterogeneous concrete activities. In capitalist societies it is the market, *qua* instrument of interpersonal coordination, the social mechanism that acquires prominence in that respect. Moreover, not only are market mechanisms deployed to coordinate those various activities but, also, most agents implicated will secure their livelihood through their involvement in market relations as well. However, recognizing the higher-order relevance that capitalist processes show in appraising contemporary societies' historical becoming and internal tensions should, by no means, lead us to downplay the decisive contribution effected by the former's non-capitalist conditions of existence (Fraser 2014). Crucially, a vast array of reproductive activities needs to be continually deployed for workers to be able to participate in capitalist labor markets, including, on the one hand, state-provided goods and services and, on the other, the multifarious activities provided (by women, more often than not) in the private realm of families and households. These manifold tasks and labors provided and/or undertaken in these two separate social spheres are not of any secondary importance whatsoever but, on the contrary, represent the ultimate condition of existence of capitalist activity for, as noted long ago by Polanyi (1957), any society whose reproduction were to be secured exclusively through market-based interactions (i.e. the liberal fantasy *par excellence*) would be necessarily driven towards its own self-destruction. Hence, the separation between public and private spheres which, in the last instance, grounds the very distinction between productive and reproductive activities, reflects no inner ontological difference among the latter, but, on the contrary, merely constitutes the 'particular historical form of appearance in which capitalism as a process posits itself' (Bhattacharya 2017b).

For social reproduction to take place, these various heterogenous activities need to be symbolically codified, that is, structured through mutual relations of hierarchy, commonality and exclusion. In this sense, we understand a social order to be a stratified symbolic network that simultaneously delimits locations within the social (i.e. social groups, classes, identities), types of activities, and the various relations articulating them which, together with the institutions and norms establishing conditions of properness and visibility, constitute the ultimate basis for social coordination. While the distribution of material rewards and responsibilities will be irremediably inegalitarian, a certain degree of consent from those enjoying a comparatively worse lot from existing social arrangements needs to be secured (either through symbolic recognition, certain material compensations, or through a minimal degree of social participation). Moreover, some others will be radically excluded from existing social arrangements, utterly deprived of symbolic recognition and civil participation. Insofar as the very line delimiting social exclusion will be marked by perennial instability, both symbolic and coercive means will need to be deployed in order to secure their effective ostracism.

Any social order's actual shape at a given historical moment will not be the phenomenal appearance, in a mirror-like fashion, of any sort of essential element underlying it. On the contrary, we situate ourselves in what Marchart (2007) has termed a 'post-foundational' approach to social theory. That is, while we forcefully reject positing any underlying social entity that would account, in the last instance, for society's phenomenal diversity (i.e. we depart from metaphysical/foundationalist approaches to social processes), we equally reject doing away with the very notion of ground altogether (as certain strands of postmodern social theory would urge us to). Instead, we understand that the very impossibility of positing any ultimate single ground, valid for every conceivable present social formation, represents itself the very possibility of positing partial and contingent grounds for regulating social difference. This means that while some sort of institutionalization, and thus some sort of systematic articulation among elements, is a necessary precondition for social interaction to be possible, its nature will be necessarily contingent and, hence, ever subject to social contestation:

> The pluralization of grounds and of identities within the field of the social is the result of a radical impossibility. [...] The ultimate grounding of a system is not impossible because the latter is too plural and our capacities are limited, but because there is something of a different order, something

> lacking, which makes pluralization itself possible by making *impossible* the *final* achievement of a totality.
>
> (Marchart 2007: 15–17, original emphasis)

What we have, therefore, is neither a social diversity that can be referred back, in the last instance, to the operation of some eternal essence, nor a multiplicity of practices unable to be submitted to scientific scrutiny. Instead, what we are left with are but continuous attempts to consolidate social practices into more or less stable institutional constructs, whose indefinite reproduction will nonetheless remain an ontological impossibility. The fact that no ultimate ground for the social exists means that the existing web of social relations will be always contingent (meaning that their existence cannot be derived from any essential entity transcending them). If the social lacks any ultimate ahistorical essence, then it follows that any social order's self-reproduction is intrinsically 'performative' (see Butler 1990), that is, it is individuals, through their (re)iterative (inter)action, who yield a sense of permanence and stability to institutions which, in turn, are but the result of their coordinated and repeated interaction itself. These iterative practices, as noted, tend to coalesce into various institutional forms with different degrees of resilience and causal effectivity. By institutions we understand stable constructs of social practices which regulate social interaction by both enabling and constraining human action, being themselves the result of pacification of previous social struggles. Moreover, while institutions structure and channel ongoing social conflicts, they are nonetheless continually haunted by quarrels over the very mode of social interaction they institute. Nevertheless, no assessment of their robustness and durability can be made from the strict recognition of their contingency. Some institutions, such as the existence of wage-labor, have endured for centuries, whereas some others, such as cell phones' mass consumption, might be infinitely more transient.

In order to think about the dynamics of institutionalization of social practices, we consider Laclau's (1990a: 34) distinction between the social and the political to be of the utmost importance. To recap, the 'social' refers to the domain of 'sedimented forms of objectivity', that is, ensembles of social practices that have become naturalized to the extent that their ultimately contingent origins has been forgotten. However, the emergence of social antagonisms contesting their mode of operation implicitly reveals their ultimately contingent origin. This revelation represents the very nature of the 'political'. Moreover, while the very distinction between the social and the political is constitutive of social relations (i.e. it permits both its ordered reproduction and its internal subversion), the dividing line between the two is nonetheless constantly displaced and renegotiated. Therefore, rather than considering the existence of social conflict as some sort of anomaly resulting from a social order's malfunction, it is the latter which is deemed to be the result of an incessant and never-ending process of pacification of manifold social struggles.

Social conflicts are then an ever-present feature that social orders ought to channel and contain so that its own self-reproduction is not compromised. On the one hand, a certain level of inequality of outcomes and demands over the population is constitutive of any social order, so that the possibility that the worst-off might contest their mode of inclusion is ever-present, even if, for a relatively long time, such conflictive substratum is successfully prevented from coming to the fore. On the other hand, every social order is grounded upon some kind of exclusion. That is, some element has to be expelled from it for any sort of interiority to emerge. While symbolic and material means need to be deployed to ensure their continuous exclusion, the possibility remains nonetheless that the excluded will somehow re-appropriate the means they are not supposed to have, and the words they are supposed not to know, to contest their symbolic non-existence (Rancière 1999). In sum, social orders and social conflicts are mutually constitutive. While social conflicts need to be appropriately confronted if a social order is to be successfully instituted, the particular shape the latter takes will in turn foster new rounds of social contestation over the very inequalities it institutes.

Every (capitalist) social order is irremediably constituted by two dualities it simultaneously has to deal with, and which, in turn, throw light upon its ultimate mode of operation. The first one, relating to the nature of social inequalities, is encapsulated in the pair '*accumulation and recognition*', which points to, on the one hand, the need to secure capitalist conditions of existence (in terms of fostering a suitable environment for ongoing capital accumulation), while simultaneously responding to manifold individual aspirations irreducible to monetary expression and, on the other hand, to the dual requirements of social consent related not only to the provision of material welfare but also of appropriate identitarian recognition. While political economy's foremost concern has traditionally been the first pole, regarding how economic surplus is first produced and then distributed among competing claims, the other one has received much less attention in comparison. However, if it is agreed that politics cannot be reduced to the interaction among already-constituted social identities but, on the contrary, should also be concerned with the processes through which heterogeneous social yearnings and aspirations are converted into actual political subjects, then it follows that politics is also an activity revolving eminently around the conditions determining social visibility and recognition. In our view, the author who has best analyzed this 'aesthetic' dimension of politics is, undoubtedly, Jacques Rancière (1999; 2004b; 2007). The term he uses to refer to the configuration of social orders is 'police'. Radically distinct, albeit certainly not wholly unrelated, to the common usage of the term, Rancière's *police* refers instead to:

> An order of bodies that defines the allocation of ways of doing, ways of being, and ways of saying, and sees that those bodies are assigned by name to a particular place and task; it is an order of the visible and the sayable that sees that a particular activity is visible and another is not, that this speech is understood as discourse and another as noise.
>
> (Rancière 1999: 29)

According to Rancière, every social order is thus a configuration of bodies and practices that delimits its internal relations in terms of what is proper or appropriate to each, that regulates a 'normality' against which social interaction takes place, that holds every single element to its apportioned place, that distributes goods and services as well as roles and occupations. However, prior to this distribution of material outcomes resides an aesthetic operation delimiting whose voices and claims are to be considered when deciding upon the former, determining the conditions of visibility and intelligibility among subjects and activities that, from the very beginning, regulate social interaction. Rancière names this regime of (in)visibility the 'distribution of the sensible' (*partage du sensible*), which stands for:

> The system of self-evident facts of sense perception that simultaneously discloses the existence of something in common and the delimitations that define the respective parts and positions within it. [...] This apportionment of parts and positions [i.e. a police order] is based on a distribution of spaces, times and forms of activity that determines the very manner in which something in common lends itself to participation and in what way various individuals have a part in this distribution.
>
> (Rancière 2004: 7)

Therefore, behind the visible confrontations among already-constituted subjects to determine the effective distribution of economic surplus among the members of the community, there is a subterraneous and never-ending struggle over a prior distribution of statuses and recognitions, which determines which voices are to be heard and considered and which others are not, whose sounds are to be recognized as legitimate voices and whose will be considered but noise. Every visible political contention, including the very constitution and recognition of social actors as such, is ultimately dependent upon such an underlying framework of intertextuality, constitutive itself of social meaning for, as noted by Rancière (2014: 94), '[i]f words serve to blur things, it is because the conflict over words is inseparable from the battle over things'.

Rancière's understanding of social orders as 'police' orders leads us straight to the second duality constitutive of the former – that between '*naturalization and normativity*'. As noted above, the various elements constituting any social order will only acquire actual existence as long as its participants act them out, behaving as if their institutional form owed its existence to some other cause external to themselves. That is, their contingent roots ought to be effaced if they are to be successful in effectively coordinating social interaction. In other words, they ought to become 'naturalized'.[2] In this respect, Laclau's distinction between the social and the political remains utterly relevant for our purposes. However, a well-functioning social order is not only required to 'buy' consent among its subordinate members (e.g. through appropriate material rewards) but also to 'manufacture' it, that is, to legitimate the various hierarchical inequalities it is based upon. Rancière's police order is, above all, a 'regime of properness' which simultaneously describes and prescribes a 'system of distribution and legitimation' that not only distributes roles and places, but also attributes specific functions and activities to each. In sum, every 'normality' contains a certain degree of 'normativity', and vice versa, conflating in its mode of operation that which is, and that which should be.

How do Rancière and Laclau's understanding of social orders, upon which we are mostly relying upon in our account, relate to our previous indications regarding the social theory we are striving for? Their implicit rejection of the level of the economy as one to be considered in their respective accounts of how social orders are instituted and subverted undoubtedly falls short of what we have previously termed the 'middle ground' position. While capitalism, in both their theoretical schemes, is virtually reduced to a fetishized notion with little to no explanatory value, the causal effectivity of material (re)production processes has to be acknowledged. In this sense, we fully share Žižek's reservation to Rancière (and Laclau's) approach:

> The 'political' critique of Marxism (the claim that, when we reduce politics to a 'formal' expression of some underlying 'objective' socioeconomic process, we lose the openness and contingency constitutive of the political field proper) should thus be supplemented by its obverse: the field of economy is *in its very form* irreducible to politics – this level of the form of economy (of economy as the determining form of the social) is what French 'political post-Marxists' miss when they reduce economy to one of the positive social spheres.
>
> (Žižek 2006b: 56, original emphasis)

Žižek argues that the relation between the fields of politics and the economy are like 'the well-known visual paradox of the "two faces or a vase": one either sees the two faces or a vase, ever both of them – one has to make a choice' (Žižek 2006b: 56). One can hardly imagine a more eloquent description of the 'middle ground' position between economic determinism and political pluralism/voluntarism we are advocating, that is, the recognition of the ultimate impossibility of granting due space to both political and economic logics in appraising social becoming while, nonetheless, simultaneously committing oneself to the possibility of not downplaying one pole in favor of the other.

In order to integrate these 'post-Marxist' insights regarding the constitution of social orders within a holistic political economy approach, the category of 'social demand' may provide a valid entry point. While Laclau himself has made of it a central category of his later writings (e.g. 2005b; 2005a; 2006), certain theoretical inconsistencies nonetheless spring from his reticence to consider economic processes as co-constitutive of social objectivity (see chapter 3). It is our view, however, that the category of 'social demand' may be useful in linking capital accumulation's institutional requirements with the vagaries of social orders without ultimately reducing one to the other. On the one hand, situating the category of 'social demand' at the center of the analysis offers the possibility of interrogating the conditions of visibility and intelligibility affecting any proffered social request, not only in terms of how various demands may relate to one another at a given conjuncture (the foremost terrain of Laclau's hegemonic logics) but also in terms of how the excluded might irrupt into a social arena where they were not expected (Rancière's understanding of politics). On the other hand, it points to the institutional configuration through which capitalist dynamics are instantiated in a given temporal-spatial location: Firstly, because dealing with a social demand, either through satisfaction or through repression, involves deploying resources susceptible to having been allocated to some alternative use; secondly, because the ongoing reproduction of the institutional environment framing such demands will be more dependent on certain social dynamics as opposed to others, in turn affecting both the potentially transformative character of the demand in question as well as the existing scope for its eventual satisfaction. The rest of this chapter will attempt to relate the various above-indicated insights regarding the nature of social orders to the study of capitalist dynamics enabled by SSA theory.

Social orders and well-functioning SSAs

When analyzing social formations, our basic unit of analysis will be that of 'social process', which, existing in a constant state of tension and contradiction among themselves, foster the social totality's continuous internal transformation (Resnick and Wolff 1987). We use the term 'institutions' to refer to ensembles of social processes that have become, for a certain time, somehow interlocked, in such a way that their mutual interaction reproduces the modality of interaction itself. While these processes will tend to coalesce among themselves into relatively stable assemblages (i.e. institutions), the continual interaction among themselves, as well as with other social processes not directly implicated in the former, will set them continually into motion. In capitalist societies, several among these processes will govern, to a greater or lesser extent, society's material reproduction in line with capitalist reproduction's internal requirements. In this sense, we understand an SSA to comprise the ensemble of institutions that, within a given spatio-temporal context, shape and structure profit-making activity in the long run. However, not every institutional assemblage qualifies as an SSA. In order to do so, it must satisfy several conditions.

Firstly, in order to secure capitalist profit-making activity over the long run, its various composing institutions ought to coat and safeguard the different stages of the circuit of capital (e.g. the provision of necessary raw materials and energy inputs; a system of labor qualifications; technological systems; various legal regulations; domestic and international markets' structure; and so on), thus securing a minimum of predictability and institutional stability in each so that economic activity may proceed without recurring blockages. Aggregate levels of capital accumulation, therefore, should not be included within the SSA's own definition, insofar as they are a by-product of manifold decisions adopted (separately) by individual capitalists (Wolfson and Kotz 2010).

Secondly, relations of complementarity ought to emerge among its various institutional realms, so that the internal dynamics of each do not compromise the ongoing reproduction of co-existing ones, this way fostering systemic self-reproduction over the long run. If the nature of an SSA's composing institutional blocks is historically contingent, then it follows that the nature of the manifold relations of complementarity and/or dissonance existing among its various components ought to be considered historically contingent as well. Moreover, while isolating the relations among two (or more) separate spheres from the overdetermined totality where they are ultimately located might be useful for heuristic purposes, the diachronic evolution of the latter affects the existing internal relations among the former, so that, it follows, relations of institutional complementarity among institutional spheres are not only contingent but also transitory.

Thirdly, a well-functioning SSA must not compromise its own conditions of existence, among which crucially stand all the care-related activities which, occurring mainly within the private realm, play a crucial role in ensuring society's successful reproduction. While these social processes may not be included within the list of SSA's internal components, the diachronic evolution of the latter must not, under any circumstances, compromise the successful reproduction of the former. Virtually everywhere, these various activities which remain the most crucial for social reproduction but which, notwithstanding, are not necessarily mediated by market interactions, are governed and/or regulated by 'gender norms'. By this we understand a cultural-symbolic construction which assigns individuals to one among the two positions of a binary matrix – masculine versus feminine.[3] This gender matrix codifies certain activities, ways of seeing and being seen, and types of conduct which are appropriate to each gender. Individuals, through repeating those normative prescriptions in their daily interactions, end up naturalizing the attributes assigned to each in such a way that, having become sedimented, these gendered prescriptions become 'naturalized'. Once these gender norms are internalized by individuals, they appear to the latter, paradoxically, as radically external to them, a pre-existing force to which they ought to submit. While these gender norms operate transversally, interacting with most other social processes comprising a social formation at a given point in time, some of them will be inherently overdetermined by existing gender norms, while others will be affected by them in a merely tangential manner. These various processes co-governed by gender norms tend to show a certain coherence in their mode of interrelation, so that the gendered nature of these processes tends to be reproduced over time. For instance, while the processes regulating labor market exit/entry, care provision to the elders, and the codification of bodies within TV shows, are ultimately irreducible to each other, they do show nonetheless a great amount of internal coherence, reinforcing one another through their iterative repetition. This coherence is due to them being governed, in the last instance, by a shared gender matrix. Insofar as their reproduction is reinforced by their mutual interaction, they tend to coalesce into relatively stable assemblages – i.e. a gender order, suitable of sustained and systematic theoretical investigation and analysis.

Regarding the institutions to be included within a given SSA, no axiomatic list can be provided for the limits of the latter will always be blurred. In the end, all social processes may be rightly considered each other's conditions of existence (Resnick and Wolff 1987), so that the pertinence of including one given institution within the SSA cannot be inscribed within the process's own conceptual definition but should depend, instead, upon the subjective evaluation of the analyst in relation to the specificities of the current conjuncture. The 'imprecise and hence inevitably arguable nature of [an SSA's] outer boundary' had already been noted by Gordon et al. (1982: 25) in their seminal contribution, when asserting that, while 'any aspect or relationship in society potentially and perhaps actually impinges to some degree upon the accumulation process, nonetheless, it is not unreasonable to distinguish between those institutions that directly and demonstrably condition capital accumulation and those that touch it only tangentially'. Besides dropping the references to capital accumulation, we would only add that the bases for such distinction are both subjective and contextual.

Lastly, the specific form these various institutions take at a given moment will tend to favor the welfare, material, and/or symbolic, of certain social groups over others. The various conflicts emerging from their interaction will need to be correctly pacified for ongoing capitalist activity to continue or, at least, to be channeled 'in directions that are not unduly disruptive of accumulation' (Kotz 1994a: 55). We do not mean that such conflicts ought to be eradicated but, instead, that they ought to be confronted with the appropriate institutional mechanisms for their indiscriminate proliferation to be prevented, precluding in turn the possibility of them coalescing around some single goal liable to further advance them all. These conflicts are manifold and heterogeneous among themselves, stretching well beyond the production process, even if strongly overdetermined by the latter. While the relevance of the conflict between capital and labor (class struggle), as well as that between individual capital units (capitalist competition) is beyond all dispute, social objectivity is nonetheless the end result of a variegated process of pacification of contingent social struggles irreducible to the former. As noted in the previous chapter, essentializing class struggle and competition carries the risk of overestimating the actual degree of institutional coherence of a given ensemble by referring its phenomenal appearance to one single center. If, instead, the plurality of struggles at stake is acknowledged, manifold dissonances among the various parts of the social will come to the fore, in turn throwing some light upon the potential lines of fracture within a given institutional ensemble. Moreover, if social conflicts are both heterogeneous and ubiquitous, and institutions derive their form from their temporary pacification, precipitating into sets of shared understandings, conventions and expectations that efface the ultimately contingent nature of their emergence, then it follows that particular institutions are context-specific, so that, in consequence, the SSA in which the latter coalesce will be also contingent and historically unique.

Therefore, there is a two-way relation between institutions and social conflicts. On the one hand, institutions may be understood as the end result of an unending process of conflict pacification. On the other, the mode institutions work tends to generate in turn various other conflicts as they invariably benefit some social groups at the expense of others (e.g. conflicts among generations, among genders, among types of occupations, among races, etc.) However, the crucial thing to note is that these conflicts will never find symbolic expression in an automatic and straightforward manner. On the contrary, in order to constitute themselves into socially intelligible demands, they will be crucially dependent upon a constitutive process of political mediation, overdetermined itself by the remaining social processes. While these demands will be inherently heterogeneous, some sort of relation among some of them is to be drawn for them to become socially intelligible in the first instance, that is, they need to be transitorily articulated in such a manner that the potentially conflictive component of each does not disrupt the stability of the relation itself (see Laclau 1996). This process of articulation, through which the particular content of each is made to recede while some dimension of commonality emerges among them, is what Laclau and Mouffe (2001) refer to as hegemony.

Every SSA, as noted above, is composed of various institutions, each of which tends to favor the material/symbolic welfare of certain groups over others. Their interaction and coalescence into relatively stable assemblages will then consolidate manifold social cleavages, which will remain in need of being symbolically articulated. While every SSA relies upon an existing group of beneficiaries, that is, an amalgam of social groups who have an interest in reproducing the *statu quo*, their constitution as such is neither straightforward. On the one hand, the fact that social conflicts are both manifold and ubiquitous means that people will be affected by several of them simultaneously, whose relative importance at each time will be ultimately determined by the nature of existing hegemonic articulations. On the other, these same people will also hold to different criteria when judging the existing state of affairs (e.g. some will be interested in employment opportunities, some in the availability of leisure time, others in the ethnic homogeneity of their surroundings), among which some sort of internal unification ought to be produced so that their respective views may find some common anchoring points. Hegemonic (re) articulations will be never-ending, as the various institutions' inner workings will contribute to generate and/or modulate the various expectations through which the current situation is to be judged. The potential disjunction between these various expectations and institutional outcomes will give rise to various new demands around which the hegemonic struggle will mainly revolve. Depending on the reach and nature of existing hegemonic articulations, these newly emerging demands may either be successfully blocked or, perhaps, precipitate further social change. However, as already noted, the translation of the conflict-ridden nature of institutions into a set of socially intelligible demands is not a straightforward process. Being able to advance one's own claim into the public sphere requires having at own's disposal the appropriate means, both material and symbolic, which the prevailing institutional structure may block.

In sum, hegemony refers to this process through which different coalitions of interests emerge that sustain and reinforce the *status quo*. While the configuration of each SSA favors the material well-being of certain groups of society while simultaneously marginalizing others, it is necessary that broader coalitions of interests between dominant and other subaltern groups emerge to support the ongoing reproduction of the existing order, the nature and extent of such coalitions being one of the main objects of contention within the hegemonic struggle itself. We are not arguing that all agents with an interest in maintaining existing social arrangements will receive a proportional share of the social output, but that institutional conditions ought to be established for each group to be satisfied with the differential position assigned to each in the existing social order. While both the existing alignments among social demands and the actual content of each will be the result of hegemonic articulations, those who occupy a subaltern position within the latter ought to comply as well with their respective roles in the social fabric. Moreover, those that had been excluded from them also have to be prevented from challenging the institutional basis of their exclusion. Therefore, despite this operation of building up social consensuses being eminently political in nature, it is ultimately dependent upon the social processes governing material (re)production underlying it.

As long as the conflict-ridden substratum of the existing social order is satisfactorily pacified, and the internal relations among those enjoying some degree of social visibility attain some relative stability, a minimum level of 'social peace' will then ensue, which, in turn, constitutes a necessary prerequisite for sustained economic activity. Continued profit-making activity in conjunction with sufficiently low levels of social unrest would then signal the effective operation of a well-functioning SSA. Economic expansion will favor the ongoing reproduction of already-existing social positions. Moreover, as continuous, if not rapid, growth permits to expand progressively the material base of society, a partial satisfaction of certain previously unsatisfied demands might be afforded, thus not only reproducing, but also expanding, the material conditions of existence of the existing order's base of beneficiaries.

Social order decomposition and SSA decay

While an SSA is an integrated whole articulated through relations of complementarity and co-constitutivity among its various spheres, nothing prevents some of its composing institutions from harboring markedly contradictory dynamics when considered in isolation. Nonetheless, such contradictory dynamics may be successfully contained during the expansion phase thanks, precisely, to the various relations of synergy and complementarity emerging among them. Indeed, it is precisely such capacity to counterbalance internal contradictions through their very interplay, rather than their erasure from the social field, which signals the operation of a well-functioning SSA. However, such homeostatic functioning of the SSA will at some point come to a halt, in turn causing a process of gradual institutional decomposition. This is so because every institution is subject to contingent struggles over its mode of operation, internal malfunctions, and changes in its external environment. While the various institutional blocks will undergo continuous internal transformation, their respective rhythms and direction of change will certainly not have to be coordinated. At some point, the respective changes undergone by the various institutions implicated will end up undoing the internal coherence of the SSA provided by existing relations of complementarity, thus blocking further profit-making activity in turn. The integrated nature of the SSA means that blossoming malfunctions will reverberate all throughout its internal equilibria, giving rise to a phase of gradual institutional decomposition. Partial amendments introduced in some of its key institutional buttresses will not serve to restore the institutional conditions needed for further profit-making activity. Instead, restoring favorable institutional conditions to capitalist enterprises will strictly require fully-fledged transformation of the whole institutional environment (including, crucially, the manifold relations of complementarity among its individual components). These moments represent, therefore, the systemic crisis of each SSA, which in turn signal a turning point between different stages within capitalism (McDonough 2011).

The dysfunctional nature of such institutional assemblage will be further compounded by existing hegemonic alliances, which may shift from repressing social change to fostering widespread SSA transformation as a response to perceived malfunctions within the latter's mode of operation. The social consensuses that had regulated social objectivity up to that moment start to crumble as a result of internal problems directly affecting the material base on which they had been grounded. The necessity to re-draw the institutional structure framing the accumulation process throws into light the inherently contingent character of those diverse alliances that had supported the reproduction of previous institutional equilibria. While sustained, if not rapid, economic growth allows various subaltern groups to receive a part of an 'expanding pie', a decaying SSA encounters a diminishing surplus through which to satisfy those same groups' requirements, so that it necessarily has to leave aside certain demands which, during its previous expansion phase, could have been dealt with through existing institutional channels and mechanisms. In contrast, while every well-functioning SSA leaves some demands unsatisfied, these either lack symbolic strength to significantly modify the existing order, or their exiguous number allows the institutional order to push them into the background. In sum, the institutional structure that had permitted the accommodation of different groups' demands over an 'expanding pie' progressively turns into its opposite, an 'accumulation of demands over a shrinking pie' which cannot but reinforce further SSA decline.

Therefore, the social field becomes increasingly fragmented, and the isolated character of each demand becomes increasingly visible, as the social consensuses that used to bind them together are progressively eroded. Fixed expectations start to crumble, old loyalties show themselves to be ultimately contingent, and the social alignments that for a time had been sedimented into a society's 'common sense' no longer manage to make the situation intelligible to the different groups involved. The previously held 'naturalness' of social facts suddenly becomes questioned, thus entering into what Marchart (2007) terms the 'moment of the political', when the ultimate contingency of any social order is made manifest. In sum, systemic crises eventually turn into organic crises.

In this context of fragmented loyalties and expectations, hegemony refers, precisely, to this process of political articulation among heterogeneous unsatisfied demands into wider political projects, such that an element of commonality is produced among them that, despite not pre-existing this process of articulation, can nonetheless form the basis of a new solidarity. As the process of SSA decay worsens due to the 'accumulation of unsatisfied demands', the need for their re-articulation through what Laclau (2005a: 77–83) terms a 'chain of equivalence' becomes the most pressing. Various social groups, holding different criteria for evaluating the current situation, will seek to promote institutional changes directed towards restoring previously existing social conditions. However, the integrated nature of the decaying SSA will prevent that possibility from taking shape. As long as economic outcomes worsen, economic imperatives foregrounding the necessity of social change will accentuate, especially on the side of capital, but they will necessarily have to impregnate themselves with non-economic demands and expectations if successful social transformation is to be attained.

The nature of the previous phase of expansion is expected to have empowered certain social groups over others, and also to have yielded an institutional environment which, despite undergoing gradual dissolution, will remain nonetheless favoring certain groups over others regarding their relative capacity to advance their own claims in response to the current situation. Therefore, the main contradictions of the decaying SSA will pose limits to the possible outcomes of the struggle, as well as to the character of its actors. Depending on which were the imbalances that led to the occurrence of the systemic crisis in the first instance, some outcomes will be more likely than others, and some political alliances will have more chances to materialize themselves than others. Moreover, the various social conflicts acquiring prominence during the crisis phase, as well as the possible alliances that may be built around them, will be crucially affected by the particular set of beneficiaries of the decaying SSA, whose relative shares of material and symbolic resources, respectively, will condition the potential lines of fracture and recomposition in terms of political action.

Although the exact form of its articulation will remain undetermined *a priori*, for economic activity to be resumed in a sustained manner new loyalties and coalitions will have to emerge that materialize into a common project. It can either happen that old actors manage to incorporate these disaffected demands into a common project with many degrees of continuity with the previous period, or that those unsatisfied demands might give rise to a new hegemonic bloc based upon their common rejection of the previous *status quo*. What the outcome will be, between these two extreme cases, will be the result of the hegemonic struggle itself. Laclau's understanding of the hegemonic struggle postulates that these various unsatisfied demands, initially tied to concrete claims and yearnings, will inhabit a constant tension between their strictly particular content and their aimed universal aspirations. Some of them will gradually empty themselves of their sectorial connotations to start functioning as surfaces of inscription of further unsatisfied demands, thus becoming gradually hegemonic. In the limit, as more and more individual demands take the former as the frame of reference through which their expression will be made intelligible to the remaining social groups, they will turn themselves into 'empty signifiers', that is, particular demands which, having emptied themselves of their own particular content, start functioning as the embodiment of the community's aspiration of fullness, i.e. a future devoid of conflict and antagonism (Laclau 1996c). In sum, while Laclau's conception of hegemony says nothing about the progressive character of future articulations, it does shed some light upon how the struggle among contending groups in a fragmented social field takes place while, for its part, SSA theory helps to conceptualize the constraints of the necessarily uneven terrain where such struggle for institutional redefinition inevitably occurs.

The formation of a new SSA implies that favorable conditions for surplus value extraction and accumulation need to be established, comprising, among other things, a new institutional fix for the capital–labor contradiction. Although the relative importance enjoyed by various political identities during the hegemonic struggle for institutional redefinitions cannot be ascertained in advance, some sort of resolution to perceived impediments to continuing capitalist activity will have to be offered. However, the new institutionalization of the capital–labor relation and associated capitalist institutional requirements may emerge by strict indirection in the course of the hegemonic struggle's resolution, in which it is perfectly possible that explicitly class-related identities and demands might not even be explicitly at stake in the very terms of the contention.

The concrete shape the upcoming SSA will take (as long as some post-capitalist form of social organization does not materialize) will bear the imprint of, firstly, the various social conflicts acquiring centrality during the previous organic crisis's resolution, that is, it will be affected by the character of the various contending subjects (whose nature will be molded in the course of the hegemonic struggle itself); secondly, the drive of capital to restore institutional conditions favoring further profit-making activity; thirdly, historical contingency; and, lastly, various other social processes which, in the last instance, might be considered exogenous to the SSA in place. A new SSA will consolidate itself, perhaps even inadvertently from the perspective of the main actors implicated in the hegemonic struggle, when conditions are set that permit profit-making activity to continue in a relatively undisturbed manner, and various institutional blocks emerge whose individual continuation is favored by their joint co-existence. Resurgent capitalist accumulation will further the existing material ground through which to attempt a partial satisfaction of several demands among the many involved within the hegemonic struggle. Not only will this help consolidate and solidify the existing alliances at the roots of the ongoing process of institutional construction but, crucially, will also help broaden its reach by incorporating other disaffected demands not articulated from the outset.

Concluding comments

The synthesis between SSA theory and Laclau's hegemonic logics that has been presented is intended to respond to certain aspects identified in each which we found in need of further theoretical elaboration. Let us recap our respective lines of criticism. Regarding SSA theory, it was argued that one of the main shortcomings it had to face was its marked underdevelopment of the terms in which the political contention for institutional redefinition is both framed and undertaken. It is our view that most of the literature so far has seemed to assume a relatively straightforward constitution of collective subjects derived from the position agents occupy in the capitalist production process, which, in turn, greatly complicates a correct apprehension of the actual stakes in the political battle. Instead, we argue in favor of introducing a theoretical hiatus between the conflict-prone nature of capitalist institutions and the actual struggles among already-constituted political subjects, a hiatus we intend to grasp theoretically through Laclauian categories. Moreover, by paying close attention to actual institutional configurations, a more nuanced treatment of the laws regulating the differential degrees of visibility enjoyed by various social strata can be obtained.

Regarding Laclau's post-Marxist account of hegemony, certain theoretical impasses were identified in chapter 3, derived from his lack of proper consideration of capitalist institutional requirements and dynamics. Firstly, we had noted that Laclau's adoption of the category of social demand as the primary unit of social analysis, while definitely a productive move in debunking essentialist and/or economicist narratives of political interaction, carried with it several other theoretical complications. On the one hand, it precluded a correct understanding of how the manifold conflicts pervading any capitalist society could be translated into socially intelligible demands in the first instance, that is, how such conflict-ridden magma is 'individuated' into separate claims. We intend to solve that matter by grounding such a process upon the underlying institutional structure governing socio-material (re)production. Having the possibility to advance one's own claim requires having at one's disposal the appropriate material and symbolic resources, as well as organizational capacities, whose inegalitarian distribution over the population is greatly overdetermined by the underlying institutional structure. If demands are adopted as the primary unit of analysis, one runs the risk of neglecting the relevance of the institutional environment in configuring an uneven field of visibility, which in turn makes some voices more likely to be heard than others. On the other hand, doing away with any notion of overarching social structure altogether prevents a correct appreciation of the differential anti-systemic capacity each of them may enjoy at a given point in time. The specific configuration of the institutional structure constraining and structuring political interaction makes some demands more difficult to assimilate without in turn compromising the former's self-reproduction.

Secondly, we had argued against Laclau's univocal treatment of 'class' as just one mode of collective identification, on the grounds that it prevented appreciating the historical specificity of capitalism. Denying any sort of direct transposition between class-in-itself and class-for-itself does not lead us to discard the former in favor of the latter, as Laclau seemingly does, but to postulate that, despite the need to find some sort of institutionalization to capital–labor relations if capitalism is to work properly, such an institutional fix will be overdetermined by a political struggle where class-related motives and slogans might not even be present at all. Moreover, the particular configuration of the wage relation will have crucial effects upon distributive patterns in society at large, which, in turn, will greatly affect the modality of prevailing social consensuses (a line of inquiry explored at length in the following chapter).

Thirdly, we had complained about Laclau's understanding of the temporal evolution under capitalism. While his distinction between the 'social' and the 'political' results of great value to apprehend the processes through which social orders are both instituted and subverted in a strictly non-teleological and non-essentialist manner, it needs to be supplemented with an account of why, in capitalist societies, periods marked by relative institutional stability alternate with others marked by widespread deinstitutionalization. Only by paying close attention to the institutional requirements imposed by the capitalist accumulation process can one accurately grasp the nature and form of systemic crises, which in turn underlie the differential historical rhythms undergone by the twin processes of institutionalization and deinstitutionalization Laclau aims at grasping. Moreover, only an analysis that recognizes the varying degrees of institutional thickness of a given institutional structure can properly account for the different degrees of resilience and causal effectivity enjoyed by the former. The last set of issues we called attention to concerned Laclau's understanding of populism. The next chapter, concerned with the existing relation between the modality of institutional breakdown when a systemic crisis emerges and the way existing social consensuses are dislocated in return, will tackle those issues in detail.

Notes

1 See O'Hara (1995) and Gillespie (2013), who have attempted to explore the role of the family as an SSA's constituent institution.

2 As noted in our previous discussion of Laclau in this chapter, while politics emerges whenever their ultimately contingent origin is brought to the fore through a quarrel

over its mode of operation, not all elements will be shattered at once. However, as the upcoming discussion will hopefully illuminate, it is possible to go beyond Laclau's theoretical agnosticism regarding the extent to which the political haunts the social at a given time by relating it to political economy insights.

3 Gender norms are not derived in any sense by the biological nature of the subjects concerned. We use the term 'sex' to refer to biological factors, while reserving the term 'gender' for cultural-symbolic inscriptions of the above-mentioned sexed nature of human beings.

6 Grounding populism upon political economy

This chapter has two separate albeit interrelated objectives. Firstly, it is concerned with examining the character of organic crises in relation to the reformulation of SSA theory advanced in the previous chapter, that is, how social consensuses get shaken once core capitalist process find their reproduction irremediably compromised. To that extent, it will make use of the distinction drawn by Wolfson and Kotz (2010) between Liberal and Regulated SSAs in order to examine the nature of the ensuing political struggle once the underlying SSA shows undisputable signs of exhaustion. It is argued that, while both institutional environments may ensure a level of 'social peace' high enough for economic activity to take place in a sustained manner over time, important differences between the two types concern their effects upon the accumulation process, the different actors they empower during its expansion phase, and the crisis tendencies borne by each. These differences, in turn, will be shown to greatly affect the terms of the political struggle once fully-fledged institutional transformation becomes a structural imperative, the character of the contending subjects, and the ultimate nature of its resolution. In order to substantiate this claim and draw its various implications, we will interrogate the last two systemic crises of US capitalism, namely, that corresponding to the demise of the Postwar SSA (a Regulated SSA) during the 1970s and 1980s, and the one corresponding to the decay of the Neoliberal SSA (a Liberal SSA), spanning from 2008 up until the present moment.

Secondly, it seeks to offer a theoretical resolution to some of the aporias previously identified in Laclau's understanding of populism. In order to do so, a conceptual distinction between 'populist situations' and 'populist interventions' will be introduced, explicitly aimed at relating the higher or lesser degree of success enjoyed by populist phenomena, on the one hand, with the characteristics of the social environment through which capitalist dynamics appear instantiated in a given spatio-temporal setting, on the other. In that respect, it is argued that systemic crises associated to Liberal SSAs should be assimilated to the aforementioned 'populist situations' which, in turn, favor the emergence of populist phenomena of various types. Grounding populist phenomena in its socio-material conditions of existence, it is argued, remains crucial to understanding populism's historical specificity, and hence to counteract certain misusages of the term in contemporary discussions. Lastly, the chapter concludes by making a case for a 'left-wing' populist strategy in the current historical juncture, a rejection of which would seriously reduce the capacity of those of the Left to affect the various processes of institutional transformation already in course.

The historical specificity of populism

From Donald Trump's 2016 presidential campaign in the US and the 'Brexit' referendum in the UK, to the rise to power of SYRIZA in Greece, the emergence of Podemos in Spain, the Front National in France or the '5 Stars' Movement in Italy, the term 'populism' has been widely deployed by the mainstream Western media to characterize these otherwise heterogenous movements and political processes, arguably on the grounds of them sharing a self-consciously vague, oversimplistic, and opportunistic communicative that interpellates the popular masses in an inherently demagogical manner. Nonetheless, besides such normative usage of the term, generally deployed to discredit political opponents rather than to illuminate their defining features, the conceptual category of 'populism' has gained full theoretical weight in the hands of Laclau (2005b; 2005a). To recap, Laclau recasts populism as a particular political logic whose specificity would refer not to the *content* articulated in a given political discourse but, on the contrary, to the very *form* adopted by such articulation. Nevertheless, while his formalistic account of populism remains undoubtedly useful to combat several common misunderstandings regarding what populist logics ultimately stand for, it is our view that, if Laclau's formalistic conception of populism is to gain full analytic and strategic/political value, it needs to be supplemented by a more nuanced understanding of how capitalist dynamics shape the social environment where populist logics ultimately operate.

Let us briefly recap our argument in this regard. According to Laclau, populism refers to a formal logic through which political identities are generated in times of intense institutional decomposition, marked by the simultaneous and widespread emergence of heterogeneous demands which the existing order cannot deal with individually in an orderly and successful manner. A new 'popular' identity might then be consolidated among the latter based not on any sort of essential quality these demands might share but, on the contrary, on their common dissatisfaction with the current state of affairs. In our opinion, however, two interrelated issues deserve reconsideration. Firstly, it is by no means clear what it is that fosters such process of institutional decomposition in the first instance. In other words, if the widespread emergence of heterogeneous unsatisfied demands is deemed to be a necessary precondition for populism, an explanation should be offered of what the causes are of both their simultaneous emergence and the existing order's incapacity to address them satisfactorily. Secondly, and intimately linked to it, Laclau asserts, on the one hand, that the political enjoys ontological primacy in structuring social relations and, on the other, that an element of populism pertains to the very core of politics (Laclau 2005a: 67). Were both premises accepted, it should follow that populist logics would be self-sufficient in destabilizing a given social order, thus resulting in a pan-politicist social ontology starkly at odds with the position we are here arguing for (Jessop 2019). In order to provide a more nuanced understanding of how the existing scope for political interventions is either constrained or enhanced by the institutional shape characterizing a given conjuncture, two qualifications ought to be introduced to Laclau's original account of populism. On the one hand, populist logics should not be considered the political logic *par excellence* but, rather, one particular and well-differentiated political logic (De Cleen 2019). On the other hand, it must be recognized that the higher hegemonic depth shown by populist logics in gathering together heterogeneous disaffections with the existing social order has specific socio-historical conditions of existence, intimately linked to capitalism's internal dynamics. To that extent, an analysis of the laws of motion of capitalism-in-general would nonetheless be too abstract a level of analysis for such a task (Kotz 2015), requiring instead an analysis of the concrete institutional form through which capitalist dynamics are instantiated at a given place and moment.

In order to clarify these issues, a conceptual distinction between 'populist situations', on the one hand, and 'populist interventions', on the other, needs to be introduced. In this context, we use the term 'populist situation' to refer to a social context marked by sharp institutional disintegration as well as by the simultaneous emergence of a wide variety of heterogeneous unsatisfied demands the existing order cannot deal with individually, whereas by 'populist intervention' (Panizza 2011; Retamozo 2014) we refer to, precisely, those attempts willing to address those 'unsatisfied demands' into a new 'chain of equivalence' that, through invoking a yet-to-be-constructed *people*, draw a dichotomous division within the social field in which an antagonistic frontier emerges between the existing order and those who, by virtue of being rejected by it, aim at subverting it. While the occurrence of a 'populist situation' emerges as a necessary pre-condition for a 'populist intervention' to be successful in re-shaping the social order, the latter is to be considered but one among the many possible resolutions, certainly not the only one, of a 'populist situation'.

Firstly, the occurrence of these 'populist situations' constitute precisely that 'degree of crisis in the old structure' that Laclau (2005a: 177) refers to, a mapping of which may be provided by an analysis of the interplay between capitalist dynamics, on the one hand, and the institutional environment where the latter appear instantiated in a given spatio-temporal setting, on the other. Secondly, as already noted, a 'populist intervention' refers to the formal logic through which various heterogeneous demands can be drawn together into a single popular identity. It thus follows that no specific ideological content is inherently associated to it. While constructing a 'people' requires drawing an internal antagonistic frontier within the social, the ultimate character of such construction will ultimately depend on which specific difference is emphasized in such a construction (Miró 2017). Equivalential logics, in order to operate successfully, depend on postulating an 'Other' in opposition to which the resulting popular construction will acquire its ultimate character. For instance, whereas a 'people' that achieved internal unity by emphasizing its difference with respect to the financial elites would probably show a progressive and inclusive character, one that was configured in opposition to immigrant groups would surely be a reactionary one.

It is our contention that 'populist situations', involving both widespread institutional disintegration and a constitutive inability on the side of the existing order to provide satisfaction to proliferating unsatisfied demands, are intimately related to capitalism's systemic crises. However, as noted above, an abstract analysis of capitalist dynamics does not suffice to identify a 'populist situation'. Instead, an analysis is required of how the interruption of ongoing capitalist dynamics affects, and is affected in turn, by the specific configuration of the overarching institutional structure through which capitalist activity appears instantiated in a given spatio-temporal setting. To that extent, we contend that Wolfson and Kotz's (2010) distinction between Liberal and Regulated SSAs enables a more nuanced understanding of how such interplay between capitalist dynamics and the various social consensuses supporting its ongoing reproduction is ultimately mediated by the configuration of the existing institutional order.

Both types differ with respect to the actors each tends to empower during the expansion phase, the nature of the institutional breakdown ensuing once capitalist reproduction is interrupted, and the mode of emergence of unsatisfied demands following the latter. In consequence, the link between the occurrence of a systemic crisis (an interruption of capitalist reproduction requiring fully-fledged institutional transformation for capitalist activity to be resumed in the long run) and a concomitant organic crisis (the breakdown of social consensuses hitherto supporting previous institutional equilibria) differs among the two types. By help of an analysis of the two last stages in US capitalist history, the two next sections will argue that organic crises ensuing from a Liberal SSA's internal breakdown may be rightly assimilated to what we have previously termed 'populist situations', whereas the opposite holds in relation to their Regulated counterparts. This, in turn, would hold the key to explain the pervasiveness of populist expressions at the current historical juncture.

Expansion and crisis in Regulated SSAs

In order to apprehend the nature of the organic crisis corresponding to each SSA it is necessary to understand the existing relation between the problems endogenous to the production process and the 'accumulation of unsatisfied demands' ensuing, insofar as the nature of the former conditions the development and unfolding of the latter. Each systemic crisis involves a recomposition of existing social orderings and hierarchies, through which the diverse alignments among different groups that had sedimented during the prior phase of expansion reveal their ultimately contingent character. While every process of SSA demise and change involves a transformation of its underlying group of supporters, as well as the relations of hierarchy existing among them, the way in which the processes of accumulation and profit-making had been framed and organized during the previous phase of expansion conditions the nature of the systemic crisis ensuing, the type of agents acquiring prominence in the struggle for institutional re-definition, and the potential outcomes resulting from the latter.

One of the main differences of Regulated SSAs in relation to their Liberal counterparts concerns the different implications each carries with respect to the aggregate rate of capital accumulation. Two among the most salient features of Regulated SSAs, namely, a tendency towards co-respective competition among individual capital units and a more cooperative stance towards organized labor, tend to have positive implications for capital accumulation. While the former tends to lengthen the temporal horizon under which investment decisions are made, the latter favors the eventual realization of the surplus value previously generated in production, encouraging the re-investment of money-capital into the productive process rather than into inherently speculative activities. Despite Regulated SSAs promoting social stability over the long run by progressively broadening the material base over which different groups' demands can be offered partial satisfaction, the existence of coordination problems within the capitalist class may prevent its implementation at a given conjuncture. Although economic growth and accumulation do not incorporate diverse groups into an SSA's base of beneficiaries on an equal footing, they do provide a material base for various subaltern groups to accept their particular mode of inclusion within the social fabric.

While the exact form of its institutional appearance will be idiosyncratic to each particular case, the manner in which its different institutional blocks fit each other shows a certain coherence, consisting in the 'active regulation of economic relations and behaviors by various types of institutions other than market forces' (Kotz 2013a: 340). The oligopolistic nature of capitalist competition, together with a higher implication of other social actors in running the economy, favors a more egalitarian distribution of social output among the actors involved. Insofar as a broadening base of beneficiaries ensures that increased accumulation will find its necessary counterpart in a progressively growing aggregate demand, the eventual occurrence of a 'realization crisis' is generally not a serious threat to the existing social order. Moreover, it also permits the accommodation of different demands over an 'expanding pie', as well as the gradual inclusion of different groups whose demands were not taken into account in the initial 'relations of equivalence' that had supported SSA's establishment at its early stages.

Systemic crises of Regulated SSAs tend to take the form of a relatively long period of macroeconomic instability, manifested through a gradual descent of the average rate of profit from peak to peak of successive business cycles, rather than through a sudden crash of economic activity (Kotz 2013a: 342). Constitutive features of Regulated SSAs favor the spread of various demands over existing profits during the expansion phase, in turn gradually compromising the conditions needed for sustained surplus value creation. For instance, the climate of cooperation between capital and various subaltern groups that is at the core of a Regulated SSA's institutional edifice empowers the former so as to progressively put further pressures on the existing social output.

The process of 'accumulation of unsatisfied demands' and the gradual decline in profitability should not be understood as independent social processes. On the contrary, the very conditions that had promoted profitability during the expansion phase underlie the emergence of this set of 'unsatisfied demands' that will eventually reinforce the process of SSA decay. In a nutshell, eventually, success breeds failure. Whereas the initial stages of a new SSA require diverse groups to show their consent towards their respective positions in the social order, the gradual improvement of their material conditions of existence sets the terrain for a growing contestation of their subordination in those specific areas where generalized subservience is a *sine qua non* condition for ongoing capitalist reproduction, namely, capital's absolute prerogatives over the organization of the production sphere.

In sum, Regulated SSAs, through their normal functioning, endogenously generate a growing mass of unsatisfied demands during its phase of expansion that end up accelerating economic decline by putting additional pressures on existing profits. This 'accumulation of unsatisfied demands' over existing profits during the phase of expansion does not manifest itself through a sudden crash of economic activity but through growing macroeconomic instability. On the one hand, different stages of the circuit of capital suffer from pressures for institutional change according to various groups' requirements, thus impeding economic activity to proceed as it used to. On the other hand, dealing with these demands (either through satisfaction or through repression) implies additional costs over existing profits.

The Postwar SSA in the United States provides a very accurate example of these dynamics. Gordon et al. (1987) list four main institutional pillars that had sustained economic activity in the postwar order: US international dominance (*Pax Americana*); a Capital–Labor Accord; a Capital–Citizen accord; and the moderation of inter-capitalist competition. Over time, a variety of 'unsatisfied demands' gradually emerged out of the 'normal' development of these constituent institutions, which thus put under increasing stress the existing institutional structure as well as its capacity to ensure both 'social peace' and sustained economic activity over time.

On the one hand, problems internal to the accumulation process emerged as the role played by the US as the industrial leader of the new world order started to be challenged by growing competition from European and Japanese manufacturing (Brenner 2006). Increasing penetration of Japanese and European imports into the national market gradually led to a growing excess of capacity in the US industrial sector that, in turn, contributed to lower the average rate of profit in manufacturing. Therefore, the surplus generated by the US economy through which to be able to satisfy the material requirements of various subaltern groups gradually came under growing restraint. On the other hand, several groups that had occupied a position of subalternity *vis-à-vis* US capital progressively manifested growing dissatisfaction with existing social arrangements. Firstly, third world countries began to struggle against US domination in the 1960s, thus compromising the steady supply of raw materials needed for the latter's industrial production. Secondly, the 'Capital–Labor Accord' became increasingly contested. Increasing material security, associated with the decreasing influence of unemployment as a disciplinary device, enabled the spread of diverse demands from an increasingly militant labor movement. From demands related to workplace safety to a blunt rejection of Taylorist discipline and its associated lack of autonomy, capital had to incur increasing costs to safeguard the social stability needed for economic activity to continue.

Thirdly, the Capital–Citizen Accord gave way to a climate of increasing contestation of the capitalist order. The anti-war, feminist, environmentalist, or civil rights movements were but multifarious expressions of a general climate of rejection of a social order ultimately subject to the vagaries of capitalist self-reproduction. On the one hand, this situation forced an increase in the costs capital had to incur through various regulations that limited its scope for action. On the other hand, the multitude of expressions in which this movement of social rejection was reflected opened the possibility of a system-wide 'equivalence' among various conflicts susceptible to have questioned the capitalist order as such.

In sum, a gradual 'accumulation of unsatisfied demands' took place due to the steady empowerment of various groups that had been assigned a subsidiary role in the social order *vis-à-vis* capital, so that the increasing 'costs of keeping people down' (Bowles et al. 1990) capital had to incur eventually put further pressures on an increasingly compromised accumulation process. When these are considered alongside the internal problems that capital was experiencing at the time as a result of growing international competition in manufacturing, it is rendered clear that the institutional conditions that had secured capitalist domination during previous decades, and thus sustained capital accumulation and economic growth, were increasingly fragile. The institutional structure that had permitted to accommodate different groups' demands over an 'expanding pie' progressively turned into its opposite, an 'accumulation of demands over a shrinking pie' which could not but reinforce SSA decline.

The manner in which systemic crises derived from Regulated SSAs unfold ultimately constrains the different scenarios its eventual resolution can give rise to. Kotz (2010) argues that several factors explain why systemic crises derived from Regulated SSA's internal contradictions tend to be 'milder', thus limiting the existing possibilities for radical systemic transformation. On the one hand, the oligopolistic nature of inter-capitalist competition characteristic of Regulated SSAs tends to generate a climate of cooperation among the capitalist class that makes it easier for them to act as a unified agent when the political struggle for redefining the contours of the next SSA arrives. On the other, the State has recent experience in managing the economy so that, when problems eventually become insurmountable, it has the means to bring the crisis to a quicker resolution along continuist lines. This means that a transition to a liberal form of capitalism is a more likely outcome than radical systemic transformation.

As already noted, Wolfson and Kotz (2010) hypothesize that there might be a natural tendency for Regulated and Liberal SSAs to alternate. As the latter are mainly based on enshrining market principles within various social institutions, building up a Liberal SSA out of a decaying Regulated SSA basically amounts to deconstructing the old institutional structure. This is an inherently easier task to be effected than having to build complementarities anew among different institutional spheres. Using Hirschman's (1970) terminology, while Regulated SSAs are based on 'voice', 'exit' is an ever-present possibility for capital when things are not going as expected (Streeck 2014a). Moreover, as argued by Moseley (2013: 382), there might be a deeper reason favoring the succession of a decaying Regulated SSA by a Liberal one. Capitalists' refusal to significantly devalue wide masses of capital in order to restore the rate of profit, supported by the organizational capacities they had developed during the previous phase of expansion, would enable them to shift the burden of adjustment towards workers' wages so that, 'in a dynamic, long-run sense, a falling rate of profit may evolve into a realization problem' (Moseley 2013: 382).

While the reasons just indicated mainly refer to capital's capacity to block a process of radical transformative change by favoring a transition towards a Liberal SSA, we nevertheless disagree with Kotz (2010: 377) in presuming that increasing standards of living accruing to the working class during the previous expansion phase make an anti-capitalist stance towards the existing social order less likely. Not only did the (uneven) improvements in the material conditions of existence of the working class enable increasing contestation of the institutional bases grounding their subordination but, most importantly, the wide variety of democratic demands that spread through many Western economies during the 1960s and 1970s accounted for a *de facto* condemnation of the capitalist social order, although 'Anti-capitalism' might not have been the slogan under which oppositional movements had grouped at the time. System-threatening social upheavals find no privileged locus in class-related social identities but, on the contrary, crucially depend upon, firstly, an over-determined translation of multifarious conflicts into incommensurable social demands and, secondly, an 'equivalential' relation to be developed among the latter through the hegemonic struggle itself.

In relation to our discussion of populism, two main features of the 'legitimation crisis' (Fraser 2015) corresponding to a Regulated SSA's decomposition impede its qualification as a 'populist situation' in the above-mentioned sense. On the one hand, demands tend to emerge gradually during the phase of expansion, being susceptible to be dealt with in a relatively orderly and sequential manner by an institutional order that still retains strong competences to accomplish such a task. Despite the period of macroeconomic instability being relatively lengthy, the basic institutional foundations regulating the social order, although widely contested, will not be shattered at once. On the other hand, the absence of an abrupt institutional breakdown prevents political identities developed during the phase of expansion from suddenly losing their legitimacy, so that political struggle is likely to take the form of a combat between already-consolidated forms of identification rather than a confrontation in order to produce new ones. Although the strong capacities retained by the ruling classes in order to defer from existing social pacts make a transition towards a Liberal SSA a more likely outcome than a transition to some non-capitalist mode of social organization, the ultimate resolution of the political crisis will be partly dependent upon the hegemonic struggle itself. However, it is presumed that populist interventions will not be a determinant element of such struggle.

Recent US experience exemplifies this scenario. After the turbulent years of the 1970s, active measures were taken in order to restore capital's supremacy over labor, a political program which Bowles et al. (1983) succinctly termed the 'Great Repression'. These measures included a new oppositional stance towards organized labor, including lowering minimum wages, reducing social benefits, and policies actively confronting unions (Rosenberg 2010); dismantling industries where unions were the most powerful and/or using the threat of relocation to curb labor's power (Wallace and Brady 2010); and a Federal Reserve's restrictive monetary policy aimed at restoring mass unemployment as a key disciplinary device. The final outcome was a new institutional structure, with few links to the former one, which reinstated capital's dominance over other social groups. In a sense, the 'accumulation of unsatisfied demands' that had emerged during the expansion phase of the Postwar SSA was no longer a problem to social stability after the early 1980s. However, it was not due to a partial satisfaction of the growing popular discontent. On the contrary, demands waned from the public arena because the ground upon which they were made eventually crumbled, and the horizon with respect to which those demands addressed an absence virtually disappeared.

Expansion and crisis in Liberal SSAs

Systemic crises fostering the disintegration of a Liberal SSA yield a sharply different scenario from the one presented above. Contrary to Regulated SSAs, key features of Liberal SSAs tend to result in lower levels of aggregate capital accumulation. On the one hand, the prevalence of cutthroat competition among individual capital units shortens the temporal horizon of investment, thus making inherently speculative activities more attractive. On the other, rising inequality along different social dimensions jeopardizes potential demand for expanding productive capacity. In sum, aggregate levels of (productive) capital accumulation tend to be rather low. However, their lower ability to generate a surplus to be then distributed among diverse groups does not necessarily compromise its capacity to generate a material basis for the social consensus that is needed.

Liberal SSAs are characterized by the 'expansion of market forces at the expense of other forms of economic regulation' (Kotz 2013a: 341), thus reinforcing the power of capital in various spheres of social life. Generally, despite favoring surplus value creation, its institutions tend to simultaneously compromise the latter's eventual realization. While this is a crucial contradiction in terms of every Liberal SSA's systemic reproduction, any successful SSA needs to generate certain institutional mechanisms that postpone the eventual occurrence of a systemic breakdown. Otherwise, the former could not be qualified as an SSA in the first instance. Hence, the contradiction between the conditions necessary for surplus creation and those needed for its ulterior realization might never present itself as such, as it might give rise endogenously to other contradictory tendencies that, at a later moment, might as well cause a systemic breakdown, although one of a significantly different nature. Therefore, rather than postulating a hierarchical ordering of social contradictions, it is necessary to appraise the ways in which diverse social processes co-exist among themselves in a permanent state of tension and contradiction.

Attaining long-lasting social stability requires these various social processes to mutually sustain each other through their common interaction despite them being potentially contradictory. That is, for the whole set of their relations to be sustained over the long run, their joint interaction ought to contain their potentially explosive character. Recent US experience under neoliberalism provides an accurate example of the ways in which a latent realization crisis tendency may endogenously give rise to different trends that postpone the eventual actualization of the former: 'Neoliberal capitalism was able to operate as an SSA for the very reason that its institutions were able to prevent a crisis of underconsumption for 25 years' (Kotz 2013b: 287). Growing profits in the face of stagnating wages not only fostered the occurrence of various asset bubbles but also increased levels of household indebtedness among the working classes. While the former encouraged increasing consumption through the operation of a wealth effect among those holding assets, the latter permitted upward consumption patterns despite sluggish wage increases. In sum, despite growing concentration of wealth and income, aggregate demand might grow in line with productive capacity for a long time through the operation of these unsustainable trends. While these trends were unsustainable in the long run, it was precisely their joint occurrence that corrected their inherently contradictory nature and permitted the system's reproduction over decades.

The means through which a latent realization crisis tendency has been postponed gave way, in the US, to a different type of crisis tendency, namely one of 'asset bubble-induced over-investment' (Kotz 2013a; 2013b), as a 'latent' excess of industrial capacity was not revealed as long as consumption kept growing in line with GDP thanks to increasing levels of household indebtedness.[1] The latter could be expanded, despite stagnant wages, as long as a housing bubble allowed a risk-prone financial sector to keep lending them money using households' appreciating assets as collaterals, and so on. However, once the housing bubble eventually deflated, and consumer spending returned to a normal relation to disposable income, it was revealed that the whole institutional edifice was dependent upon certain trends whose endless reproduction was merely a chimera.

Therefore, a social order was indeed successfully reproduced under neoliberal capitalism, although one of a significantly different nature than that corresponding to Regulated SSAs. Liberal institutional edifices are generally not based on compromises reached between capital and other subaltern groups, nor do they tend to gradually empower the latter through a steady improvement of their material welfare. As their constituent institutional elements tend to reinforce the power of capital in the process of surplus value extraction, it is unlikely that a proliferation of unsatisfied demands during the expansion phase would manage to disrupt the normal functioning of the production process. Therefore, the interaction between the emergence of unsatisfied demands and the evolution of capital profitability ought to be sought elsewhere.

While surplus value realization is generally a contradiction at the very core of each Liberal SSA, the mechanisms generated to postpone it tend to make the eventual crisis worse (Kotz 2010b: 370). As noted above, a set of unsustainable trends may provide mutual sustainment to each other so that social stability is attained for a relatively long time. However, the potentially contradictory character of each of the main components of such institutional architecture implies that the disintegration of one of them tends to carry with it the breakdown of the whole institutional assemblage, rather than just one of its individual components. Those that gives stability to the whole are but the relations of complementarity existing among its components so that, by the time these mutually sustaining trends can no longer sustain each other, a sudden crash of economic activity ensues rather than a long period of macroeconomic turbulence (Kotz 2013a: 347). In sum, Liberal SSAs 'tend to eventually produce a *severe* structural crisis of accumulation' (Kotz 2010b: 368, emphasis added) because, in order to resume economic activity, the whole institutional edifice needs to be restored (chiefly including the relations of complementarity existing among its various components), rather than just some of its single elements.

The analysis presented above concludes that systemic crises derived from a Liberal SSA's collapse tend to last longer than those corresponding to Regulated SSAs. Under the presumption that Liberal and Regulated SSAs tend to alternate with each other, Kotz (2010b; 2013a) argues that, because Regulated SSAs usually take longer to be built up, the corresponding period of institutional indetermination is comparatively more prolonged. On the one hand, Liberal SSAs tend to weaken the managerial capacities of the State as well as to undo a general climate of cooperation within the capitalist class, so that a unified response by the ruling classes is less likely to be straightforward. On the other, prevalent trends of impoverishment and indebtedness among private households leave private aggregate demand with little sources to keep on fostering production growth during the recession phase. Furthermore, while Liberal SSAs may be established by merely deconstructing a previously existing Regulated SSA, the opposite case does not prove true.

Regarding the nature of its eventual resolution, systemic crises of Liberal SSAs yield, *a priori*, a more indeterminate scenario. Kotz (2010b) speaks of a paradoxical situation regarding the existing possibilities for radical systemic transformation. Despite the severity and duration of the crisis period, there might not be an already-existing political subject ready to give a political battle worthy of the name as a result of those trends that had governed the previous expansion phase. However, despite potentially transformative movements having been systematically weakened, the necessarily long period of institutional recomposition grants the possibility of that subject emerging during the period of political struggle itself.

As already noted, in order to shed some light upon both the nature and likely resolution of each systemic crisis, it is necessary to analyze the co-implication between those problems internal to the production process and their effects upon the disintegration of the social consensuses that had framed and supported it during the previous phase of stability. Under Regulated SSAs unsatisfied demands tend to emerge during the expansion phase as the disciplinary mechanisms of capitalism progressively lose their grip on various subaltern social groups. The latter's contestation of their respective roles in the social fabric amounts to growing pressures over the various stages of the circuit of capital, which translates into increasing macroeconomic instability. Liberal SSAs yield a radically different scenario. Despite its relative inability to generate a growing surplus through which to accommodate 'different demands over an expanding pie', a social order may be maintained thanks to the operation of a set of inherently unsustainable trends. Systemic crises corresponding to Liberal SSAs thus involve a sudden crash followed by a long period of stagnation, due to the sudden implosion of several social processes, intrinsically contradictory, that had regulated social objectivity so far.

While a social order is the result of a hegemonic struggle through which some groups are differentially integrated while others are simultaneously relegated to a radical ostracism, the reproduction of this differential integration is ultimately dependent upon the successful operation of certain social dynamics that enable each group to receive a given portion of the social product. Of course, the portion that ought to accrue to each group in order to show satisfaction with existing social arrangements is a perennial object of contention within the hegemonic struggle itself. However, once the already mentioned unsustainable trends cannot be reproduced any longer, a sudden crash gives way to an abrupt process of institutional decomposition. As the economic situation worsens, certain groups that had been successfully integrated into the social order are suddenly faced with the precarious character of their mode of inclusion. Moreover, the relative absence of a climate of cooperation among social actors during the expansion phase favors the adoption of defensive measures by economic elites. Hence, several groups that had been successfully integrated in the social order are abruptly expelled from their differential positions. The 'naturalness' with which each group understood their differential inclusion within the social order is violently shattered, the sedimented relations among them are shown to be contingent, and their shared worldviews start to disintegrate. Therefore, an abrupt breakdown of social cohesion ensues, throwing underlying social divisions abruptly into light.

The economic crash is thus followed by an intense and simultaneous proliferation of unsatisfied demands, radically heterogeneous in nature and without already-constituted relations among them. On the one hand, the impossibility to deal with them in an individual and orderly manner, together with the inability to generate a material surplus in the short run to offer them a new material integration, yields the possibility of a new alliance among those that had been rejected on the basis, precisely, of their common rejection of/by the *status quo*. On the other hand, the dislocatory effects of the crisis upon social identities are not restricted to one single area of the social but affect instead very different latitudes of the social order. The implosion of the several processes that had been regulating social objectivity makes the 'unsatisfied demands' ensuing inherently heterogeneous in nature. In short, it is the inherently heterogeneous character of those unsatisfied demands as well as the abrupt and simultaneous character of their emergence that permits us to qualify the ensuing scenario as a 'populist situation'.

For economic activity to be resumed in a sustained manner, new alliances and coalitions ought to emerge in order to establish the institutional bases that will regulate the next period of long-lasting stability. For radical social transformation to be accomplished, it is strictly necessary that a political subject emerge during this period of institutional re-definition. On the one hand, new elements are needed that enable the recently excluded to constitute themselves as a political subject capable of taking part in the ongoing political struggle, as their differential positions in the previous social order prevent them from having already drawn relations of solidarity among themselves. On the other, for the reasons already offered, the political struggle for institutional redefinition will be necessarily long, so that there is a possibility that such movement will emerge in the course of the struggle itself.

'Populist situations' signal that 'populist interventions' will show much higher hegemonic depth in their attempt to reshape the social order, relative not only to other historical periods when a successful SSA operates but also to those corresponding to a systemic crisis of a Regulated SSA. Current US experience provides a good example of these dynamics. Two antithetic dichotomizing narratives can be found spreading through the social body, both aiming at collapsing a wide range of unsatisfied demands into a new popular identity. One could be found in the thread linking the Occupy movement to the 2016 US presidential campaign of Bernie Sanders, whereas the other one would be associated with the Tea Party through to Donald Trump's eventual presidential election. This exemplifies how populist logics can serve very different political projects, for it is not the content articulated which makes them populist but, rather, the very form of such an articulation. One that attempts to build a 'people' in opposition to the financial elites and their connivance with their political counterparts would surely be one ready to advance progressive goals towards a fairer and more inclusive society, whereas one that built a 'people' in opposition to certain dispossessed groups would certainly stand by the former's very opposite. This example highlights the relevance of correctly apprehending the exact terms on which the political struggle is to be conducted. In particular, for those on the Left, populist logics ought to be consciously studied, rather than just be considered a degraded and misguided version of truly emancipatory politics. The structural terrain upon which the political struggle is currently being conducted is one conducive to populist interventions, so that those refusing to accept the constraints imposed upon the hegemonic struggle by the nature of the underlying material processes will be necessarily doomed to fail in their attempts to re-shape the social order.

Left-wing populism after the Great Recession

The analysis presented above attempts to throw some light upon the contours and characteristics of the social field where political struggles for institutional redefinition are currently being conducted. At times when sustained capital accumulation and economic growth are the norm, existing coalitions supporting the reproduction of the *statu quo* find an enlarging material base for their continued reproduction, in turn constraining the available scope for radical political transformation. Capitalism's systemic crises, on the contrary, give rise to a sharply different scenario. Once internal malfunctions accumulate to the point that the existing institutional order no longer manages to promote further economic growth and capital accumulation, pressures for institutional redefinition intensify as dominant coalitions see their material support severely curtailed. Wide-ranging institutional transformation thus becomes a systemic imperative. While the periodic alternation between periods featuring relative institutional stability and others marked by social turmoil and institutional transformation is a perennial feature of societies where capitalism is the dominant mode of production, such an alternation is nonetheless mediated by the specific institutional form through which capitalism appears instantiated at a given time and place. In that respect, Wolfson and Kotz's (2010) distinction between Regulated and Liberal SSAs provides a useful starting point to explore how the ensuing political struggle is affected by the character of the institutional structure undergoing disintegration.

As explored in detail in the previous section, the scope, timing, and intensity of the institutional breakdown characteristic of a Liberal SSA's internal implosion can be readily assimilated to what we had previously termed a 'populist situation', namely, a social context marked by a sudden, abrupt, and relatively simultaneous emergence of unsatisfied demands which, while having no *ex ante* relations drawn among them, clash with the inability of the existing order to provide them satisfaction. Such a scenario corresponds with the one ensuing after the onset of the Great Recession. Moreover, because of the widespread dislocatory effects derived from the latter, affecting very different latitudes of the social, old forms of socio-political identification do not manage to make the new situation intelligible to the various groups involved. As a result, the current political struggle prominently takes the form of competing, and potentially antithetic, attempts to produce such new forms of identification through which to gather the aforementioned heterogeneous dissatisfactions with the current state of affairs, i.e. a new 'popular' identity whose defining character cannot be predetermined *a priori*.

SSA theory contends that, for sustained capital accumulation to be resumed again in the long run, a new favorable institutional environment, articulated through contingently developed relations of complementarity among its core building blocks, needs to be established. The ultimate character of such SSA cannot be determined *a priori* but, on the contrary, will be dependent upon the eventual resolution of the current hegemonic struggle for institutional redefinition, which, we argue, will prominently take the form of competing attempts to consolidate a new 'popular' identity through which disparate yearnings and aspirations will be articulated on the grounds, precisely, of their shared dissatisfaction. In sum, the core political struggle nowadays would then be that among different competing attempts to construct a 'people', whose character will shape the process of institutional restructuring already in progress while, simultaneously, being in turn shaped by it.

Asserting that the current political struggle prominently involves potentially antithetic 'populist interventions' refers exclusively to the formal logic through which such heterogeneous dissatisfactions with the current state of affairs can be drawn together. In order to elucidate what the actual stakes would be in such a contention among competing 'populist interventions', the distinction between 'left-wing' and 'right-wing' populist interventions provides a useful starting point (e.g. Stavrakakis and Katsambekis 2014; Kioupkiolis 2016; Mouffe 2018). While, because of the strictly formal character of Laclau's account of populism, no absolute, clear-cut demarcation can be offered between 'right-wing' and 'left-wing' populist interventions, respectively, according to one of its foremost proponents the difference between the two 'owes to the fact that the former tends to restrict democracy while the latter works to extend and radicalize democracy' (Mouffe 2017). The 'people' implicit in a left-wing populist intervention would then be a construction 'whose unity is secured by the identification with a radical democratic conception of citizenship and a common opposition to the oligarchy, the forces that structurally impede the realization of a democratic project' (Mouffe 2018: 80), 'asserting inclusion rather than exclusion, advocating an egalitarian vision of society, fighting inequalities and opposing strict hierarchies' (Katsambekis and Kioupkiolis 2019: 13). In that respect, a valid criterion of demarcation to differentiate 'left-wing' from 'right-wing' populist interventions might be obtained, in our view, from an examination of Rancière's (1999; 2014) own understanding of populism. Laclau (2005a:

244–9) had criticized Rancière's approach to populism (rightly, in our view) for insisting on ascribing a particular content to it, namely, the political irruption of the previously excluded. While a strictly formal approach to populist logics (such as Laclau's) enhances the analytical value of the latter, Rancière's normative stance nonetheless provides a valid criterion of demarcation to identify 'left-wing populist interventions', namely, the inclusion of the previously excluded, through which the voiceless regain the voice they are not supposed to have in order to contest the symbolic and material inequalities through which their very exclusion is enforced in the first instance.

Insofar as several among the defining features of the current conjuncture enhance the capacity of populist logics to reshape the socio-symbolic field, actors willing to affect the ongoing process of institutional restructuring will need to engage seriously with populist logics. Nevertheless, a marked distrust towards populist interventions is singularly prevalent among those on the Left who, speaking from a Marxist standpoint, argue against the very possibility of a (truly) socially progressive populism on the grounds that, arguably, populist interventions cannot but constitute a self-conscious distortion and manipulation of social antagonisms utterly incompatible with truly emancipatory politics (e.g. Žižek 2006a; Fassin 2018; Bidet 2019). In our view, those holding such a theoretical position miss the fact that no social relation (including, of course, capitalist relations of production), however contradictory it may be, enjoys an in-built tendency to acquire expression in the socio-symbolic field, and much less to be converted into the dominant social antagonism in a given conjuncture.

In that regard, it is our contention that not only is there no inherent incompatibility between populist interventions and the promotion of anti-capitalist politics but, also, that advancing the latter in the current conjuncture strictly requires engaging with the former (Bray 2015; Formenti 2017; Sotiris 2019). Despite capitalist relations of production containing the ever-present possibility to be politicized, in order for the former to become so in a progressive manner an active process of political mediation is required that constructs a social antagonism along an anti-capitalist direction. Every social antagonism (including, of course, the one between capital and labor) needs to be actively constructed. Irrespective of whether particular social dynamics exist providing a material basis for the social antagonism under consideration, such an act of political mediation is ultimately constitutive of the latter.

Populist logics, we contend, ought to be considered a privileged tool to construct such social antagonism along anti-capitalist lines. On the one hand, key features of the current political landscape favor the operation of populist logics in fostering the reconfiguration of the socio-symbolic field. On the other hand, the strategic value of populist logics in gathering together heterogenous struggles is significantly enhanced by a social context featuring marked social fragmentation and a generalized discredit of collective identities as a result of decades of neoliberal hegemony. Despite no particular social dynamic enjoying a privileged route of access into the socio-symbolic field, the dichotomizing nature of 'populist interventions' does have a correlate in current trends of increasing social inequality, through which social wealth is being concentrated in increasingly fewer hands, and the diachronic evolution of top incomes shows an enlarging gap with that corresponding to the rest (e.g. Piketty 2014; Milanovic 2016).

Moreover, spurred by worldwide capital profitability problems in tradable sectors, several areas previously protected from commodification have been increasingly brought within the reach of capitalist processes, such as housing, health provision, or tertiary education systems, for instance. Capital's drive for self-expansion thus increasingly overdetermines the increasing precarization of labor relations, ongoing ecological destruction, existing pressures for privatizing public health and education systems, the disruption of traditional family arrangements, or the reproduction of traditional gender relations to subjugate women to their role as 'natural' carers. Despite there being no essential commonality fostering the symbolic articulation of these separate struggles, they do share a common material overdetermining factor. As argued by Sotiris (2019: 31):

> instead of treating these common political signifiers as the processes of articulation of diverse and not necessarily connected social demands, one might say that the opposite dynamic is at work: common conflicts and antagonisms, having to do with the offensive of capital and the dominant classes, brought together by the contradictions of capital accumulation, enable this translation into radical democratic demands.

Nevertheless, while such commonality does not enjoy any sort of privilege regarding its capacity to enter the socio-symbolic field, a populist articulation might create a shared solidarity among them despite their initial constitution as demands appearing detached from their material social determination. Were such articulation successful, it would reinstate the ongoing relevance of class struggle at a time when the social influence of capitalist dynamics expands well beyond the strictly productive sphere. Confronting the pervasive effects upon living conditions of 'capital-as-a-whole' (Bray 2018), there would now stand an expanded working class, comprising 'everyone in the producing class who has in their lifetime participated in the totality of reproduction of society – irrespective of whether that labor has been paid for by capital or remained unpaid' (Bhattacharya 2017: 89). Therefore, at a time when capital's self-valorization needs increasingly compromise the very sustainability of social life, an anti-capitalist stance can no longer be considered a merely sectorial demand. Nonetheless, such a stance needs to be actively constructed. Against the total subordination of social life to capital's valorization needs, all power to the people!

Acknowledgments

Parts of this chapter have already been published as 'Grounding populism upon political economy. Organic crises in Social Structures of Accumulation theory', in *Science & Society*, 83 (1), 2019. The author thanks Guilford Press for granting permission for re-printing them here.

Note

1 See Bakir and Campbell (2015) for an opposite view on whether over-investment should be considered the key crisis tendency under neoliberalism in the U.S.

Part II

The case of contemporary Spain

7 The Spanish 'Mediterranean' Liberal SSA

A characterization

The remaining three chapters are devoted to analyzing, by help of the theoretical framework hitherto developed in previous chapters, how social reproduction has been (and continues to be) secured in the Spanish social formation since the early 1990s up until the present moment. To that extent, our main concern will be to analyze the internal workings, as well as its overdetermined relation with its external conditions, of the institutional environment structuring capitalist activity in Spain, which we characterize as a Mediterranean Liberal SSA. This chapter will limit itself to delineating its main contours while offering a preliminary justification of why we choose to characterize it as such. The next chapter will examine the period of socioeconomic expansion spanning from the early 1990s up until the onset of the Great Recession, focusing on the institutional bases supporting and structuring the economic expansion until 2008; the various internal contradictions such an institutional ensemble harbored; and the reach, limitations, and blind spots characterizing the various co-existing social consensuses. The last chapter, in turn, will analyze the phase of ulterior decay, spanning from 2008 up to the present moment, one that appears characterized by the latter period's obverse, namely, a breakdown first, and a slight recovery later on, of capitalist activity; reverberating malfunctions all over the institutional structure; and widespread social contestation in an increasingly polarized social scenario. Far from representing two historical periods deserving separate analytical treatment, the abruptness and intensity characterizing the recessionary period will be shown to constitute but the underside of the apparent vigor and strength shown by the previous phase of expansion. Identifying the various factors at play underlying the image of success the Spanish political economy managed to project in the years leading to the Great Recession remains all the more crucial, therefore, to apprehend the limits and imbalances haunting the Spanish political economy in its aftermath.

As noted above, a well-established SSA has been successful in promoting and structuring capitalist activity in Spanish territory since the early 1990s up until the onset of the Great Recession, in 2008. Nonetheless, while it delivered impressive results for certain key macroeconomic indicators, it was not free from internal contradictions. Quite on the contrary, it was precisely the proliferation of internal imbalances, together with the development of contingent relations of mutual reinforcement among them, which animated, in the last instance, the remarkable pattern of economic expansion meriting such laudatory appraisals at the time. Moreover, while the deleterious social consequences derived from several among these key social processes seemed conducive, at least apparently, to have given rise to wide-ranging social contestation, it was the relations of mutual support and reinforcement developed among the former which, precisely, enabled the worst social effects derived from each to be partially attenuated, in turn preventing them from being overtly politicized. Nevertheless, the virtuous relations developed among these social processes did not serve to mitigate, much less to erase, their inherently contradictory and ultimately self-defeating character. Far from it, their contradictory nature was accentuated through and through over the course of the economic expansion so that, once internal contradictions could no longer be kept in check, the whole institutional assemblage could not but crumble down, in turn depriving existing social consensuses of their necessary conditions of existence.

Such pattern of economic expansion was drastically reversed in 2008. Despite being concurrent with the onset of the Great Recession at a worldwide level, the implosion of the institutional structure regulating socio-economic reproduction in Spain until that moment had mainly internal roots, as mounting internal disequilibria were already driving the whole Spanish social formation towards an inevitable collapse. Nonetheless, while the Spanish model was already showing signs of exhaustion as early as 2007, the onset of the Great Recession at the world scale did act as a catalyst, amplifying the abruptness and intensity shown by the ensuing economic breakdown. Once the overarching institutional structure found its self-reproduction irremediably compromised, the various social agreements, common understandings, and shared expectations the former had helped consolidate could not but follow suit. Barely a couple of years sufficed to put an end to the greatest expansionary phase in the recent history of Spanish capitalism, thus giving rise to a new historical stage marked by institutional breakdown and widespread social conflict.

This chapter is organized as follows. The next section provides a justification of the characterization we are proposing, that is, firstly, why the institutional environment through which capitalist dynamics have been instantiated in Spanish territory ought to be considered a SSA; secondly, why, according to Wolfson and Kotz's (2010) distinction between Liberal and Regulated SSAs, respectively, the SSA under consideration should be assimilated to the former type; and, lastly, why certain constitutive features of it ought to be considered as inherently 'Mediterranean'. The final section enumerates some arguably idiosyncratic traits of Spain's recent historical experience which, in our view, justify its in-depth exploration from a political economy perspective.

Why an SSA?

The institutional assemblage governing socio-economic reproduction in the Spanish social formation during the last two decades and a half ought to be considered, we contend, an SSA. While the period corresponding to its expansion phase, when it managed to promote expanding capitalist activity without compromising the latter's conditions of possibility (both reproductive and political), spans only from 1995 until 2008, the following decade should nonetheless be understood as a (still unfinished) process of gradual decomposition and transformation of the social structure that had hitherto governed the previous phase of expansion. To recap, the reasons that, in our view, justify our considering such an institutional environment as a well-functioning SSA refer to the limited geographical reach of its mode of operation; an identifiable temporal span; its ability to develop various internal complementarities and synergies; and, lastly, its capacity to attain a level of social peace high enough to support ongoing capitalist activity. We will analyze each in turn.

Geographical and temporal reach

Regarding the institutional determinants of the economic expansion leading to the Great Recession, one of the features that most immediately comes to light is the markedly self-centered character of its core economic processes, in the sense that the diachronic reproduction of its core institutional components and social dynamics was secured, to a great extent, through the various synergies developed within the SSA itself. While the next chapter will substantiate this claim in detail, it suffices to point out, for now, how domestic demand constituted itself as the main driver of economic growth during those years; how households' aggregate consumption levels rose in line with GDP throughout the period, in turn helping cement existing social consensuses; how a massive housing bubble, the ultimate foundation of the SSA's diachronic reproduction, was mostly fed by rising internal demand while having a crucial and devastating impact upon the national territory; or how the Spanish State played a paramount role not only in helping Spanish capital restructure itself, but also in 'manufacturing' the above-mentioned housing bubble.

We are well aware of the various dangers implicit in reifying the national level of analysis, thus losing sight of its necessary interrelation with several other social processes operating out of the national boundaries in question. Not only, at a very high level of abstraction, every social process can be rightly considered to partake of the conditions of existence of any other social process under consideration (Resnick and Wolff 1987), but, most relevantly to our purposes, several among the Spanish SSA's constituent processes have an indisputable extra-national character, such as, for instance, the extent to which the vast amount of international liquidity that helped fuel the housing bubble was ultimately enabled by Spain's integration within the European Monetary Union (EMU); the process of international expansion, chiefly in Latin America, undergone by Spanish capital during those years; or the large swathes of immigrants who arrived from the early 2000s, without which a 'care crisis' likely to seriously compromise systemic reproduction would have probably materialized. Nonetheless, we do contend that a framework of analysis that prominently focuses upon institutional dynamics operating within Spain's national borders, while simultaneously acknowledging its overdetermined relation with transnational processes, is justified by the nature of the interrelations among the former as well as by strictly heuristic purposes.

Regarding its actual timespan, two well-differentiated historical stages, corresponding to the SSA's expansion and decay, respectively, are identified. While the effects of a well-functioning SSA are mostly qualitative in nature, having recourse to quantitative information remains nonetheless crucial to properly differentiate the upswing from the downturn. Moreover, every isolation of social processes for analytical purposes is crucially dependent upon the analyst's subjective appreciation, insofar as every SSA contains several social processes which, despite their potentially central role in sustaining social reproduction, might have different historical origins, some clearly predating the beginning of the expansion phase while others not even being in place at the moment of the SSA's early consolidation. In our view, the strength shown by some core social processes during the phase of expansion (in terms, for instance, of GDP growth, capital accumulation, or employment growth) as well as its very long duration (especially considering the ultimately precarious nature of its foundations) merit its treatment as a coherent whole whose inner workings are worthy of in-depth theoretical scrutiny.

From 2008 onwards, the various synergies fostering the previous expansion were rapidly undone, in turn submitting social reproduction to increasing blockages. Nonetheless, despite the proliferation of internal imbalances and the impossibility to reproduce previous levels of social peace in the aftermath of the Great Recession, no alternative institutional arrangement has yet been successfully implemented. Social reproduction is, to date, still being governed by an SSA undergoing gradual dissolution, unable to reinstate previous synergies though, nonetheless, still firmly in place. In that respect, as explored in detail in the last chapter, the downturn comprises so far two different periods, one featuring sharp institutional decomposition and widespread social contestation (2008–2013), another one marked by a slight revitalization of previous virtuous dynamics and receding social conflict despite persisting internal contradictions and imbalances (from 2014 onwards).

Regarding the periodization we propose, one last precision should be made. Some of the SSA's core elements were already in place during the last phase of economic growth between 1986 and 1991, such as the crucial role played by asset price bubbles in sustaining the expansion of aggregate demand or the dominant role played by finance capital over industrial capital. However, its temporal duration was much shorter, the level of social contestation was considerably higher and, especially, the level of internal coherence achieved by then, as well as its capacity to prevent internal contradictions from disrupting existing institutional equilibria, much lower. Of course, it could be argued that the starting point of the SSA under consideration should be set at 1986, in turn considering the recession between 1992 and 1994 to be merely a short-lived blockage of an otherwise ascending two-decades-long trajectory. However, we understand the period 1986–1991 to constitute the 'exploration phase', in Gordon et al. (1982) terminology, of the upcoming SSA, a period when the institutional mechanisms that were to ground the upcoming economic expansion were being tentatively set up. The years 1995–2008 would thus constitute the SSA's 'consolidation phase', a period when the main social processes governing economic expansion had already been established, its joint occurrence being further reinforced by the emergence of several internal synergies and complementarities. As explored in greater detail in the next chapter, several elements still present during the 1986–1991 period prevented the incipient complementarities springing up among various social processes from acquiring full intensity, such as, for instance, a deindustrialization process which had not yet been completed; the continuing presence of organized labor as a relevant actor within the political arena, as manifested in the general strike of 1988; and a national currency easing the translation of internal contradictions into external disequilibria.

Internal coherence

The next chapter will provide an in-depth exploration of the way in which the various social processes implicated in social reproduction managed to secure each other's reproduction during the whole expansion phase. Now, it suffices to indicate that systemic reproduction during the upswing was articulated through several relations of complementarity and mutual constitution among several social processes which, when they are considered in strict isolation (that is, without reference to the actual social context where they had actually been developed) indubitably show a markedly contradictory character but which, nonetheless, did effectively manage to secure each other's conditions of existence thanks, precisely, to the way their joint occurrence provided each other mutual support. As shown at length below, economic expansion between 1995 and 2008 was ultimately grounded in several trends whose indefinite reproduction was not only socially undesirable but also radically impossible to attain, such as, prominently, a housing bubble of massive proportions, soaring levels of indebtedness among private agents, a distorted accumulation process or rising consumption levels in the face of widespread real wage stagnation. In that respect, it is crucial to stress the extent to which their intrinsically contradictory character not only was no impediment for their respective individual reproduction but acted instead as a driving force of their mutual co-evolution. Indeed, their contradictory character was not erased, not even attenuated, during the expansion phase thanks to their idiosyncratic modality of interrelation but, on the contrary, actually accentuated through and through during the whole upward phase. Such dynamics, in turn, contribute to explain the singular virulence shown by the ensuing systemic crisis.

In this sense, the notion of complementarity we are here entertaining crucially refers to the joint dynamic evolution of the social processes considered. When we speak of a relation of complementarity among two institutionalized social processes, we refer neither to a situation where 'the presence (or efficiency) of one increases the returns from (or efficiency) of the other' (Hall and Soskice 2001: 17), nor to one where the 'components of a whole mutually compensate for each other's deficiencies' (Crouch in Crouch et al. 2005: 359). Rather, we understand a relation of complementarity among two separate institutional spheres to have emerged when the ongoing reproduction of the internal dynamics borne by a given institutional sphere is favored by the continuing reproduction of the internal dynamics borne by the other one, and vice versa. These relations of complementarity are thus not external to already-constituted institutional blocks. Rather, they refer to the tendential dynamics undergone by each, which, in the course of their own development, might even transform the nature and form of the underlying institutional blocks themselves. Thus, when we speak of complementarities we do not imply any sort of healthy interrelation whatsoever among those spheres. Rather, we point to the means through which a whole institutional edifice manages to reproduce itself despite internal contradictions not only not balancing each other out but, potentially, being accentuated through and through.

That is, we are not interested in whether the specific institutional configuration of, say, the Spanish financial system increases or not the expected returns of a sharply dual labor market, but, instead, on whether the intrinsically contradictory dynamics borne by each do reinforce or not similarly contradictory developments in co-existing institutions. Take, for instance, a situation where a distorted accumulation process primarily driven by asset revaluation dynamics co-exists with rising levels of private indebtedness for a relatively long time. Such a situation would be rightly considered counterproductive insofar as a deteriorating productive structure increasingly complicates future debt repayments. However, recent Spanish experience illustrates how these two processes did reinforce their mutual occurrence over the long run, inasmuch as rising housing prices incentivized rising private leverage in the expectation of obtaining future rents in the midst of a process of self-revaluation, while rising debt-financed demand supported rising housing prices, in turn animating further rounds of indebtedness. While their mutual interaction did certainly not serve to compensate for each other's deficiencies, the dynamics harbored by each did nonetheless foster their joint occurrence over time, despite enhancing their intrinsically contradictory character when considered in isolation.

While the sound macroeconomic performance the Spanish 'Mediterranean' Liberal SSA managed to deliver during its expansion phase, together with the wide social consensuses it did effectively manage to sustain, testify to the successful interaction developed among its key components during these years, the various relations of mutual constitution and reinforcement emerging among these contradictory developments does also explain the sudden and fully-fledged character of the ensuing recession. In sum, the very mechanisms that ensured its joint reproduction for a certain time also acted as catalysts for the subsequent institutional breakdown.

Conflict pacification

The last requirement for an existing institutional assemblage to be qualified as a well-functioning SSA concerns its capacity to prevent widespread social contestation over its mode of operation. As already noted, we do not mean that social conflicts ought to be eradicated, nor even that they should be either minimal or transitory, for an SSA to be reproduced over time. Rather, we consider social conflicts to be an ineradicable feature of any contemporary society, derived from the asymmetric conditions of visibility and recognition enjoyed by the agents involved, from the necessarily unequal share of outcomes and responsibilities accruing to each regarding socio-material reproduction or, more commonly, from the combined effects of both sources of hierarchical stratification. Therefore, while the proliferation of social conflicts of various types will be an ever-present feature of any social formation under consideration, it is not a matter of suppressing them but, rather, of articulating and channeling them in such a manner that their public expression does not compromise the ongoing reproduction of the key social processes governing socio-economic reproduction. To that extent, underlying dissatisfactions with the existing social order need to be articulated around certain themes and issues which do not politicize, either explicitly or implicitly, those social processes being the most crucial for the diachronic reproduction of the whole institutional assemblage governing socio-material interaction while, at the same time, fostering widespread social consensuses that rationalize and naturalize existing social inequalities. The dominance of capitalism in a given social formation, however, makes the ongoing reproduction of the differential positions a social order consists of to be ultimately dependent upon the continuing reproduction of capitalist activity so that, once the latter results are structurally compromised, the former appear deprived of their material conditions of existence.

The Spanish SSA under consideration did certainly manage to promote widespread acceptance of the existing order during the upswing. Nevertheless, several among the SSA's key social processes, whose joint occurrence and interrelation remained crucial to ensure the reproduction of existing institutional equilibria, as well as the social dynamics the former helped bring into existence, were inherently antagonistic in nature. However, as shown below, it was precisely their joint occurrence and mutual interaction which prevented their conflict-prone nature, when considered in isolation, from giving rise to political expressions able to compromise existing institutional equilibria. In that respect, various social consensuses were effectively manufactured, relative to, for instance, the desirability of developing a massive housing bubble; the redefinition of middle- and working-class statuses as dependent on consumption patterns instead of labor market outcomes; the normalization of widespread labor precariousness and welfare state underdevelopment; or the pro-growth orientation of subnational governments and municipalities. Moreover, symbolic and material means were equally deployed to deprive the worst-off from enjoying the necessary means to make their respective voices heard in the public arena.

Nevertheless, as soon as the mutually reinforcing character of its main institutional blocks came to a halt in 2008, the homeostatic functioning of the institutional structure could no longer be secured. In that respect, the fact that the underlying SSA was a Liberal one, as argued below, did strongly condition the form and tempo in which a systemic crisis was converted into an organic crisis, as explored in chapter 6 above. Between 2008 and 2013, when the process of institutional decay was the most intense, the inherently antagonistic dimension of the Spanish SSA came abruptly to the fore, giving rise to widespread social contestation which, in turn, further reinforced the interruption of the above-mentioned institutional mechanisms. Nonetheless, from 2014 onwards, a gradual recovery of capitalist activity broadened the capacity of the existing order to counteract the uncontrolled proliferation of social antagonisms that had dominated the Spanish social formation in the immediate aftermath of the Great Recession.

Why Liberal?

Drawing upon Wolfson and Kotz's (2010) distinction between Liberal and Regulated SSAs, we argue that the SSA still under operation in Spain ought to be assimilated to the former type, insofar as the ultimate coherence of the Spanish structure under consideration is provided, in the last instance, by the dominance of capital over other subaltern groups in several separate social spheres. To recap, Wolfson and Kotz (2010) list five main areas along which Liberal SSAs differ in relation to their Regulated counterparts, namely, a marked dominance of capital over labor, anarchic inter-capitalist competition, a relative autonomy of financial capital over industrial capital, a receding role of the State in regulating economic activity, and a dominant ideology advocating a 'free-market' version of capitalism. While not all of them apply to the Spanish case, it is argued that, on the one hand, the internal coherence of the resulting institutional structure is derived, above all, from the gradual reinforcement of the power of capital in various different social spheres while, on the other hand, the underlying crisis tendencies of the resulting structure closely resemble those typically associated with Liberal SSAs.

Firstly, the capital–labor relations instituted by the Spanish SSA have been markedly antagonistic, as exemplified by several structural features of the Spanish labor market in recent decades such as, for instance, the pervasiveness of precarious forms of employment (singularly, fixed-term contracts), the low levels of trade union density to European standards, or the flat profile shown by the evolution of real hourly wages throughout the whole expansion phase. Secondly, Liberal SSAs tend to feature cutthroat competition among individual capital units. The Spanish experience deserves in this respect, however, a more nuanced treatment, insofar as the Spanish capitalist structure is markedly dual. In this sense, whereas a few firms, globally competitive and heavily dependent upon close connections with the State apparatus, enjoyed a markedly oligopolistic position in their respective markets (e.g. telecommunication, utilities, construction, etc.), in this sense closely resembling the type of muted competition characteristic of Regulated SSAs, they did nonetheless co-exist with myriad small and medium enterprises (SMEs), technologically backward, with little capacity to undertake product differentiation, and thus too dependent upon wage containment and external flexibility practices in order to compete among themselves in terms of prices rather than quality. The type of competition characteristic of this latter group of firms does closely resemble the anarchic, cutthroat competition Wolfson and Kotz identify as distinctive of Liberal SSAs. Thirdly, in stark consonance with Liberal SSAs' paradigmatic features, financial capital has been (and continues to be) relatively autonomous, to say the least, over industrial capital. Indeed, Spanish capital underwent, in the course of the 1980s and 1990s, a strong process of relocation from industrial to chiefly financial activities which, in turn, has greatly shaped the resulting institutional architecture. Moreover, as shown below in much greater depth, many among the most relevant social processes sustaining systemic reproduction during the upward phase have been derived, in one way or another, from such stark predominance of finance capital over not only other subaltern social groups, but also over other competing fractions of the capitalist class itself (e.g. mounting indebtedness, a massive housing bubble, stagnant wages, etc.).

However, the two remaining structural features of Liberal SSAs, in Wolfson and Kotz's (2010) account, depart strongly from the Spanish experience under consideration. On the one hand, the role played by the State was certainly not one of self-subtraction from actively regulating economic activity. On the contrary, it played a crucial role in securing Spanish capital's gradual centralization and internationalization, both through widespread privatization processes of previously State-owned enterprises and through various State-sponsored programs aimed at accelerating its shift from industrial activities to chiefly financial ones. On the other hand, the dominant ideology was definitely not subsumable under the eminently individualist ideology Wolfson and Kotz point out. While we strongly disagree with the possibility of characterizing ideological process under such a simple banner, in case we were forced to do so, we would rather point out the crucial role played by EU integration in legitimizing successive changes in conjunction with an eminently 'familialist' ideology that posits the family as the main locus of social solidarity.

While the internal structure of Spanish capital was plagued by several internal disequilibria which severely compromised its international competitiveness, it was precisely the situation of dominance it retained over remaining social groups which enabled it to enjoy such a long period of success. The eventual manifestation of its manifold internal problems was effectively postponed for a long time thanks to the emergence of several contradictory dynamics (some of which emerged involuntarily, by indirection, whereas others were explicitly sought and reinforced, not only throughout the expansion phase, but also during the early stages of the crisis period). While the widespread emergence of unsatisfied demands over existing profits was unlikely to interrupt systemic reproduction, at some point in time the underlying problems in capital valorization were bound to come to the fore, undoing in turn the very mechanisms that had guaranteed its temporary postponement in the first instance.

Regarding the characterization of this institutional environment as 'Liberal', one last clarification is due. In truth, it may be argued that the use of the term 'Liberal' to characterize recent Spanish history might be a bit of a misnomer. On the one hand, among the most perfidious effects of the Francoist period one should count, undoubtedly, an absent culture of public involvement in social affairs, a systematic lack of transparency in State-related matters, and a general perception among the population of political participation being a futile, if not dangerous, enterprise. On the other hand, there has never been a truly liberal form of capitalism within Spanish territory, in the sense of manifold individual capitalists competing among themselves in a state of fair competition. On the contrary, one of the main social traits inherited from the Francoist regime has been, precisely, a business culture all too accustomed to profit from their links with State representatives and their access to privileged information as the key basis of new business opportunities. As nicely summarized by Naredo and Montiel (2011: 40–1), the 'liberalism' preached by Spanish elites is but 'an elitist liberalism, which defends the *laissez-faire* only for the powerful, so that they can promote at their will various megaprojects and other real estate enterprises in order to obtain fortunes'. This lack of a well-established liberal tradition results in a generalized 'narrow conception of citizenship' (Torns et al. 2013) where social responsibility in governing the public sphere is absent more often than not, a feature leading us straight to the third term in our characterization of the SSA, still awaiting justification. In sum, we retain the term 'Liberal' in order to call attention to certain morphological parallelisms relative to the socio-institutional organization of the circuit of money-capital. However, as shown in following chapters, the ultimate source of its success was to be found in several markedly illiberal social practices which resulted, at best, in little more than an asymmetric and predatory liberalism (Naredo 2019).

Why 'Mediterranean'?

The term 'Mediterranean', in the particular sense we are using it here, originates from the Welfare Regimes literature (Esping-Andersen 1990; 1999) and refers to a cluster of countries (Portugal, Italy, Spain, and Greece) which arguably share some common traits regarding the mode of integration of their labor markets, families and welfare state mechanisms, respectively, in securing social reproduction (Arts and Gelissen 2002). It has been argued that those countries share several socio-historical characteristics, such as a common historical trajectory marked by a late and incomplete industrialization linked to a shared authoritarian past (Mingione 1995); sharply dual labor markets, where relative employment protection offered to 'core' workers (read 'male') stands in stark contrast with the very high levels of precariousness experienced in the external labor market; a patchy and fragmented network of social protection, biased towards the needs of 'core' workers and the elders at the expense of peripheral workers and the young (Ferrera 1996; 2010); universal entitlements to a public healthcare system; a welfare state with particularly low redistributive reach, affected by high levels of clientelism and patronage in the delivery of social benefits; high incidence of the black/informal economy; and, above all, the constitution of the family as the main locus of social solidarity and welfare provision. In the words of Ferrera (1996: 21), '[w]hat gives some coherence to this kaleidoscope, somehow extenuating its potential excesses and contradictions, is the "southern family", still largely operating as a social clearing-house, mediating the difficult relationships between a variegated labor market and equally variegated income maintenance systems'.

In our view, it is precisely the idiosyncratic role played by the family institution in securing social reproduction within the Spanish social formation which merits the inclusion of the tag 'Mediterranean' in our own definition. Building upon well-established traditional gender norms, this prominent situation of the family regarding both care provision and social cohesion is reproduced by a situation of 'implicit familialism' (Leitner 2003) in the configuration of public policy, where the State does not explicitly encourage families to take up care responsibilities but, precisely through its very inaction, leaves them as the only available alternative regarding care provision. In the words of Flaquer (2001: 21):

> The specificity of Southern European countries in the field of family policy [is found] in the assumption that families are crucial in providing support and services to dependent people. [...] Southern family policy, through its inaction, implicitly nurtures and reproduces the assumption that the family is the main provider in society.

As long as the crucial role Spanish families play in securing social reproduction, both in strictly material, affective, and symbolic terms, is not properly acknowledged, it remains virtually impossible to apprehend, on the one hand, how the key trends governing social reproduction in 1995–2008 behaved in the way they did and, on the other, perhaps more crucially, how widespread social cohesion was secured in face of such antagonistic institutional grounds even after the Great Recession made its entrance into History. Regarding the systemic relevance of social interactions within the family and, crucially, of women's unpaid household and care work, its crucial contribution in satisfying the dual requirements of any social order's successful reproduction, which we have encapsulated in the pair 'accumulation and recognition', need to be highlighted.

On the one hand, Spanish families are forced to undertake several activities on whose successful accomplishment wholesale social reproduction crucially depends.

Being articulated around very rigid, traditional, and resilient gender norms, their female members are mostly responsible for the manifold tasks needed for the household's ongoing functioning, generally unpaid and guided by a strong sense of moral obligation towards other family members. Moreover, not only are routine household tasks systematically allotted to them but, also, they are forced to carry, on their own more often than not, the heavy burden of providing for unsatisfied care needs among the 'extended family' members. This situation of 'dependence within the household' (Bettio and Villa 1998), in conjunction with a labor market and a social protection system that systematically discriminates against women in favor of their male counterparts, configures women as second-order workers, susceptible to being submitted to greater time demands and precarious working conditions in the expectation that they will happily accept them, thus reinforcing the 'low road' pattern of economic development underwent by the Spanish SSA throughout the whole period.

On the other hand, Spanish families are characterized both by high levels of internal cohesion and by strong dynamics of solidarity throughout the life cycle, reaching well beyond the nuclear family structure to cover intergenerational transfers within the 'extended family' network as well. The worst social effects of an inherently antagonistic labor market (either psychological, physical, emotional, or material) which deliver great levels of precariousness and time-strenuousness to all but the 'core' workers, could only be attenuated, in the absence of a sustained and equitable system of social protection, by the intense dynamics of solidarity that characterize Spanish families, materialized in the various affective, emotional, and material exchanges taking place within the extended family throughout the life cycle. Were families not acting as 'social clearinghouses' helping cover those manifold social needs left unsatisfied by both State and markets, the various widespread consensuses that accompanied the long decade of SSA expansion might have been undone well before the period of SSA decay eventually consolidated itself. In sum, it is our contention that Spanish women stood as the ultimate sustainers of existing social equilibria during the expansion phase. However, as shown below, soaring female labor market participation in the face of a very resilient domestic division of labor constituted one of the great internal contradictions the Spanish SSA had to deal with, one whose diachronic evolution could not but further aggravate.

The idiosyncratic character of recent Spanish experience

The recent historical evolution of the Spanish social formation offers many valuable insights regarding how, from a political economy perspective, social reproduction may be secured in a given spatio-temporal setting. In our view, several lessons ought to be drawn from recent Spanish experience regarding the scope of social processes to be considered when undertaking political economy analyses concerned with analyzing social reproduction, on the one hand, and the existing relation between capitalist dynamics and co-existing socio-political interactions, on the other.

Firstly, it shows the extent to which the main institutional dynamics promoting the expansion of capitalist activity for a long time may spring up in an entirely unintended manner. In that respect, two key features of the process of economic restructuring undertaken during the 1980s and early 1990s seemed to preclude a future pattern of development driven by the expansion of internal demand insofar as, on the one hand, recovering capital profitability was done at the expense of disempowering organized labor and, on the other hand, the adoption of the common currency placed severe restrictions upon the State's future capacity to undertake discretionary expenditures. However, the ensuing institutional environment gave rise to several unplanned social dynamics (e.g. increasing private consumption levels supported by wealth effects and rising indebtedness rather than by rising labor incomes, capital investment driven by rent-seeking expectations rather than by strictly productive motivations, etc.) that contributed, contrary to initial expectations, to consolidate internal demand as the main driver of economic growth during the expansion phase.

Secondly, recent Spanish experience reveals the extent to which a given SSA's phases of expansion and decay, respectively, ought to be analyzed as an integrated whole. SSAs are institutional assemblages whose success demands not the suppression of whichever internal imbalances and contradictions they might harbor within but, rather, the development of contingent relations of complementarity and mutual constitution among the latter so that the respective internal dynamics of each are prevented from undoing the articulated whole in which they take part. In the Spanish case, the strength shown by the phase of expansion was not due to the eradication of internal contradictions but, on the contrary, it was precisely the proliferation of the latter which lent momentum to the former in the last instance. However, while their interlocked character permitted their ongoing reproduction for more than a decade, it did also account for the singular virulence shown by the subsequent breakdown for, once their virtuous interaction finally came to a halt, internal contradictions mutually reinforced each other, thus amplifying their effects all over the institutional structure.

Thirdly, it shows how capitalist processes present in a given social formation are necessarily interlinked with other nonmarket processes that not only act as the former's own conditions of possibility but which, also, play a crucial role in either accelerating or attenuating the former's own internal dynamics. Positioning the manifold labors deployed in the private sphere without monetary compensation, as well as other income sources not captured in conventional National Accounts (such as those derived from asset price revaluation), on an equal footing relative to market-based processes, opens a way to study social reproduction in a way that, while acknowledging the higher-order relevance enjoyed by the latter in capitalist societies, nonetheless recognizes the utmost relevance of the former in affecting the historical evolution of the social formation under consideration. Indeed, the evolution of Spanish capitalism during the last decades would remain impossible to apprehend were the contribution effected by these non-capitalist processes ultimately neglected.

Lastly, the Spanish case provides a case in point to analyze the complex relations existing between the evolution of capitalist dynamics, on the one hand, and the promotion of generalized social acquiescence towards the actual configuration of the existing order, on the other. During the phase of economic expansion widespread social consensuses were effectively sustained, despite the markedly conflict-ridden nature of the main social processes driving the former, thanks to the mutual support provided by their interaction. However, once their joint reproduction was no longer possible, a variety of unsatisfied demands irrupted into the public arena which, indeed, appeared intimately linked to the underside of the social processes governing the previous economic expansion in the first instance. In sum, whereas the domain of socio-political interactions is not independent of that of capitalist dynamics, it is neither a passive reflection of the former. Recent Spanish experience, we contend, brings to the fore the extent to which capitalist dynamics shape the uneven institutional environment where hegemonic logics operate in a historically punctuated manner.

8 The 'Mediterranean' Liberal SSA's expansion phase: 1995–2008

This chapter is devoted to exploring the very idiosyncratic manner in which systemic reproduction was secured during the whole expansion phase of the Spanish 'Mediterranean' Liberal SSA. Our core thesis is that its macroeconomic success, on the one hand, and the manifold internal contradictions it nevertheless harbored, on the other, ought not to be considered as disparate events. On the contrary, it is the latter that accounts, in the last instance, for both the apparent strength and ultimate fragility of the former. Moreover, such a model of development did gain widespread social acceptance. On the one hand, the inherently conflictive nature of the Spanish SSA's main institutional blocks was prevented from coming to the fore thanks to the relations of mutual support provided by their joint interaction. On the other hand, social conflict was effectively channeled along lines ultimately unrelated to the institutional underpinnings of the economic expansion, thus leaving the latter immune from its utterly conflict-prone bases. In this regard, it is contended that an idiosyncratic 'regime of visibility' which, following others, we term the 'Culture of the Transition', played a crucial role in delimiting the issues suitable to undergo public debate, on the one hand, while legitimizing and rationalizing the manifold social inequalities the Spanish SSA harbored, on the other.

This chapter is organized as follows. Before dealing in detail with the shape of the Spanish SSA in the period 1995–2008, a brief review of its previous 'exploration' phase will be offered, so that lines of historical rupture and continuity can be properly identified. Subsequently, after having briefly reviewed the institutional underpinnings of the Spanish model by paying attention to both the productive and reproductive spheres, respectively, its main underlying contradictions will be scrutinized in detail, namely, the imbalances affecting the capitalist accumulation process, the existing disjunction between soaring consumption levels and stagnating real wages, and, lastly, the growing strenuousness to which Spanish families were submitted in the absence of public support in that regard. Then, the extent to which the main dynamics sustaining the economic expansion supported each other will be analyzed, together with the support they lent to each other in preventing their respective undersides from undergoing overt politicization. Lastly, we will analyze the hegemonic social consensuses structuring socio-political interaction until the onset of the Great Recession.

Some tentative explorations: The years 1982–1991

The period 1982–1991 constitutes the 'exploration phase' of the upcoming SSA (Gordon et al. 1982), that is, a period in which various contending social actors made tentative moves so as to shape the process of institutional transformation in course, even though key elements of the previous institutional environment still persisted, and internal synergies and complementarities had not yet been well developed. For analytical purposes, two different sub-periods are identified. The first one, corresponding with *PSOE*'s first term in office (1982–86), was marked by the implementation of a strict adjustment program aimed at addressing existing macroeconomic disequilibria. The second one, ranging from 1986 to 1991, corresponds to a period of economic growth where the institutional traits that would guide future economic expansion were mostly consolidated (or, at least, in the process of becoming so), although internal dysfunctions and institutional maladjustments, from the perspective of systemic reproduction, nevertheless persisted.

After four decades of authoritarian rule, General Franco's death in November 1975 triggered a gradual transition towards a liberal parliamentary regime. The crisis of the State was concurrent with a fully-fledged crisis of the Spanish productive apparatus, as the effects of the global over-accumulation crisis in manufacturing were heavily aggravated by the dependent and subsidiary character of Spain's industrial development during the previous two decades (López and Rodríguez 2010). Nevertheless, it would be a mistake to understand the economic crisis, on the one hand, and the decomposition of the Francoist regime's state structures, on the other, as disparate events. Rather, the transformation of the State apparatus, on the one hand, and a regressive distribution of the costs of productive adjustment, on the other, were but different elements of the same process of socio-institutional transformation. In this sense, as noted by Rodríguez (2015: 36, emphasis added), 'the economic crisis is not the background of the Transition, it is, rather, *the problem* of the Transition'. Charnock et al. (2014: 55) express themselves along similar lines: 'Increasingly, then, the struggle waged by the Spanish working class within the institutional form of the fascist state became a broader struggle over the very form of the state'.

The process of transition was concluded with the victory of the Socialist Party (*PSOE*) in the 1982 general elections. Immediately after assuming office, the newly elected Socialist government implemented an 'orthodox' adjustment program aimed at correcting the various macroeconomic disequilibria derived, in the last instance, from the intense crisis of over-accumulation the Spanish productive structure was by then going through. The Socialist administration held to the belief that, in order to fully consolidate the newly implemented democratic regime, social transformation had to fully respect not only existing capitalist relations of production but, also, the privileged role Spanish capital had traditionally enjoyed in dictating economic policy's main guidelines (Etxezarreta 1991). To that extent, securing Spain's accession to the European Community (EC) was to be the government's main priority, a goal which, in turn, placed the requirement of gaining international competitiveness center stage (Montes 1993). The government, however, exposed a restricted understanding of international competitiveness by equating it, unilaterally, with price competitiveness. Discarding from the outset the possibility of competing in terms of either product quality and/or productive diversification, wages were thus prominently configured as a production cost to be contained, rather than as a primary source of aggregate demand (Recio and Roca 1998). Hence, among the several macroeconomic disequilibria to be confronted, stabilizing inflation, the exchange rate and balance of payments' disequilibria would take absolute priority over restoring economic growth and/or employment levels (Etxezarreta 1991). Exposing a strong belief in supply-side explanations dominant at the time, the recovery of profit margins at the expense of labor costs and conditions was thus to be the government's foremost concern (Albarracín 1991).

To that extent, a harsh and socially regressive adjustment program was implemented.[1] Firmly based upon monetarist principles, it included a sharp devaluation of the *peseta* in 1982; an increase in fiscal revenues, mostly through an increase in indirect taxation; stringent monetary policies; social concertation strategies with unions directed at submitting wage increases below expected levels of inflation (which, in turn, were systematically lower than actual inflation levels); and an 'Industrial Reconversion' plan which, with the help of copious public funds, aimed at restructuring Spanish manufacturing in the expectation that it could, eventually, be competitive according to new international standards (Gómez Uranga 1991).

By 1986, the policies implemented had been successful both in curbing inflation levels and in correcting balance of payments' disequilibria, while the severe attack on labor conditions had succeeded in reducing the wage share by 4 percentage points during those years (González i Calvet 1991: 186).[2] However, recovering profits had been mostly used by firms to rationalize their productive structures and/or to alleviate their respective financial leverage, while, moreover, the investment expenditures actually undertaken were driven towards further restricting their labor needs (Albarracín 1991). As a result, while Spain could successfully join the EU by January 1986, unemployment remained above 20 percent and economic growth had barely been resumed (Hernández Marco 2012). Adjusting to the new competitive scenario at the European level encouraged the dismantling of an industrial sector affected by serious over-capacity problems, energetic dependency, and technological backwardness. Abandoning industrial development altogether, in turn, significantly reduced the scope Spanish capitalism had to generate a material surplus to then be distributed among competing social groups, thus accentuating the antagonistic character of the ensuing institutional assemblage. Moreover, by relocating to economic sectors significantly protected from international competition, Spanish capital was capable of systematically transferring cost increases into market prices, thus giving rise to pervasive inflationary pressures which only a sustained attack on labor remunerations could successfully attenuate.

In this context, several among the institutional changes undertaken during those years were already paving the way for the construction of a Liberal SSA in Spanish territory, among which a thorough process of capitalist restructuring supported by a targeted and gradual process of privatization of previously public enterprises crucially stands out (Etchemendy 2004). On the one hand, in sectors such as telecommunications, oil, and energy production, the State resorted, first, to a process of restructuring, centralization and vertical integration aimed at building 'national champions' able to be internationally competitive in the future. Then, a gradual process of privatization was initiated, where the State kept 'golden shares' in the affected companies in order to prevent foreign capital from taking dominant positions in their respective ownership structures (Juste 2017). As a result, big capital could successfully relocate to those sectors, in the guise of a small number of globally competitive firms enjoying highly oligopolistic market structures in the domestic arena (Recio 2009).

On the other hand, the State governed the process of rationalization and adjustment of manufacturing firms to then sell them to international competitors (Etxezarreta 1991). The weakness of the industrial bourgeoisie, together with the new competitive scenario derived from European integration, favored the entry of foreign capital into those sectors. In key manufacturing sectors, such as steel production, shipbuilding or home appliances, the State implemented several 'reconversion plans', where copious funds were deployed both to subsidize laid-off workers and to offer monetary compensation to firms experiencing profitability problems. However, the State did neither intend to nationalize private firms nor to keep ownership of already public enterprises. In this sense, no restrictions were offered to the penetration of international capital in their ownership structures, in stark contrast to the more protected sectors mentioned above (Gómez Uranga 1991). Therefore, the neoliberal restructuring of the Spanish economy cannot be understood without taking into consideration the crucial role played by the State in protecting and organizing the process of capital restructuring. Were this process actually developed according to strictly 'free-market' principles, domestic capital would not have been able to resist international pressures in securing its dominant positions at home (Etchemendy 2004).

In this context, disarticulating organized labor emerged as a crucial element within Spanish capital's strategies to remain competitive in the new European scenario – not only in order to transfer to labor conditions the adjustment costs derived from the aforementioned process of industrial restructuring but, crucially, to prevent future workers' 'undisciplined' wage demands from undoing Spanish firms' fragile competitive position within the European arena. To that extent, a variety of policy measures and institutional changes were introduced. Firstly, the implementation of stringent monetary policies, in the guise of high interest rates, served to reinforce mass unemployment as a disciplinary mechanism upon the working class. Moreover, orchestrating social concertation strategies aimed at keeping wage increases not only below actual rates of inflation, but also below annual productivity increases, served to systematically skew the income distribution in favor of capital, in turn disempowering the working classes through and through by negatively affecting the material grounds upon which they could have confronted the dominant policy guidelines. Secondly, a legislative modification of the Workers' Statute [*Estatuto de los Trabajadores*] was passed in 1984 which, under the presumption that high unemployment levels were but a by-product of existing institutional rigidities in the labor market, gave employers the possibility of signing fixed-term contracts without explicit justification. Initially aimed at improving employment levels in the short term, the reform ended up consolidating the recourse to temporary contracts as Spanish firms' preferred mechanism of adjustment to market fluctuations and, implicitly, as a weapon to further fragment the working class (Toharia et al. 2005). Thirdly, a strong 'underground' sector was consolidated during these years, as it kept absorbing part of the labor contingents made redundant in manufacturing by widespread industrial shutdowns. Such expansion of the informal economy would in turn reinforce, in the years to come, the markedly dual character of the Spanish productive structure, insofar as 'the process of industrial restructuring had, in short, provided a fresh supply of low-wage labor to Spain's small capitals and on the basis of flexible work contracts, competing to supply to larger, foreign-owned capitals engaged in production in geographical proximity' (Charnock et al. 2014: 61). In sum, various strategies to contain labor costs were deployed, as the dismantling of the manufacturing sector in conjunction with the new competitive scenario derived from European integration left labor costs as the only variable upon which economic policy could successfully intervene in order to maintain international competitiveness.

By 1986, when Spain finally acceded the EC, economic growth had been eventually resumed, both inflation rates and balance of payments' deficits had been severely curtailed, and the competitiveness of certain key industrial sectors had been significantly improved after years of painful restructuring (López and Rodríguez 2010: 161). Animated by the effects of trade liberalization, internal demand experienced a strong upsurge. Imports, mostly driven by the thrust of final consumption goods, grew considerably faster than exports, a situation that would have apparently called for a gradual devaluation of the *peseta* to prevent balance of payments' disequilibria (Montes 1993: 95). However, while inflationary pressures were moderately low during 1986 and 1987, they kicked back again in 1988, a time by which social concertation with unions had definitely unraveled (a general strike being called by the two main union confederations that same year). In order to curtail both inflation levels and trade unions' institutional power, the government decided to maintain high interest rates and an over-valued *peseta*. Such policy decisions, in turn, were crucial to continue attracting external funds with which to fund soaring current account deficits.

This policy of maintaining high interest rates reinforced the pattern of restructuring already in course, insofar as an over-valuated currency could not but forever foreclose the possibility of developing a competitive industrial sector within of the EC, promoting in turn a further shift of available financial resources towards both non-tradable sectors and consumer credit. Such transfer of resources, in turn, accentuated inflationary pressures within the Spanish economy, as sheltered sectors could successfully translate cost increases into higher market prices (Pérez 1999). Moreover, high interest rates served to attract not only long-term FDI flows directed towards acquiring strategic positions in the manufacturing sector but, also, intense short-term speculative flows which, besides accentuating inflationary dynamics, served to cover for rising current account deficits. These latter flows supported the emergence of an asset price bubble in the real estate sector which, in an environment featuring markedly high rates of homeownership, enabled increasing indebtedness among the population by using the latter as collaterals (Naredo 1996). Once these funds are partly diverted to finance increasing consumption patterns, self-reinforcing dynamics emerge that allow consumption demand to be further pushed forward through strictly financial mechanisms, that is, without support from enlarging productive capacities. These 'atypical' means to sustain internal demand growth, which will be explored at length in the rest of this chapter, will constitute the very kernel of the upcoming Spanish SSA's path of diachronic development.

The growth period initiated in 1986 was short-lived nonetheless. Growth rates started to recede by 1989, when macroeconomic disequilibria became more acute and the real estate bubble started to deflate. However, high levels of public investment in infrastructures animated by the funds received from the EC, in conjunction with the increase in public spending during those years as a result of the organization in 1992 of the Olympic Games in Barcelona and the World Exposition in Seville extended the growth phase until that year. An intense recession finally ensued between 1992 and 1994, characterized by skyrocketing unemployment and three successive devaluations of the *peseta*. Nevertheless, the institutional bases of the next period of economic growth, however fragile and self-defeating, were already in place. On the one hand, the relocation of Spanish capital towards sheltered sectors, such as telecommunications, oil and energy, had already been accomplished. On the other, organized labor was no longer in a situation to effectively revert its markedly subordinate position.

The 'Spanish miracle': 1995–2008

By the time a timid recovery was initiated in 1994, future prospects were definitely bleak. The deindustrialization process undertaken during the 1980s, through which big capital had sought refuge in sectors protected from international competition, and where securing expanding demand was more dependent upon conserving close ties with high-ranking State officials than upon improving underlying competitive capacities, offered little sources of competitive production to international standards (Recio 2009). Moreover, this problem was further aggravated by the signature of the Maastricht Treaty in 1992, which paved the way for future monetary integration among EU members. On the one hand, by establishing a fixed exchange rate between the *peseta* and the remaining currencies of the European Monetary System, it foreclosed the possibility of devaluating the national currency in future recessionary periods. On the other hand, by limiting fiscal deficits and public debt levels, potential state support in reorganizing the production process along more socially progressive and/or competitive lines was severely compromised. In sum, Spain was in the process of entering a wider economic area affected by significant productivity differentials and heterogenous productive structures, with little capacity to compete in terms of industrial production, and with the possibility to have recourse to recurrent monetary devaluations in order to offset increasing productivity differentials forever foreclosed. However, this was no impediment to an impressive boost in economic activity between 1995 and 2007, as manifested in the evolution of real GDP (+54.7 percent), employment growth (+56.2 percent), or female labor force participation (+23 percent). Surprisingly, these phenomena did take place over a decade in parallel with stagnating hourly real wages (−2.5 percent) and labor productivity (−1.1 percent).

In the absence of protectionist measures, internal devaluation strategies (prominently, wage repression) were thus left as the only possible source of macroeconomic adjustment. To that extent, building up a Liberal SSA suited Spanish capital's valorization needs, inasmuch as it could ensure widespread wage containment capable of compensating for potentially worsening productivity differentials, on the one hand, and real exchange rate appreciation, on the other, with respect to other European Monetary Union (EMU) members. This strategy could have been coherent, considering underlying technological deficiencies, with an export-led growth path. However, the most vigorous component of aggregate demand was not exports but internal demand, within which, moreover, private aggregate investment stood as its most dynamic element. Therein lies the ultimately paradoxical character of the Spanish model.

How could a Liberal SSA, plagued with internal disequilibria and thoroughly dependent upon internal devaluation strategies achieve, firstly, such economic vitality over more than a decade while, secondly, positioning internal demand as the main driver of economic growth where, thirdly, private investment became the most dynamic component despite virtually irrelevant increases in labor productivity throughout the whole expansion phase? The answer is to be sought, we contend, in the very idiosyncratic way in which underlying valorization problems gave way to several social processes which, despite indelibly showing a highly contradictory character when considered in isolation, did nevertheless manage to offer each other support in such a way that their joint occurrence was reinforced over time. The truly tragic dimension of the ensuing Spanish model lies in the fact that such internal disequilibria, whose respective manifestations managed to coalesce into a relatively coherent whole for more than a decade, did not attenuate their intrinsically contradictory character by partaking of the latter but, on the contrary, saw it increasingly exacerbated along the economic expansion. Before examining the way in which social reproduction was secured in Spain during the years 1995–2008, it is first necessary to outline the broad institutional underpinnings of the Spanish model.

The institutional underpinnings of the Spanish model

In order to analyze the institutional contours of the Spanish 'Mediterranean' Liberal SSA, we introduce separately the strictly productive sphere, in the sense of being directly implicated in the capitalist valorization process, on the one hand, and the reproductive sphere, where most activities directly involved in securing living conditions are undertaken, on the other. This division, nonetheless, serves merely heuristic purposes. Regarding the former, we will focus on the internal structure of Spanish capital, the way capital–labor relations have been institutionalized, and the role the State has played in securing profit-making activity. Regarding the latter, we will focus on the institutional configuration of the welfare state and the socio-economic configuration of the family institution.

The productive sphere

As a result of the industrial restructuring process of the 1980s, aimed at devaluing large masses of over-accumulated capital in manufacturing, the already well-established sectors of tourism and real estate gained further prominence as the cornerstones of Spain's productive specialization. These are sectors singularly labor-intensive, traditionally low-paid, over-reliant upon informal labor arrangements, and with little scope for productivity gains. Paradoxically, this situation was no impediment for an impressive upsurge of investment throughout the period under consideration (accounting for 21.5 percent of GDP in 1995, it reached 30.7 percent in 2007). Highly motivated by asset valorization dynamics, it tended to concentrate in those sectors featuring the lowest levels of labor productivity (Mateo and Montanyà 2018; Mateo 2019).

The internal structure of Spanish capital reinforced its dualism throughout the period. On the one hand, big capital consolidated its shift away from industrial activities by concentrating itself in a few number of firms, globally competitive but with few technological spillovers, anchored in highly sheltered sectors such as construction, telecommunication and utilities, and heavily dependent upon protection from the State (Banyuls et al. 2009; Ramiro and González 2019). On the other, it co-existed with numerous SMEs, very dependent upon domestic demand, which deployed a weak technological endowment and were too accustomed to external flexibility practices (mostly through fixed-term contracts) as their preferred means of adjustment to market fluctuations. In sum:

> a few key industrial sectors made the jump to the world market [though] only to a limited extent, and on the basis of a parallel and related expansion in a number of small capitals competing to supply low-tech inputs and employing low-wage, casual labor.
>
> (Charnock et al. 2014: 67)

Its general inability to consistently improve labor productivity throughout the period left extensive growth as the only development strategy available, that is, a model in which absolute rather than relative surplus value stood as the crucial ingredient of its diachronic expansion (Buendía 2018b). Moreover, this strategy was further incentivized by the presence of a vast industrial reserve army throughout the whole period. Whereas the unemployment rate reached above 20 percent at the beginning of the growth phase, it took more than ten years of uninterrupted economic growth, in 2005, for it to drop below 10 percent. This situation found its counterpart in a very dual labor market, in which high levels of protection offered to core workers, generally corresponding to the 'male breadwinner', were matched by very high levels of precariousness to those populating its external layers, mostly women, young and immigrant workers. What some authors have referred to as a 'culture of temporality' (Toharia et al. 2005) had thus less to do with a socio-cultural trait of Spanish society, and much more with the extension of precariousness as a rudimentary form of workers' control and fragmentation (Cano 2007). While many authors have long complained about the alleged rigidity of the Spanish labor market (e.g. Bentolila and Dolado 1994; Conde-Ruiz et al. 2011; Estrada et al. 2009), were it not for the protection offered to core workers in combination with the internal redistribution of resources that characterize Spanish families, anything resembling a social order would have probably been simply a chimera (Bettio and Villa 1998; Marí-Klose and Moreno-Fuentes 2013). Moreover, linked to this sharp dualization of the workforce in terms of job protection, a very polarized workforce regarding educational attainment found itself in growing contradiction with a productive model with notable difficulties to generate jobs fitting those qualifications (Karamessini 2008). While the spread of tertiary education certificates played a key role in preserving middle-class aspirations of upward social mobility, this contradiction was bound to explode as soon as widespread asset revaluation stopped disguising the relentless precarization of the younger layers of the workforce.

The reproductive sphere

Sharp welfare state expansion during the 1980s took place in an international arena already flooded by the neoliberal tide. However, despite having attained significant achievements (singularly, quasi-universal access to health and education), the application of the Maastricht criteria drew the homologation process relative to the European core to a sudden halt. Since the mid-1990s the main aim of successive reforms has been to achieve fiscal balance, thus consolidating a fragmented, geographically uneven welfare system, with a limited redistributive reach (Buendía et al. 2018; Guillén 2010; Rodriguez-Cabrero 2011) in which a low tax base was translated into public services underdevelopment rather than into fiscal deficits (Banyuls and Recio 2012).

Spanish welfare architecture's numerous lacunae could only be attenuated by the role of the family, the foremost institution regarding social reproduction within the Spanish political economy. Exiguous commodification of care services together with very timid public efforts to unburden women of care responsibilities continued to deliver a situation of 'implicit familialism' (Leitner 2003; Saraceno and Keck 2010), where families were forced to undertake numerous care responsibilities not necessarily out of will but of sheer necessity (Moreno Mínguez 2007). Intense intra-familial transfers marked by strong intergenerational solidarity constituted the family as a primary 'shock absorber' (Tobío 2013), where relatively strong protection offered to the 'male breadwinner' in conjunction with low-to-moderate old-age pensions served to attenuate the worst effects of the modality of labor inclusion predominantly offered to women and the young. The ultimate pillar of the model were thus the 'Spanish Super-women' (Moreno 2004) who, forced by stagnating wages to enter paid employment, found themselves in growing difficulties throughout the period to fulfill the functions that a very asymmetric division of domestic labor kept on assigning to them (Gálvez et al. 2011). The gravity of this latent contradiction, and the ways it was provisionally superseded, will be explored in greater detail in the following section.

The road to success: Mutually sustaining contradictory trends

Once the institutional contours of the Spanish SSA between the years 1995 and 2008 have been delineated, an explanation is due of how, despite being built upon such seemingly fragile foundations, it did manage nonetheless to become the envy of its European neighbor countries regarding its macroeconomic performance. In our view, its sound economic performance during those years cannot be understood to have occurred in spite of the various internal disequilibria it did harbor. On the contrary, it is precisely the proliferation of contradictory dynamics within itself which accounts for its apparent and temporary successes. To a great extent inadvertently, at least from the narrow perspective of orthodox economics, various social processes were operating at the time which, despite showing a markedly contradictory character when considered in isolation, did manage nonetheless to offer support to each other during more than a decade in such a manner that their simultaneous occurrence secured their individual reproduction. That is, relations of complementarity and mutual reinforcement did definitely emerge between some of its key institutional blocks, although the mutual support offered to each other did not serve to attenuate, much less to erase, their contradictory character. Rather, internal contradictions were further aggravated in the course of the whole phase of expansion, driving the whole social formation towards an inevitable internal implosion.

These mechanisms closely resemble those identified by Brenner (2006) or Crouch (2009), among others (López and Rodríguez 2010). Common aspects include the centrality of asset bubbles in assembling the various elements of the institutional structure, as well as the relevance played by debt-financed private consumption in sustaining aggregate demand. However, the scale of the housing bubble, its spread over the social body, and the role families played in attenuating its most devastating effects, must be accounted as idiosyncratic features of the Spanish experience. Among these contradictory trends, three of them are singled out due to their higher relevance regarding the continuing reproduction of the institutional edifice, namely, an increasingly distorted accumulation process, rising consumption in the face of stagnating wages, and an over-burdened family. Each will be analyzed in turn.

An increasingly distorted accumulation process

The fate of the Spanish capitalist accumulation process during the whole period under consideration has been paradoxical, if not tragic. As noted above, the main driver of economic growth during this period has been internal demand, within which the most vigorous component has been private investment. Despite the gross profit rate showing a markedly downward trend throughout the period, very low interest rates derived from European monetary integration served to attenuate existing valorization problems (Mateo and Montanyà 2018; Mateo 2019).[3] However, they simultaneously contributed to give rise to a housing bubble of massive proportions, which managed to constitute itself as the very central node around which the whole institutional architecture was articulated (López and Rodríguez 2010).

Breaking up data on gross fixed capital formation (GFCF) by type of asset, it is made apparent how most of those expenditures found their rationale not in the drive to increase labor productivity but in the expectation of obtaining future rents in the midst of a process of widespread revaluation. Not only was residential investment GFCF's most dynamic component but, within productive investment itself, it is the investment in new constructions which received the bulk of new funds. As a result, around two thirds of actual investment expenditures appeared linked to the real estate complex (see Figure 8.1). If, instead, one focuses upon the economic sector undertaking those expenditures, it can be readily observed that the Construction and Real Estate Activities sectors undertook an increasing share of investment activity throughout the cycle, reaching almost half of total investment in 2007, the last year of economic expansion (see Figure 8.2). Moreover, while these two sectors, together with Transport and Storage, experienced strong price increases which animated their investment activity, their respective levels of labor productivity decreased throughout the period. This situation strongly contrasts with the dynamics experienced by Manufacturing and Information and Communications, whose

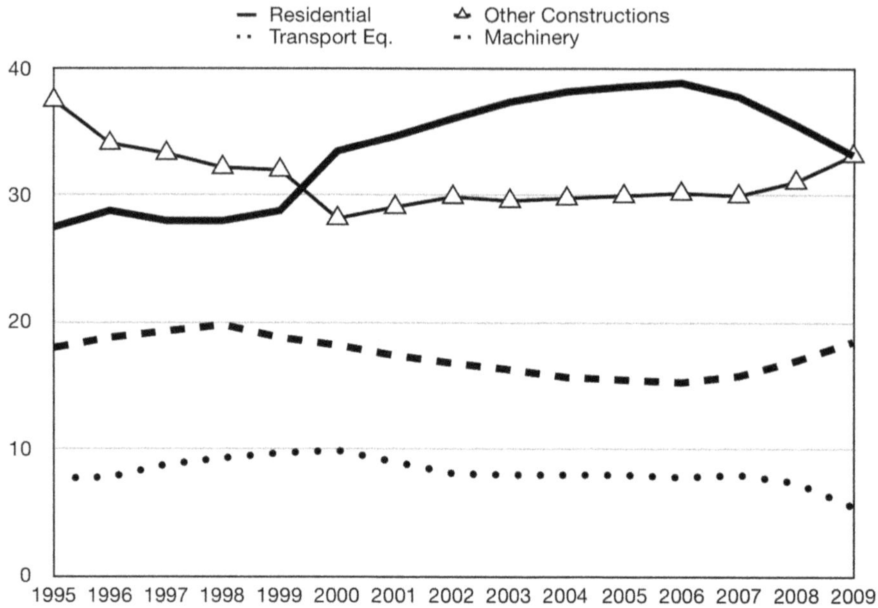

Figure 8.1 GFCF by type of asset

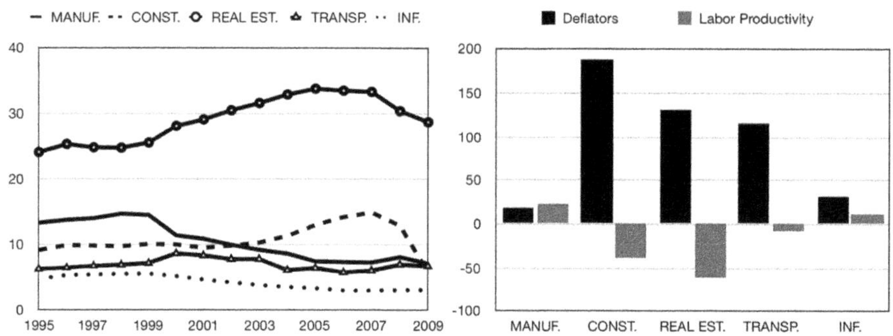

Figure 8.2 GFCF by sector of activity

relative shares within total GFCF decreased during those same years, influenced by meagre price increases, despite managing to secure small advances in labor productivity.

While the productive structure of Spanish capital was already quite imbalanced at the beginning of the cycle, leaning too much towards non-tradables and manufactures of medium-to-low technological content, the growth path followed by the Spanish economy in the upcoming decade could not but reinforce those productive deficiencies. Despite residential investments not partaking of capital accumulation, they did nonetheless have a pre-eminent influence over economic activity, as the real estate complex, however overdeveloped, did have a very strong knock-on effect upon other economic sectors (Mateo and Montanyà 2018). Moreover, beyond the sectorial shift from agriculture and manufacturing, where better possibilities exist for generating an economic surplus to be then distributed among subaltern groups, to low-quality services and the real estate complex, important internal malfunctions also affected the composition of productive investment itself (Buendía 2018a; Sánchez Iglesias 2016). As noted by Álvarez et al. (2013), Spain's production of manufactures with high technological content was not only well below the EU average during the whole period, but also decreasing through and through.

Hence, the antagonistic character of Spanish capitalism, as manifested in its utter incapacity to barely increase real hourly wages through the whole expansion phase, was ultimately grounded upon underlying productive deficiencies. Lacking the necessary means to systematically produce an economic surplus to be then redistributed among various social groups, eroding profitability placed distributive struggles at the very core of capital's strategies of survival (Nieto 2006), especially so during the second half of the upward cycle due to the declining trend of the productivity of capital (Mateo 2019). Nonetheless, this was absolutely no impediment for Spanish economic elites to profit considerably from non-orthodox processes of valorization.

Spain's productive underdevelopment relative to the European 'core' in conjunction with EMU membership constituted another core contradiction the Spanish SSA had to deal with, as current account deficits, driven to a great extent by the strength of internal demand throughout the whole decade, found their mirror-like image in Germany's increasing current account surpluses, an explosive dynamic starkly accentuated since 2001 (see Figure 8.3). However, despite this having reinforced the internal evolution of a distorted capitalist accumulation process, whose deleterious effects were to be openly manifested after the onset of the Great Recession, the incoming funds were ultimately functional to ongoing socio-economic reproduction, as they did play a crucial role in feeding a massive housing bubble well beyond existing financial resources within the Spanish territory (Fernández and García 2018; Febrero et al. 2019). The explosive evolution of housing prices represented the ultimate anchoring point of the whole institutional assemblage, and crucially underlies the upward trend followed by both private consumption and investment in the years here under consideration. In order to account for the severity and intensity of such an outstanding speculative process, however, merely pointing out Spain's traditional productive specialization is not enough. Instead, several factors idiosyncratic to the Spanish socio-economic context ought to be considered.

Firstly, ever since the late 1950s home acquisition has been actively promoted through various legislative incentives, with the rate of homeownership reaching 80 percent of households in 2007 (INE 2020b). Not only was it successful in preventing recurrent mass mobilizations by linking the latter's fate to the vagaries of the real estate complex, but it has also been strongly determined by Spanish elites' tenacity in seeking refuge in housing production in the face of economic turbulences of whatever type. In more recent years, policy

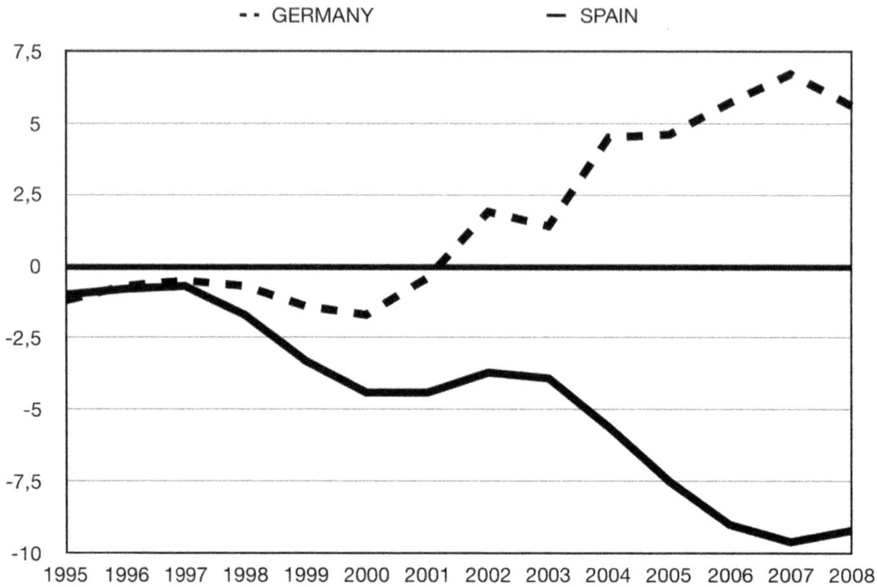

Figure 8.3 Current Account ESP–GER

interventions such as the 'Boyer decree' (1985), which introduced income tax breaks after housing acquisitions, irrespective of its future use; the removal of both rent controls in the private rented market and urban planning restrictions; or the virtual abandonment of social housing provisioning could not but reinforce Spaniards' predilection for homeownership (Coq-Huelva 2013; Pareja-Eastaway and Sánchez-Martínez 2017; Rodríguez-Alonso and Espinoza-Pino 2017).

Secondly, the adoption of the euro has played a crucial role, as it helped attract a growing pool of external liquidity, from transnational corporations' profits (Aalbers 2017), to European 'core' countries' current account surpluses (Fernández and García 2018), which found in the Spanish housing market an appropriate outlet for their desired investment opportunities. While previous asset bubbles had always ended when the scarcity of national financial resources caused a sudden hike in interest rates, thus preventing further rounds of investment, the adoption of the euro ensured that available resources were no longer restricted to those belonging to the national territory (Naredo 1996; 2009). Spanish financial capital managed to capture increasing quantities of international monetary resources in order to channel them, in increasing proportion through the whole expansion phase, to the booming construction sector (Febrero et al. 2019). This overrepresentation of housing-related activities within total investment can be easily observed in the proportion of total credit lent to the construction sector. While it represented 38 percent of the total in 1995, it grew to above 60 percent of the latter during the last years of the cycle (Bank of Spain 2020a).

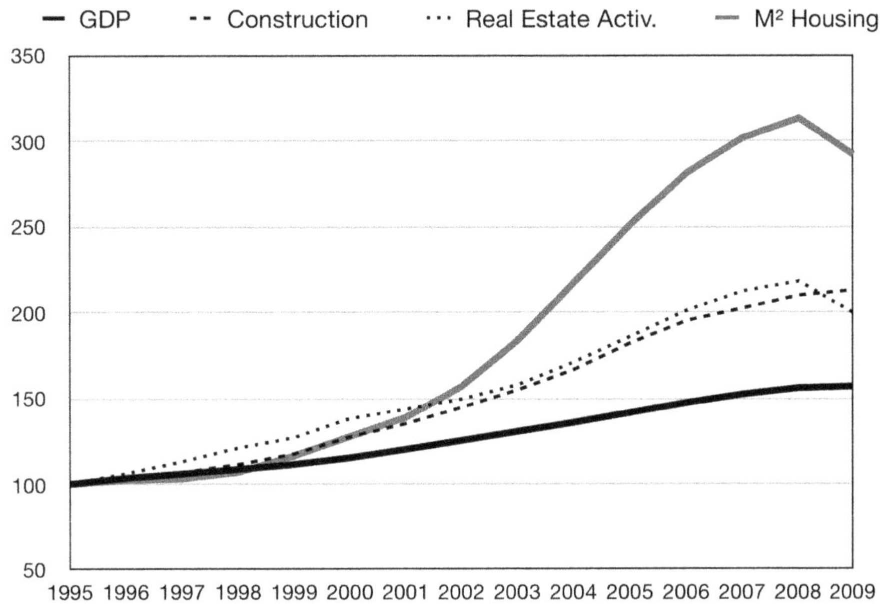

Figure 8.4 Housing bubble

Thirdly, recent Spanish experience provides a paradigmatic example of the existing trade-off between housing acquisition and welfare state development, identified by Kemeny (1981) long ago, as two alternative means of long-term insurance (see also Castles and Ferrera 1996). In this sense, homeownership has acted as a rudimentary mechanism of insurance against old-age contingencies, while also acting as an instrument for the intergenerational transmission of wealth (Trifiletti 1999). Building upon cultural path dependency and a continuing lack of alternatives, spiraling housing prices for more than a decade strongly reinforced Spanish families' preference for housing acquisition as their mechanism of long-term insurance. Housing thus became the unacknowledged pillar of the Spanish welfare architecture, the hidden element which ultimately accounted for its social effectivity. Were it not for this latent complementarity between homeownership inertia and welfare state underdevelopment, the length of the ensuing housing bubble, the extent of its social penetration, and its capacity to raise aggregate consumption levels would have been utterly impossible to attain.

Fourthly, the particular way urban planning legislation is promoted in Spain gave way to the emergence of subnational pro-growth coalitions between local and regional politicians, land developers, and financial and real estate capital, which Naredo and Montiel (2011) succinctly termed the 'triple alliance'. While urban planning decisions had traditionally been a prerogative of municipal authorities, the promulgation of the Land Regime Act in 1998 ('*Ley de Suelo*') gave them unrestrained capacities to shift land's usage at their will. Given that the ultimate capacity to effect such changes belonged to local authorities, and that huge price increases could be instantaneously generated through this process, coalitions flourished all through Spanish territory between the three types of actors mentioned above. As a result of this confluence of interests, successive rounds of urbanization were attempted throughout the Spanish territory.

Sustained revalorization of housing asset prices not only explained the impressive upsurge observed in aggregate private investment but also underlaid the upward trend of aggregate consumption during those same years. While it reinforced an impoverished productive structure increasingly incapable of fostering a more productive use of labor power, which in turn constrained the flat evolution of real wages during those years, it nonetheless permitted Spanish households to increase their consumption levels in line with GDP trends, a process to which we now turn.

Rising consumption despite wage stagnation

It has just been noted how an increasingly distorted capital accumulation process, whose 'low-road' pattern of productive specialization was reinforced throughout the whole period, conditioned the diachronic evolution of real wage levels (Mateo 2019). Despite having received a massive influx of means of payment susceptible of having improved Spain's productive capacities, internal distortions within the accumulation process placed the distributive struggle between capital and labor at the very core of the former's strategies for economic survival, manifested both in the flat evolution of real wages throughout the period and in the spread of inherently precarious forms of employment. However, these trends were no impediment for aggregate household consumption levels to rise virtually in line with GDP for these 12 years, which, in turn, was crucial to attenuate the inherently antagonistic character of the Spanish model by fostering a generalized acquiescence with the actual configuration of the existing social order (see Figure 8.5). How, then, could these two apparently antinomic phenomena be reconciled for such a long time? The answer is to be sought in the way in which the above-mentioned housing bubble allowed for the emergence of certain social trends whose mutual interrelation accounted for the Spanish model's ultimate effectivity.

Firstly, stagnating real wages co-existed with an impressive upsurge in employment of more than seven million new jobs in 1995–2008. While booming employment creation allowed the wage share to remain fairly constant throughout the whole period (Buendía et al. 2018), it also helped disguise the increasing precarization of labor relations and the temporal strenuousness Spanish workers were ultimately submitted to (Prieto and Miguélez 2009; Rey-Araújo and Fernández 2019). When analyzing the sectorial distribution of the new employment created, the reinforcement of the productive specialization pattern described above is rendered clear (see Table 8.1).

Regarding industrial employment, almost 75 percent of net job creation was in the construction sector, bearing witness of capital's flight away from

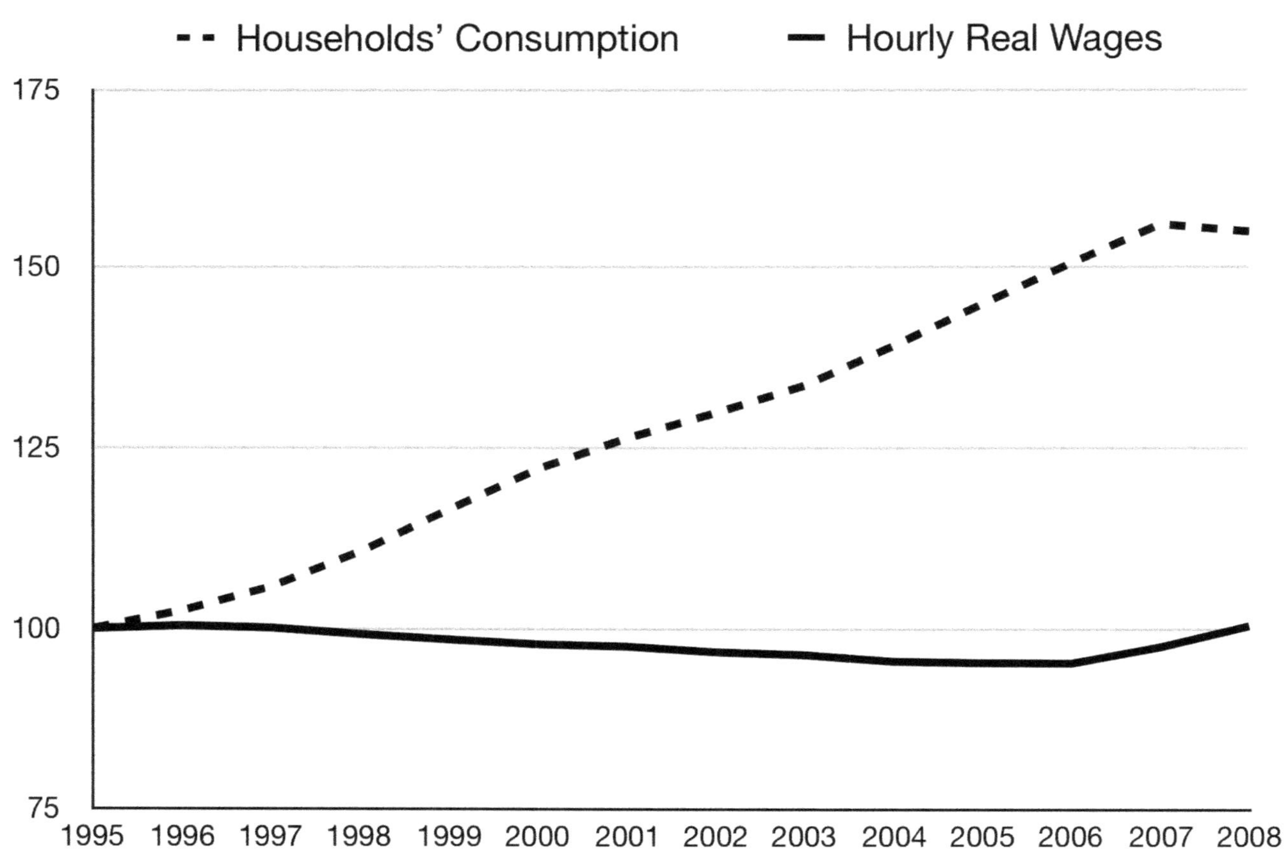

Figure 8.5 Real hourly wages and households' consumption

Table 8.1 Employment growth by sector of activity, 1995–2008

	Absolute	*%*
Agriculture	−169.4	−17.1
Extractive industries	−5.8	−11.9
Energy supply	−9.5	−17.7
Water supply	66	87.5
Manufacturing	243.7	10.2
Construction	1187	94.9
Retail	1370	58.2
Transport and storage	292.5	42.5
Hostelry	709.2	97.6
Information and communications	206.2	82.5
Financial activities	62.5	17.8
Real Estate activities	174.8	400.9
Professional activities	550	121.4
Administrative activities	953.1	292.5
Public administration	275	24.7
Education	399.3	48.1
Health	492.5	64.4
Entertainment activities	154.4	73.1
Other services	255.2	80.9
Household activities	131	20.9
TOTAL	7337.7	

Source: INE (2020c)

manufacturing, where it found itself submitted to increasing competitive pressures throughout the period, towards the oversized real estate complex. Regarding services, where the bulk of new jobs were found, the 'low-road' pattern of sectorial specialization is reflected in the impressive growth attained by tourism-related sectors ('Retail Trade' and 'Hotels and Restaurants'), as well as real estate intermediation. In sum, this pattern of sectorial specialization, anchored around the 'tourism–construction' binomial, heavily fostered the extensive pattern of development of the Spanish economy (López and Rodríguez 2010). Centered in productive areas where producing a sustained surplus was an inherently troublesome task, the antagonistic character of Spanish capitalism emerged as its necessary corollary.

Secondly, Spanish households had recourse to increasing amounts of debt during the whole period, partly in order to compensate for widespread wage stagnation, partly due to their increasing needs of further liquidity to keep on acquiring new housing properties (see Figure 8.6). The relation between the housing bubble and households' increasing leverage is twofold. On the one

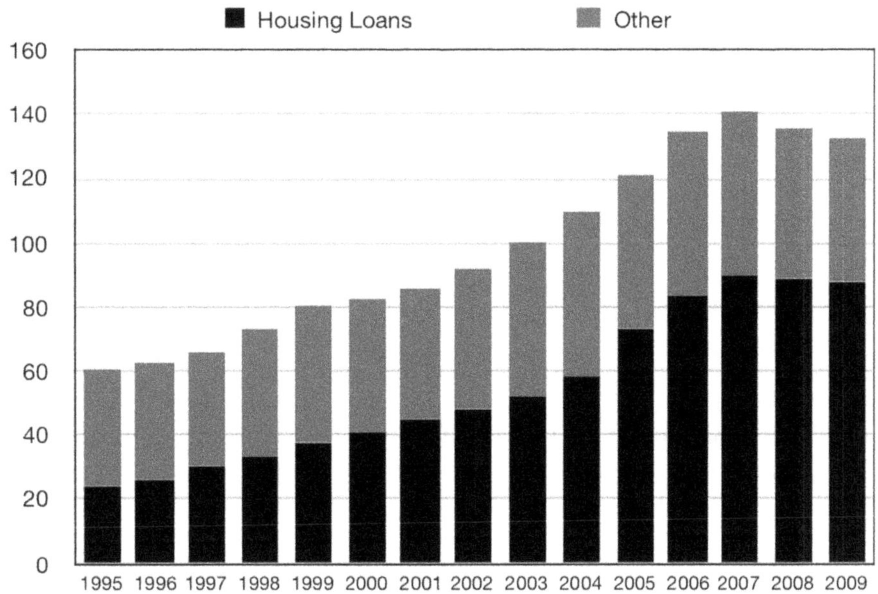

Figure 8.6 Household's debt in relation to households' income

hand, in a context in which homeownership was largely the norm, rising housing prices increased households' nominal wealth levels, which in turn allowed them to incur further rounds of indebtedness by using those same housing properties as collaterals. On the other hand, the 'reified' cultural-institutional propension of Spanish families to acquire new housing properties was compounded by the effect derived from soaring prices, thus strongly enhancing their willingness to incur higher levels of indebtedness in order to acquire new properties. While some of this new debt contracted by households was used to finance their rising consumption levels, most of it was directed to buy new housing properties during these years, housing loans representing an increasing share of households' total liabilities throughout the period, especially so during the last years of the upward phase, when revalorization dynamics were the most intense.

Thirdly, the last atypical source of income that needs to be considered, one which is not even captured by the Spanish National Accounts system, is the extent of housing prices' revalorization. According to Naredo et al.'s (2008) estimations, while they represented relatively modest amounts in relation to more traditional sources of income during the first years of the upward phase, they even surpassed total employees' compensation during the years 2004 and 2006. While not all of it could have been converted into liquidity susceptible of funding consumption expenditures, in the second half of the upward phase, when trading activity on pre-existing housing assets was the most intense, vast amounts of money could certainly have been drawn out

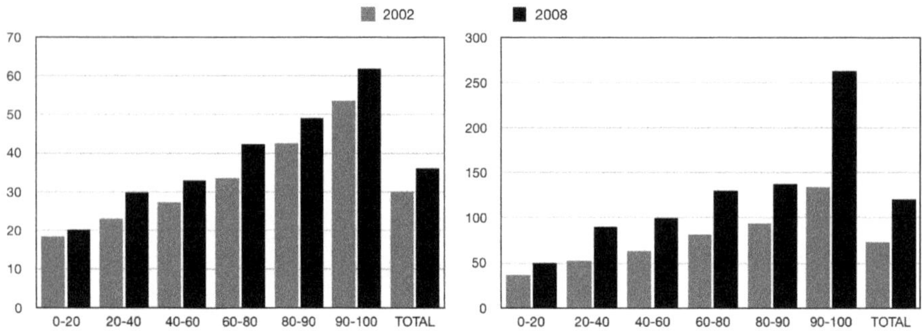

Figure 8.7 Households' multiple housing ownership

successfully. However, it is reasonable to presume that it was only those households who owned multiple properties who could actually profit from trading on them while their prices were on the rise. As seen in Figure 8.7, the proportion of households owning multiple properties heavily increased with the level of households' income, as well as the market value of those same assets. Not only did richer households profit to a much greater extent from spiraling housing prices, but they were also much better positioned to draw out money by trading on them while their prices were on the rise. Indeed, as shown by Naredo et al. (2008), around half of total expenditures in new properties' acquisition came from incomes derived from selling pre-existing properties, whereas one third of it, on average, came from households' increasing leverage.

In sum, the Spanish model, despite its many internal deficiencies and disequilibria, did manage nonetheless to give rise to other social processes, some of them unexpected, some others intrinsically contradictory and self-defeating, whose interaction, by offering each other mutual support, managed to yield an appearance of absolute success well beyond what should have been expected. In this sense, the relations of complementarity springing up among the various social processes just indicated can hardly be overemphasized. For instance, intense employment growth during those years helped prevent real wages from rising in a sustained fashion, which in turn called for higher employment participation to support family incomes in a social context marked by households' increasing leverage; stagnating wages, in conjunction with rising real estate prices encouraged further rounds of household indebtedness, which in turn encouraged rising labor market participation in order to confront existing leverage; rising consumption levels, in turn, were crucial for obliterating the gradual worsening of labor conditions and thus to secure widespread social consent with the existing order, and so on. Therefore, a virtuous cycle ensued among these various social processes as long as housing prices kept rising, offering each other support while significantly attenuating their individually contradictory character. However, despite the generalized climate of euphoria it contributed to generate during the central years of the cycle, the Spanish housing bubble, as any other asset bubble, eventually had to deflate. By constituting itself as the central element of the Spanish institutional edifice during those years, as soon as the virtuous dynamics grounding it were interrupted, the remarkable paths of both households' consumption and capital accumulation were bound to come to a halt.

Over-burdened women

The family is arguably the foremost institution regarding social reproduction within the Spanish political economy. In their role as 'shock absorbers', Spanish families cushioned the worst effects of both a dual labor market that delivered great levels of precariousness to those populating its external layers and an asymmetric and patchy system of welfare provision. Public policy, through its very inaction to relieve women from care responsibilities, served to reproduce, legitimize, and reinforce the situation itself (Leitner 2003; Saraceno and Keck 2010).

However, the contradictory growth path followed by Spanish neoliberalism ultimately compromised its own foundations, as soaring female participation in paid employment put under greater strain a welfare regime ultimately grounded in the widespread availability of women's unpaid domestic labor. Despite women's labor force participation being still relatively low compared to European standards, the change experienced during the last two decades in that respect is an unprecedented one. The rate of women's labor force participation has increased more than 13 percent in barely 15 years. However, if we confine ourselves to those women who are in the middle years of their life (25–54 years), the increase experienced in the period exceeds the 20 percent of the considered population (INE 2020a). Certainly, any social change of such an order is necessarily grounded in many other processes. While some of them may not be directly related to the specific institutional equilibria corresponding to Spanish neoliberalism (e.g. long-lasting cultural changes, increasing female enrollment in tertiary education), stagnating average real wages together with surging household indebtedness have probably acted as strong pull factors in that respect.

It must be stressed that the contradictory character of this process lies not in the absolute value female labor force participation had reached, but in the magnitude of its change in the face of a very resilient and asymmetric domestic division of labor (Gálvez et al. 2011; Sevilla-Sanz et al. 2010) on the one hand, and public policy inaction to consistently unburden women of care responsibilities, on the other (León and Pavolini 2014). Moreover, if increasing labor market participation encounters a labor market that delivers great levels of precariousness to its external layers, where labor usage flexibility is obtained prominently through the spread of fixed-term contracts instead of other types of 'flexi-time' arrangements and/or part-time jobs, and where maternity is associated with either remaining full-time or leaving paid employment altogether (Anxo et al. 2007), it is obvious that a profound 'care crisis' that could have compromised social reproduction did emerge as a serious threat (Pérez-Orozco 2014).

The eventual actualization of such a 'care crisis' was partially prevented through the operation of several social processes whose indefinite perpetuation was clearly impossible to attain. Firstly, Spanish families kept operating as 'social clearinghouses' in which intense exchanges within the family permitted a partial amelioration of work–family conflicts (Bettio and Plantenga 2004). This temporary solution did reinforce traditional gender relations, as it was mainly other women within the family who fulfilled what, in other contexts, would have been public policy duties (Moreno 2004; Tobío 2013). Secondly, myriad strategies of individual resistance were deployed, such as multitasking and, most significantly, a sharp drop in fertility. In a context marked by scarce family-oriented policies, resilient traditional gender norms and rigid labor conditions regarding time flexibility, Spanish couples opted for postponing child-rearing as their preferred means to balance the excessive temporal demands they had to deal with (Bernardi 2005). Thirdly, the entry of large swathes of immigrants, many of whom ended up working in the informal sector, provided a cheap market-based solution to unsatisfied care needs (Ibáñez and León 2014).[4] Several consecutive regularization programs in conjunction with a large underground sector constituted strong 'pull' factors for immigration (Bettio et al. 2006), fostering a reorganization of care provision in which families shifted from providing care themselves to coordinating informally hired migrant carers (Simonazzi 2009).

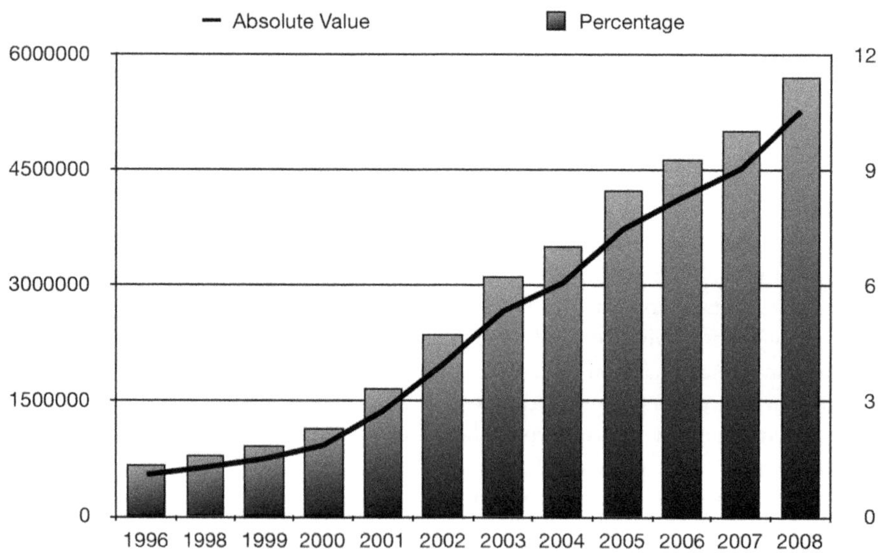

Figure 8.8 Foreign-born population

Developing complementarities among unsustainable processes

Contrary to established economic wisdom, recent Spanish experience shows the extent to which deepening underlying productive disequilibria may co-exist, for a relatively long time, with the ongoing reproduction of a widespread appearance of unparalleled macroeconomic success. To that extent, as already indicated in previous pages, it is our contention that the impressive macroeconomic record the Spanish SSA managed to deliver in certain indicators during these years was proportional, in the last instance, to the extent of its internal contradictions. Neither self-sustained revaluation dynamics in the real estate sector, nor growing indebtedness unsupported by expanding productive capacity, nor increasing current account imbalances with its main trade partners, nor an enlarging competitiveness gap with other members of the same monetary area, nor the continuous expansion of investment expenditures that did not foster a more productive use of labor power, nor rising consumption levels unsupported by rising average wages, nor rising female labor market participation unaccompanied by public policies designed to relieve women of their household's responsibilities, could ever be reproduced *ad infinitum*. These dynamics, despite showing a markedly contradictory character when considered in isolation, managed to coalesce into a precarious institutional ensemble articulated by relations of mutual reinforcement among its key components that, in turn, supported their joint reproduction. The development of such relations of complementarity and mutual reinforcement not only ensured that their respective dynamics did not destabilize the articulated whole in which they coalesced but, also, represented the ultimate source of the momentum experienced by the economic expansion itself.

For instance, the internal deficiencies affecting the Spanish productive sector did favor a continuous shift of available resources towards the financial and construction-related sectors. Common interests built around the latter in turn favored the emergence and consolidation of widespread speculative dynamics within the real estate complex, as manifested in an impressive upsurge of both housing prices and new constructions, the ultimate source of the social effectivity of the Spanish model. On the one hand, this productive specialization both needed and favored an inherently 'low-road' pattern of sectorial development which, in turn, reinforced the extensive pattern of growth adopted by the Spanish economy, much more dependent upon incorporating new labor units than upon fostering a more productive use of them (Buendía 2018a). Its dependence on continually lowering labor costs thus helped consolidate an already-strong underground sector which, among other things, acted as a strong pull factor for sizable immigration flows. The inability to consistently raise labor productivity throughout the period made securing a positive balance in its distributive struggle with labor the centerpiece of Spanish capital's strategies for survival, in turn promoting the incorporation of massive influxes of new workers, singularly previously inactive women and immigrants of various origins. Such a vigorous process of employment creation, one of the most praised achievements of the Spanish model at the time, was functional to capital valorization as it prevented widespread real wage revaluation which, in turn, fueled further new entries into paid employment, both in order to complement family incomes in light of increasing private consumption levels and as a response to soaring levels of indebtedness among households.

On the other hand, rising housing prices both required and enabled soaring levels of private indebtedness. While private firms did so in order to profit from revaluation dynamics delinked from their alleged productive activity, households could use their housing properties as collaterals in order to incur new rounds of indebtedness, a portion of which they partly diverted to keep on expanding their consumption levels while simultaneously feeding the housing bubble which, in turn, further favored rising consumption through the operation of wealth effects supported by rising housing prices. Moreover, while booming activity in the real estate complex incentivized the arrival of sizeable immigration inflows, the latter did also help sustain rising demand for housing properties by the end of the upward phase. The momentum it yielded to aggregate economic activity animated further women's incorporation into the labor market which, in turn, further expanded the existing demand for cheap market-based solutions to their care needs, a demand that was to be fed by ascending immigration flows.

In sum, self-reinforcing dynamics sprang up between households' growing indebtedness, employment expansion, financial firms' soaring leverage, wage stagnation, increasing consumption levels, growing trade deficits and ecological destruction, all these processes being ultimately knotted together by self-sustained price increases within the real estate sector. However, once the housing bubble eventually deflated, as every asset price bubble is bound to do, existing internal relations of complementarity suddenly gave way to its very opposite, that is, a precarious structure plagued with internal malfunctions, where the internal expression of each could not but reinforce analogous dynamics in co-existing domains, promoting in turn further economic decline and institutional decomposition.

The homeostatic functioning of the Spanish SSA

So far, the core social processes co-governing social reproduction in Spanish territory during the phase of economic expansion have been analyzed. While, it is argued, the key to their joint reproduction over time resided in the manifold relations of complementarity and mutual reinforcement springing up among them during those years, they were nonetheless conducive, at least apparently, to have given rise to social contestation over the social dynamics they instituted. While securing the conditions needed for sustained capitalist economic activity is a crucial feature of any well-functioning SSA, its core institutional blocks must also be prevented from undergoing widespread politicization. To that extent, social consensuses supporting the ongoing reproduction of existing institutional equilibria need to be generated and protected, while existing social conflicts need to be channeled along lines that do not interfere with the former. In sum, a social order, articulated through internal relations of hierarchical stratification and exclusion, needs to be reproduced.

To recap, a successful social order needs, firstly, to channel existing social conflicts along dimensions not directly implicated in the underlying SSA's internal mode of operation, preventing its core elements from being politicized. Secondly, some common ground needs to be generated among symbolically recognized social actors that unifies to a certain extent their initially heterogeneous aims and aspirations. Lastly, institutional means ought to be deployed to prevent those excluded from existing social hierarchies from disrupting them, reproducing their lack of symbolic and material resources with which to unsettle existing social equilibria. This section will explore the extent to which the inherently conflictive nature of the Spanish SSA's main institutional blocks was prevented from coming to the fore thanks, precisely, to the relations of mutual support provided by the remaining ones. Among the several areas around which social conflicts might have sprung during those years, three of them merit special attention in our view, namely, antagonistic labor relations, an underdeveloped welfare state, and the absence of family policies.

Firstly, the Spanish SSA has featured antagonistic labor relations all throughout the period, as the distorted pattern of capital accumulation made capitalist profitability increasingly dependent upon the result of its distributive struggle with labor. Politicizing capital–labor relations certainly represents a serious threat to any capitalist social formation irrespective of the particular form adopted by its institutional environment. However, it would have been even more system-threatening in the Spanish case due to capital's valorization dynamics. While the impressive upsurge in employment stood as one of the foremost accomplishments of the Spanish SSA, it was nonetheless obtained at the cost of widespread wage containment (manifested in the flat evolution of average real hourly wages); dramatic levels of precariousness, especially in the labor market's external layers (manifested in the pervasiveness of fixed-term contracts); and very high levels of unemployment (which never managed to fall below 8 percent of the active population in more than a decade of uninterrupted growth). To be sure, the increasing precarization and individualization of labor relations, inasmuch as they foster a generalized state of material insecurity and mutual rivalry and competition among workers, certainly constitutes a great impediment to the widespread politicization of capital–labor relations *tout court*. However, the erosion of working-class political identities' hegemonic depth, and the concomitant obscuring of class struggle as a decisive axis of social contention, cannot be properly understood without taking into consideration the support provided by other individually contradictory trends partaking of the SSA, among which real estate self-valorization dynamics definitely stand out.

In a social context featuring widespread homeownership, not only did patrimonial rents derived from real estate revalorization dynamics serve to partially compensate for wage stagnation but, also, they were crucial in providing access to credit resources that enabled consumption levels to increase beyond what the evolution of labor income would have indicated. In turn, increasing consumption levels were crucial to re-signify a new 'middle-class' status now linked prominently to consumption patterns rather than to the enjoyed modality of labor inclusion. Property income, rather than employment outcomes, was thus consolidated as the primary marker of social status (López and Rodríguez 2010). Despite being ultimately grounded in rising indebtedness and wealth effects derived from spiraling housing prices, neither of which could have been reproduced endlessly, rising consumption levels played a decisive role in helping obliterate both underlying class divides and the general degradation of labor conditions affecting many of those whose living had to be secured through their involvement in paid employment.

Indeed, degrading labor conditions were unevenly distributed over the employed population, insofar as the relatively high levels of protection enjoyed by 'core' (read male adult) workers were matched by very high levels of precariousness among those participating in the external market, that is, mostly women, young and immigrant workers. In that respect, the higher protection offered to 'core' workers in conjunction with, on the one hand, the intense internal redistribution of resources that characterizes Spanish families and, on the other, a welfare system skewed towards the needs of the elderly, were fundamental to cushion the widespread effects of labor precariousness. Were it not for the relative security offered to 'core' workers within a family institution that, despite being submitted to increasing strains, kept nonetheless showing quite high levels of internal cohesiveness, anything resembling a social order would have probably been simply a chimera. It was precisely the persistence of micro-solidarity dynamics within the family which precluded sharp labor market segmentation from being translated into fully-fledged social divides, thus preventing wider opposition towards the existing social order from those systematically enjoying the worst modalities of labor inclusion, significantly women and the young. Regarding the former, the 'narrow concept of citizenship' upon which familialist welfare regimes are grounded, by categorizing women as second-order workers, prevented wider contestation by women of their modality of labor inclusion (Torns et al. 2013). Regarding the young, on the one hand, extended family support helped obliterate existing intergenerational cleavages regarding labor opportunities, while, on the other, a middle-class status linked to tertiary education played a fundamental role in re-signifying labor precariousness as a transitional stage rather than as a clear indication of accelerating proletarianization.

Secondly, another issue around which potential unsatisfied demands might have coalesced was welfare state underdevelopment. In this respect, two main factors should be singled out. On the one hand, the ideological role played by European Union membership cannot be underestimated. Ever since the 1980s European integration has been used strategically as a symbol of progress and modernity, even after the process of convergence in terms of social expenditure drew to a halt during the 1990s (Moreno and Serrano 2011). The final adoption of the common currency in 2002, moreover, coincided with the strongest phase of housing revalorization dynamics which, in turn, were crucial to continue sustaining rising consumption levels. Despite monetary integration having significantly aggravated the underlying disequilibria of the Spanish SSA, rising consumption in hand with a social perception of generalized enrichment served to reinforce the already reified association between European integration and widespread socio-economic development. On the other hand, the classical trade-off identified by Kemeny (1981) between homeownership and welfare state expansion as alternative mechanisms of long-term saving was exacerbated by the effects derived from the housing bubble, in turn drawing out social support for further welfare state development. These dynamics contributed to reinforce the material position of older generations for, as noted by Schwartz and Seabrooke (2008: 257):

> [dwellings'] re-pricing conveys windfall gains on housing market insiders, while burdening new entrants with increased debt. Because on net nearly all insiders are older established households while new entrants are younger households, re-pricing creates a massive transfer of wealth upwards in both age and income terms.

Conversely, younger generations, were doubly affected by these dynamics, insofar as they could barely profit from speculative dynamics in the housing market, while their employment outcomes were heavily affected by the type of productive specialization the former promoted. However, it is again the key role played by Spanish families which explains their lack of social contestation, as strong intra-familial transfers helped compensate the demographic bias towards the elderly regarding both welfare spending and homeownership, thus preventing the generational cleavage from acquiring full political expression in a way that could have seriously destabilized the existing social order. Somehow paradoxically, while Spain has been among the EU countries where more extensive support for active state intervention in welfare state areas could be found (Calzada and del Pino 2011), it was so ultimately because of the operation of two crucial pillars generally unacknowledged in conventional accounts of welfare state components, namely, the housing property market and the family.

Lastly, another element around which social discomfort could have given rise to a set of unsatisfied demands susceptible to having seriously compromised social reproduction concerns the most flagrant absence in the Spanish welfare architecture, namely, family policy. A systematic lack of public policy interventions directed towards unburdening women of the care responsibilities 'naturally' assigned to them was implicitly supported by an ideological configuration of social care needs as a strictly gendered private responsibility (Serrano-Pascual et al. 2019), in which a strong sense of moral obligation prevented (and certainly continues to prevent) widespread politicization of the public-private divide upon which social reproduction ultimately rests (Bruff and Wöhl 2016). Despite family economies being submitted to increasing strains due to rising female employment participation in the face of a very traditional and resilient domestic division of labor, the arrival of large swathes of immigrants played a key role in attenuating social pressures regarding the insufficient provision of public services directed towards families and children, as the widespread availability of informal low-cost market-based care arrangements enabled dual-earner families to externalize to some extent their care responsibilities, thus diminishing the salience of work–family conflicts among the layers of the population that disposed of the appropriate material and symbolic means to actually turn it into a public issue.

In sum, the Spanish SSA was successful not only in the sense of having attained an impressive record in certain macroeconomic indicators but, also, in that it managed to safeguard its main institutional pillars from being politicized, partially because the worst social effects derived from each were temporarily attenuated and/or obliterated thanks to the support offered by other individually contradictory social processes. For instance, housing revalorization dynamics permitted a successful obliteration of both an increasingly skewed income distribution and welfare state insufficiencies from public debate; widespread expansion of credit and debt among private households reinforced a re-signification of middle-class status now linked to consumption patterns rather than to labor market outcomes; social conflicts around care provision were partially ameliorated by large immigration flows, whose entry was further induced by a booming underground economy linked to Spanish productive specialization, and so on.

It must be stressed, however, that despite the capacity of the Spanish model to draw vast layers of the population into its self-generated consensuses, not all of those who were involved had the symbolic and material resources to make their own voices heard. Among those whose (potentially critical) voices were prevented from disrupting existing consensuses one should count, among others, lower-class women, where the intersection between class and gender divides became more acute, who lacked the capacity to externalize their care responsibilities by having recourse to informal market arrangements, and whose predominant modality of labor inclusion offered little to no possibilities of upward promotion; those without housing properties, who could not benefit from asset revalorization dynamics, who had to have recourse to an insufficient and expensive rented market, and whose destinies where left to the vagaries of the labor market; the young who could not enjoy family support to face stagnating wages and rising housing prices; and, above all, the large masses of immigrant workers who, utterly deprived of both symbolic recognition and material resources, were forced to cater to the needs of the many while enlarging the profits of the few. Nevertheless, the success of the Spanish SSA in securing widespread social consensuses resided not in its capacity to fully eradicate social antagonisms but, rather, in its capacity to channel and structure social conflict in such a way that its main institutional pillars were safeguarded and unaffected by them. To that extent, the idiosyncratic regime of visibility limiting and structuring socio-political interaction in the Spanish social formation throughout the period needs to be accounted for.

The 'Culture of the Transition' and social antagonisms

Underlying any visible political interaction there is always a silent network governing what is sayable and what is not, what is arguable and what is not, which words are heard as words and which others as noise, which social actors have a right to speak and which others ought to be condemned not to have a recognized voice, and hence to have someone else speaking for them. This regime of (in)visibility, which Rancière (2004b: 7–8) terms the 'distribution of the sensible', stands for:

> the system of self-evident facts of sense perception that simultaneously discloses the existence of something in common and the delimitations that define the respective parts and positions within it. [...] It is a delimitation of spaces and times, of the visible and the invisible, of speech and noise.

Along very close theoretical lines, some authors have proposed the term 'Culture of the Transition' (see Martínez 2012) to refer to 'the whole organization of the visible, the sayable, the thinkable' dominant in the Spanish social formation since the democratic regime was finally implemented until the present moment, '[for] every social organization is first of all a symbolic and aesthetic order which configures a common perception of things' (Fernández-Savater 2013). This underlying regime of visibility has been significantly successful both in governing and regulating the terms of political contention as well as in delimiting which topics were susceptible to political debate. How does it relate to the idiosyncratic pattern of capitalist expansion detailed above?

Following Fernández-Savater (2012), the 'Culture of the Transition' ('CT' hereafter) may be characterized by three main traits. Firstly, it has been an eminently 'consensual' culture, not in the sense that it values the capacity to reach agreements from dissenting positions at the outset but, rather, in that it features a remarkable aversion to political contention of whichever type. Secondly, it is a 'de-problematizing' dispositif for it does not accept public quarrels over its mode of operation. Social contestation thus is systematically reduced to a sort of aberration utterly incompatible with (market liberal) democratic procedures, mere interruptions to an otherwise 'normal' course of events. Lastly, as a corollary, it is a 'de-politicizing' assemblage for it does not permit posing questions over the social organization of collective life, that is, not only regarding whether 'parliamentary capitalism' is the most appropriate and/or socially convenient mode of social organization but, also, regarding the idiosyncratic version of capitalism operating in Spain during those years: 'The CT is a mode of naturalizing the economy while not speaking about it, to take for granted its necessities and to de-problematize them' (Fernández-Savater 2013).

The CT is thus a symbolic dispositif which de-politicizes and legitimizes existing social inequalities by presenting them as having sprung from merely technical decisions, while configuring the consumption of commodities as the paramount marker of social status. Following Moreno-Caballud (2015: 28–9), it is a:

> technocratic and hierarchical [culture], because it understands the establishment of the social 'rules of the game' (politics and the economy) as technical or 'profound' matters to be resolved by experts and intellectuals, [as well as] a consumerist culture because it understands daily life as an individual's election and attainment of a series of desired objects.

In this sense, the CT closely resembles that which Mouffe (2005) and Žižek (2008) have termed 'post-politics', that is, an eminently technocratic mode of administration where truly political dissent is either not recognized or, if forced to do so, immediately reduced to violent outbursts lacking any sort of underlying rationality whatsoever. Society is thus assumed to be a fully self-transparent entity, whose basic coordinates are to be shared by all its participants, and where a harmonious co-existence between a plurality of different identities is ensured by the installation of a neutral framework of cooperation. As a corollary, the distribution of the social product among its participants remains but a purely technical operation.

In sum, it is the very framework delimiting both the issues suitable to undergo public debate and the social actors whose expertise on the matter is to be recognized, which is prevented from politicization proper. In that respect, absolute consensus over the main guidelines orienting economic policy stood as the hidden element whose suppression from public debate grounded, in the last instance, available political alternatives at the time. As explored above, social redistribution of both acquisitive power and consumption opportunities was largely attained through fostering massive recourse to private debt in combination with a sustained generation of capital gains derived from real estate properties' revaluation. This model successfully generated a constituency adapted to both its nature and its limits – the 'middle class' (López and Rodríguez 2010).

The 'middle class' status that became hegemonic in Spain was one increasingly dissociated from the modality of labor inclusion characteristic of the Fordist period, being more dependent in turn upon the socio-symbolic value of (mostly real estate) property *qua* vehicle to social integration and de-proletarianization. Considering oneself a member of the middle class thus meant, implicitly, accepting the basic coordinates organizing social coexistence (from validating existing social hierarchies to accepting patrimonial capitalism to be, at the end of the day, 'the only game in town') while, in return, enjoying increasing consumption levels while projecting oneself as being situated in an ascending historical continuum (Alonso, Fernández-Rodríguez, and Ibáñez-Rojo 2015; 2017). It is this general acquiescence with the existing state of affairs, irrespective of the manifold inequalities and segmentations the latter nonetheless harbored, which is reflected in the Spanish population's massive self-identification as 'middle class'. The latter contained a symbolic and aspirational dimension, inapprehensible from theoretical lenses self-restricted to strictly material conditions, which signaled a minimum level of both social recognition and representation within the public sphere, while simultaneously refusing to struggle against the very fundamentals articulating social co-existence.

However, despite it being an eminently aspirational declaration, it did have nonetheless very precise material conditions of existence which economic policy had to promote and reproduce, such as, for instance, securing widespread access to consumption credit to increasingly vast layers of the population; favoring new entries into the real estate market to ensure sustained price increases of housing assets; favoring the arrival of masses of immigrants in order both to develop an informal market for care services and to ensure wage repression in the low-quality employment niches where the Spanish economy specialized (crucially construction and tourism); a strategic use of European integration in order to further the interests of domestic elites; and so on.

Moreover, the nature of the last economic boom has accentuated some socio-cultural traits dating back to the Francoist period related to a generalized aversion to political participation, or at least a distrust of it, in a context in which every type of conflict was immediately read as an excess in need of being eradicated. The fragile and short-lived character of Spanish democracy was reflected in the fact that the type of middle-class identification it managed to spread and consolidate was an inherently individualistic and ever-threatened one for, as noted by Maura (2018: 84), in Spain, 'the surface of the middle class coincides almost exactly with the aspiration to belong/remain in it'. This perennial fear of the stubborn persistence of underlying class realities contributed to further discredit collective action in favor of individual strategies of upward mobility. This has fostered, in turn, a general climate of popular connivance with the strategies undertaken by Spanish elites, heavily dependent on having close ties with the State apparatus in order to safeguard their own productive positions (Rey-Araújo 2019). In this sense, others' personal enrichment was validated as long as it did not interfere with one's own material improvement, despite most probably both processes occurring at quite different rhythms. Widespread capital gains thus helped legitimize myriad illicit practices undertaken by Spanish elites to profit from their privileged position within the real estate business, as long they were accompanied by employment creation (despite their precarious character) and rising consumption levels (despite being unsupported by improving labor conditions). As concluded by Naredo (2019), 'the housing bubble extended the virus of speculation all throughout the social body'.

In sum, along the course of the economic expansion a symbiotic relation ensued between, on the one hand, an institutional environment chiefly articulated around inherently conflict-prone social processes and, on the other, a socio-symbolic dispositif tailor-made for the latter regarding its capacity to deactivate potential political discomfort with the existing state of affairs. Nevertheless, doing away with social conflict altogether is an ontologically impossible task. While social antagonisms were certainly not completely eradicated from the public arena, they were nonetheless systemically diverted towards issues ultimately unrelated to the main social processes sustaining the economic expansion in the first instance. As a result, the main axes of political confrontation left the core blocks of the Spanish SSA virtually untouched.

In 1996, a discursively and symbolically renovated Popular Party (PP) led by José María Aznar came into office for the first time since the democratic transition, thus putting an end to a 14-year-long period of uninterrupted Socialist government. Founded by former Francoist officials after the dictator's death, it had progressively abandoned its traditional conservative motives to openly embrace an eminently neoliberal rhetoric consonant with the general orientation of the times. The period corresponding to its first term in office, 1996–2000, coinciding with the beginning of the economic expansion, were years of relatively low levels of social contestation (Antentas 2015). Not only had the economic expansion served to calm social discontent, but its lack of absolute majority in Congress obliged the PP to initiate a politics of social dialogue with the main trade unions while also making concessions to peripheral nationalisms, on whose collaboration the government's sustainability crucially depended.

Its second term in office (2000–2004) was marked, however, by much higher levels of social contestation, especially during its second half (Carbó et al. 2005). The absolute majority obtained in the 2000 general elections enabled the party in government to pursue the main lines of their program without being constrained by the necessity to reach parliamentary agreements with other forces. During these years, a neo-conservative version of Spanish nationalism was unashamedly put forward by the PP, which revendicated a self-enclosed and essentialist Spanish nationalist identity defined, prominently, in opposition to Spain's peripheral nationalisms (Delgado 2015). The continued (although decreasing) action of the Basque terrorist group ETA thus enabled the party in government, (now increasingly dissociated, at a strictly symbolic level, from its Francoist heritage), to initiate a process of social polarization against virtually everyone who did not openly support PP's strategy to combat the so-called 'terrorist menace', which included several measures of a more than dubious democratic character.

While social protests in the streets were on the rise, especially from 2002 onwards, in turn playing a crucial role in undermining the PP's social hegemony during those years, it is nevertheless remarkable the extent to which they were, in the last instance, mostly unrelated to the specific institutional configuration governing economic expansion, with the only exception of the General Strike called by unions in June 2002, in response to a labor market reform which included several measures to further degrade labor conditions, and significantly hardened the requirements to have access to unemployment benefits. Enjoying absolute majority in Parliament, the PP no longer felt in need of continuing to develop social concertation strategies with the main trade unions, thus giving way to a response from the latter in the guise of a general strike.

Besides the 2002 General Strike, this cycle of contention had two different strands (Antentas 2015). On the one hand, previous autonomous experiences, such as a long tradition of neighborhood associations and diverse social movements, led to an emerging anti-globalization movement which reached its highest point during the European Council Summit celebrated in Barcelona in

March 2002, as well as to a resurgent *squatter* movement (Flesher-Fominaya 2007; Alonso, Betancor, and Cilleros 2015). Despite having a relatively minor impact at the time, the activist networks and occupied spaces developed during these years were to play a decisive role, some years later, in the emergence of the 'indignados' movement in 2011 (Flesher-Fominaya 2015).

On the other hand, a wave of protests took place against the neo-conservative stance espoused by the Aznar government, including, among others, widespread student mobilizations during late 2001 and 2002 against a new law promulgating university reform; protests against the government's infamous response to the sinking of the oil tanker named *Prestige* in front of the Galician coast; or the massive demonstrations celebrated in several cities against Spain's enthusiastic involvement in the US-led 'War on Terror'. This wave of mobilization was somehow concluded with the spontaneous demonstrations following the terrorist attacks in Madrid on March 11, 2004. The government's stubborn insistence to blame ETA as the ultimate designer of the attacks was rapidly contested by massive and spontaneous concentrations of demonstrations in most of the country's main cities, as all of the evidence then available pointed instead towards Islamist cells. Widespread condemnation of the government's unabashed manipulation gave the electoral victory to PSOE's candidate Jose Luis Rodríguez-Zapatero. While this protest cycle managed to undermine Popular Party's neo-conservative hegemonic stance, these various mobilizations, with the only exception of the 2002 general strike, had left the core elements of the Spanish SSA, whose politicization would have seriously compromised ongoing social reproduction, virtually untouched.

The Socialist Party was thus back in office after eight years of PP government. During its first term (2004–2008), it took advantage of a favorable economic scenario to advance some very progressive pieces of legislation regarding civil and individual rights, such as the passing of the right of homosexual couples to marry; an Integral Law to combat gender violence; a new Law of Equality, which was intended to promote gender parity in the public sphere; and, above all, a potentially revolutionary legislative intervention, the so-called 'Dependency Law', which intended to establish a universal right to care for all the persons involved in an objective situation of dependency. In an eminently 'familialist' institutional environment such as Spain's, the actual implementation of such laudable intentions would have deeply transformed Spain's social organization of care along markedly egalitarian lines. However, the onset of the Great Recession left its commendable aims in little more than ink and paper. These changes were harshly confronted by the ecclesiastic authorities, the Popular Party and its various associated collectives. Campaigning against issues such as homosexual couples' right to marriage, the legalization of euthanasia, or a new, less restrictive, abortion law, brought thousands to the streets during those years (Carmona et al. 2012). Besides these heightened social antagonisms over the PSOE's modernizing civil rights' agenda, territorial conflicts were brought again center stage as the government launched a peace process with the Basque terrorist group ETA. Moreover, a reform of Catalunya's Statute of Autonomy was passed in 2006 that broadened the region's degree of self-government. Both processes were met with stringent opposition by the PP's reinvigorated Spanish nationalism, in the guise of accusations of having 'surrendered to the terrorists' blackmail' or of 'breaking up Spain' (Sánchez-Cuenca 2012).

In sum, PSOE's first term in office was certainly characterized by heightened social tensions. During these years, two axes of social antagonization gained prominence. On the one hand, the government's civil rights agenda was confronted by recurrent neo-conservative mobilizations commanded by the PP and the ecclesiastic authorities. On the other hand, an intransigent and reinvigorated Spanish nationalism actively confronted what, in their view, were unforgettable concessions from the government to Spain's peripheral nationalisms. Again, however, the various social antagonisms capturing media attention were to a great extent unrelated to the idiosyncratic character of Spanish capitalism, insofar as a silent consensus with regard to the dominant orientation of economic policy left the core elements of the institutional environment structuring capitalist activity systematically untouched. However, by the time economic expansion was interrupted with the onset of the Great Recession, the climate of generalized social consensus that had dominated Spanish society during the years of economic prosperity soon began to unravel, throwing into light the manifold malfunctions which, during previous years, were successfully prevented from coming to the fore. To the post-2008 period we now turn.

Acknowledgments

Parts of this chapter have already been published as 'The contradictory of "Mediterranean" neoliberalism in Spain. 1995–2008' in *Review of Radical Political Economics*, 2020. The author thanks Sage Publishing for granting permission for re-printing them here.

Notes

1 It has been widely noted how the stringency with which 'monetarist' policy principles were adopted was somehow at odds with the party's social-democratic credentials. In this respect, while Recio and Roca (1998: 140) point out how the Mitterrand administration's previous failure in implementing an expansionary Keynesian program in France, as well as the need to avoid capital flight, reinforced such policy decisions, Juste (2017) underlines instead the common ideological milieux, linked to the Bank of Spain, from which PSOE's policy makers mostly came from.
2 Montes (1993) has pointed out how the government's willingness to secure accession to the EC at all costs greatly undermined its capacity to negotiate an agreement of accession beneficial to Spanish interests.
3 Mateo (2019) provides various alternative calculations of the rate of profit during these years. While the intensity of the experienced decline depends on how the profit rate is calculated, all estimates they provide invariably show a downward trend throughout the growth phase.
4 By 1998, Spain had the lowest share of immigrant population among EU-15 countries. Just a decade later, in 2008, it was already the third highest (Laparra 2011).

9 From systemic to organic crisis: 2008–2019

The vigorous expansion of capitalist activity the Spanish SSA promoted since the mid-1990s served to conceal its increasingly crumbling foundations. Moreover, widespread social acceptance regarding both the manifold social inequalities it harbored, and the idiosyncratic pattern of socio-economic development it promoted, was definitely attained. Nevertheless, at some point the virtuous interaction among its core internal dynamics was bound to come to a halt. Such a point was reached, eventually, in the second half of 2007, when residential investment, the ultimate driving force of the whole institutional assemblage, initiated a downward trend (although GDP and housing prices would not follow suit until mid-2008). Hence, while the onset of the Great Recession played a key role in magnifying internal contradictions, it cannot be held responsible for the breakdown of the Spanish SSA, insofar as internal contradictions had been driving the whole social formation towards an inevitable collapse virtually since its very inception. Once revaluation dynamics in the real estate sector could no longer be self-reproduced, co-existing social processes finding in the latter their ultimate source of support immediately followed suit.

A couple of years thus sufficed to undo the various internal relations of complementarity that had yielded momentum to the previous economic expansion. The interlocked character of its main internal contradictions, far from contributing to attenuate their respective breakdown, did further accentuate their mutual collapse. The 'Spanish miracle' soon turned itself into a collective nightmare. Moreover, existing social consensuses were radically disrupted as the material base in which they had been grounded virtually disappeared: A systemic crisis was soon turned into an organic one. An institutional structure in the course of breaking down dragged down with itself existing social consensuses, in turn giving rise to a variety of unsatisfied demands which abruptly entered the public sphere. The latter, in turn, were intimately linked to both the institutional bases that had regulated previous economic expansion and the way crisis management was attempted. The timing, scope, and intensity of such proliferation of social discontents constitutes a paramount example of what we had previously termed a 'populist situation'. Aiming at hegemonizing the latter by help of a 'left-wing populist intervention', a new political party was born in 2014: Podemos. The way the hegemonic struggle was conducted in response to such populist challenge will receive special attention in the pages that follow.

While, to date, the Spanish SSA's phase of decay is far from being concluded, two separate internal stages ought nonetheless to be identified. The first one, ranging from 2008 until 2013, was marked by wide-ranging institutional decomposition, where reverberating internal disequilibria entered into a downward spiral that mutually enhanced their joint decay. Concomitantly, social antagonisms proliferated as the ongoing reproduction of the manifold differential positions the social order consisted of was terminally compromised by the abrupt end to which the economic expansion was driven. The second phase, ranging from 2014 onwards, is marked by a partial reversal of the aforementioned process of institutional self-dissolution: GDP growth was resumed to the point of reaching, by 2017, its previous 2008 levels; some of its core internal imbalances have been partially corrected, although many old vulnerabilities nonetheless persist and, concurrently, the socio-political climate has gradually cooled down. Despite existing pressures for radical socio-institutional transformation having partially faded away, the hegemonic struggle remains far from concluded, as contemporary developments, such as the intensification of Catalunya's pro-independence movement, the emergence of the extreme-right political party *Vox*, or the recent feminist mobilizations, certainly reveal.

A fully-fledged systemic breakdown: 2008–2013

While economic crises are an inescapable corollary to any sustained process of capitalist expansion, the precise form they take is inherently dependent upon the specific form adopted by the institutional structure governing its previous expansion (Kotz 2015). Insofar as the reproduction of the Spanish model, once the utmost envy of its rival capitalist counterparts, had been supported by the relations of complementarity and mutual reinforcement generated along the expansion among self-defeating dynamics, it was just a matter of time until such manifold underlying contradictions would, eventually, lethally overflow the institutional assemblage which their very interrelation had helped consolidate (Recio 2010). Among the main social processes driving the aforementioned expansion, one of them clearly stood out due to the role it played in coordinating co-existing ones, namely, the housing bubble (López and Rodríguez 2010). As soon as it started to deflate, as every self-sustained process of asset price revaluation is sooner or later forced to, other social processes finding support in it were suddenly deprived of their material conditions of existence. A sudden and abrupt process of institutional decomposition ensued, one not circumscribed to one specific area of the social (thus susceptible to being solved through partial modifications or amendments) but, on the contrary, one which pervaded the whole institutional assemblage, demolishing it in turn.

As already noted, Liberal SSAs, by reinforcing the power of capital in several social spheres, tend to harbor intrinsic problems to generate internal demand through 'normal' mechanisms (i.e. by sharing among competing groups the surplus previously generated in the production process), giving rise to other atypical and/or unsustainable processes through which aggregate demand can be made to grow for a certain period. As a result, systemic crises derived from Liberal SSAs tend to take the form of an abrupt process of institutional decomposition, instead of a prolonged period featuring mild, although recurrent, macroeconomic turbulences. On the grounds that it is the whole institutional structure that is shattered, rather than just one of its single components, Kotz (2010b: 368, emphasis added) has argued that Liberal SSAs 'tend to produce a *severe* crisis of accumulation'. The implosion of the Spanish SSA, while definitely conforming to this pattern, nevertheless constitutes a significantly acute manifestation of it. The short timespan ranging from 2007, when the Spanish economy was enjoying an unparalleled success, to 2010, when the initial implementation of austerity policies seemed to leave it on the brink of collapse, is utterly indicative in that respect.

In a nutshell, the crisis arose once 'debt stopped renewing itself' (Buendía 2018b: 65). Despite the triggering effect derived from Lehman Brothers' bankruptcy in 2008, as well as from the European Central Bank's (ECB) sustained interest rate increases in previous years, from 2 percent in 2005 to 4.25 percent in 2008 (Garzón et al. 2018), the Spanish construction sector was already showing signs of exhaustion as early as mid-2007. Indeed, residential investment was the first component of aggregate demand to start its decline, in the third quarter of 2007, although housing prices kept on rising until the first quarter of 2008 (Mateo 2019). Housing prices revaluation could only continue in the expectation of further future price increases. Once the entry of new investors began to slow down, housing prices could not but start a sustained decline, dragging down alongside themselves the various social processes whose source of support they ultimately represented.

The interruption of revalorization dynamics in the real estate sector gradually brought down employment levels (last quarter of 2007) as well as the remaining components of aggregate demand. GFCF started its decline in the first quarter of 2008, private consumption started in the second, and GDP in the third (INE 2020b). A spiraling process of institutional decomposition and economic activity slowdown ensued, mutually reinforcing each other. In annual terms, GDP grew by 1.1 percent in the year 2008, the last one recording a positive increase in real terms prior to 2014; households' final consumption fell by 0.7 percent in 2008 and by a further 3.7 percent in 2009; imports immediately plummeted (–6.3 percent in 2008, –19.4 percent in 2009), and GFCF, the ultimate engine of the economic boom, fell dramatically by 3.6 percent in 2008 and by 17.2 percent in 2009 (INE 2020b). In sum, virtually a year sufficed to abandon the greatest expansionary phase in recent Spanish history to abruptly enter a social nightmare with no foreseeable future at the time (see Figure 9.1). The systemic crisis of the Spanish SSA was thus initiated.

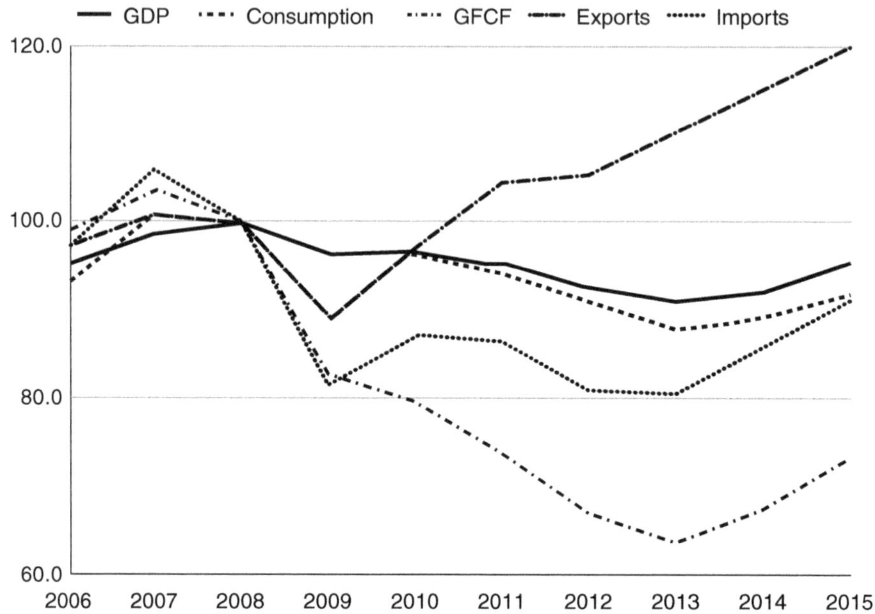

Figure 9.1 GDP and its main components, 2006–2015

Between 2008 and 2010, GDP levels did not experience a dramatic breakdown insofar as plummeting capital investment and a moderate fall in households' consumption were partially counterbalanced by a significant increase in public expenditures, on the one hand, and the sharp fall experienced by imports, in turn helping correct existing balance of payments' disequilibria, on the other. Nevertheless, the adoption of austerity from 2010 onwards could not but further reinforce the downward spiral the Spanish economy was already in. Between 2010 and 2013, with the only exception being exports, all components of aggregate demand experienced a further decline, within which the evolution of gross fixed capital formation (GFCF) clearly stands out. Private investment, the ultimate engine of the previous expansion, declined by 40 percent between 2007 and 2013 (representing 30.4 percent of GDP in 2008, it only accounted for 17.4 percent in 2013), mostly due to the sharp contraction of residential investment (INE 2020b; Mateo 2019).

In sum, far from representing a temporary slowdown of economic activity, the crisis signaled the onset of the Spanish SSA's systemic crisis which, in turn, was further aggravated by the intensity and scope of the various contradictions which had been developed and magnified during the years of expansion, and whose force was bound to be felt with unheard-of intensity in the upcoming years. Such a sudden breakdown of economic activity sparked a downward spiral of institutional decomposition, where the main dynamics supporting the previous expansion mutually reinforced their respective decay. In what follows, a brief account is offered of the extent to which those we had baptized 'individually contradictory but mutually sustaining trends' radically changed not only their sign (from positive to negative) but, more importantly, their modality of integration with the remaining ones.

From employment growth to massive unemployment

After having generated more than seven million new jobs during the previous expansion, Spain now became one of the European landmarks of job destruction. Between 2008 and 2010, 1.5 million jobs were lost, raising the unemployment rate from a low of 8.2 percent in 2007 to 19.8 percent in 2010, barely three years later. By 2013 the rates of both male and female unemployment surpassed 25 percent, with more than three million jobs having been destroyed, of which 1.4 million were in the construction sector, 0.8 million in manufacturing, and another 0.8 million in wholesale and retail trade (INE 2020a).

Such a strong upsurge in employment resulted from two key structural features of the Spanish labor market during the expansion years. Firstly, the pervasiveness of fixed-term contracts, which had underlain the flat evolution of real wages during those years, contributed to magnify the rise of unemployment due to the lack of costs associated to layoffs. The consequences of Spanish capital's sempiternal preference for temporary contracts as a means of adjustment to adverse economic fluctuations found here their most dramatic expression.

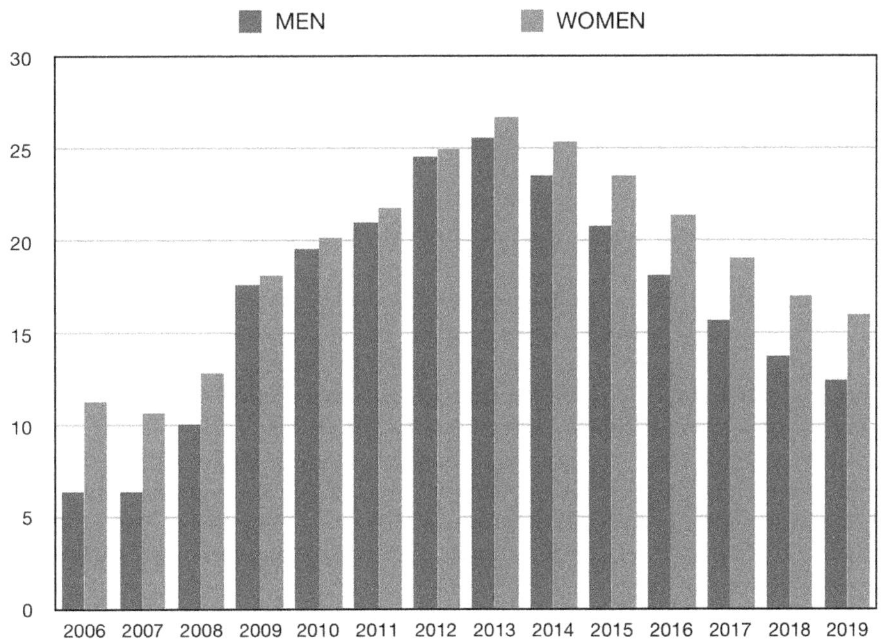

Figure 9.2 Unemployment by sex

Secondly, such an intense process of job destruction was a direct consequence of the deflation of the housing bubble. Not only was the real estate complex, the sector which first and most intensely experienced the effects of the economic downturn, significantly oversized in terms of employment (it accounted for more than 2.5 million jobs in 2007), but also had very strong carrying effects upon adjacent industries, so that its abrupt decay further accentuated employment destruction (Mateo and Montanyà 2018). Soaring unemployment further induced households' de-leveraging strategies, thus reinforcing the negative effect upon their consumption levels and, by extension, upon aggregate demand. In sum, while some job losses were due to the decline experienced by internal demand in conjunction with a labor market leaning too far towards external flexibility practices in times of economic recession, others were linked to an oversized real estate sector whose perpetuation was neither socially desirable nor economically profitable.

Initially, the most affected sectors were construction and manufacturing, where male workers significantly predominated (during 2008–2009, 64.5 percent of job losses affected male workers). However, mainstream narratives initially speaking of a 'he-cession' soon proved to be illusory, as female employment was also rapidly affected since the implementation of austerity from May 2010 onwards: During 2010–2013, women accounted for more than half of new job losses. The reduction of public sector employment heavily affected women's employment opportunities, as women still represent the majority of public sector workers, and the branches where most intense cuts were applied were precisely those where women's presence was significantly higher, such as education, health, and social services (Gálvez and Rodríguez-Modroño 2013). Moreover, its manifestation in unemployment rates was exacerbated by the divergent evolution experienced by their respective rates of activity: Between 2007 and 2013, while men reduced their labor force participation rate by 3.3 percent, women increased theirs by 4 percent in order to cope with the loss of earnings caused by their male partners' unemployment (Gálvez and Rodríguez-Modroño 2016; INE 2020a).

In generational terms, younger workers have been disproportionately affected by widespread job destruction during these years, resulting, on the one hand, from their higher exposure to temporary contracts and, on the other, from a generalized lack of policy mechanisms supporting their entry into the labor market (the unemployment rate for workers aged 20–29 stood at 40.1 percent by 2013) (INE 2020a). Even though most young adults have seen their employment prospects deteriorate during these years, class differences regarding their employment trajectories have nonetheless been amplified (López-Andreu and Verd 2020): Whereas workers with middle-to-high educational attainment levels have experienced work trajectories dominated by involuntary part-time and temporary contracts, those with low educational levels have been comparatively more affected by unemployment and inactivity (López-Andreu and Verd 2016).

The collapse of capital gains from 2008 onwards accentuated Spanish capital's dependency upon obtaining a successful outcome in its distributive struggle with labor. Under the assumption that labor market rigidities accounted for the impressive upsurge of unemployment, and that furthering internal devaluation was the only path available to regain international competitiveness, successive labor market reforms in 2010 and 2012, respectively, carried one step forward existing trends towards further labor market precarization (Muñoz de Bustillo and Esteve 2017). The one corresponding to 2010, with the Socialist Party still in office, had the declared aim of enhancing internal and external flexibility (Ruiz-Gálvez and Vicent 2018). The reform increased the grounds for fair dismissals, eased the justification of collective dismissals on the grounds of negative temporary results, raised the possibility of business opting out of wage agreements, and encouraged the promotion of indefinite contracts with lower dismissal compensation (Fernández-Rodríguez et al. 2016). The one corresponding to 2012, already with the right-wing PP back in office, was far more radical in its intentions (Banyuls and Recio 2015). It further increased the grounds for fair collective dismissals; it introduced a new type of contract where costless dismissals could be introduced during the first year; it gave a unilateral right to companies to change working conditions; and, most importantly, it introduced radical reforms regarding collective bargaining, so that now:

> company agreements take precedence over sectoral agreements; companies can unilaterally opt out of agreements; in companies with no union representative it is possible to negotiate with three employees chosen ad hoc (an excellent opportunity for companies to choose their counterparts in negotiations); and the economic effects of collective agreements cease one year after expiry.
>
> (Banyuls and Recio 2015: 54)

These reforms have certainly been successful in promoting internal devaluation (Muñoz de Bustillo and Esteve 2017). Nevertheless, wage devaluation was not directly translated into improved price competitiveness, insofar as firms used their increasing profit margins to reduce their excessive levels of indebtedness (Álvarez et al. 2019). Therefore, by reducing the scope and scale of collective bargaining while allowing for even more precarious job conditions, as manifested in the indiscriminate proliferation of involuntary part-time contracts, temporary contracts, and the generalization of the 'working poor' as the new archetypical figure in the Spanish labor market (Ruiz-Gálvez and Vicent 2018), the main effect of these reforms has been a marked alteration of the relative balance of class forces to the benefit, once again, of Spanish capital (López-Andreu 2019).

Households' painful de-leveraging

During the previous expansion, existing productive deficiencies and disequilibria, as manifested in the downward evolution experienced by the productivity of capital throughout the whole period, underlay widespread real wage stagnation (Mateo 2019). Nevertheless, households' consumption levels had grown steadily during those years thanks to, on the one hand, booming employment opportunities and, on the other, soaring indebtedness levels. The latter, in turn, were both enabled and motivated by ascending housing prices in a social environment featuring markedly high homeownership rates. As explored in the previous chapter, while much of that new debt contracted by households was driven towards the acquisition of already-existing housing properties, it did nonetheless enable a sustained rise of consumption levels by diverting some of those extra funds towards the satisfaction of other households' consumption needs.

The deflation of the housing bubble suddenly made manifest the excessive level that households' private indebtedness had reached. Moreover, besides the absolute levels of debt, another crucial imbalance resided in the asymmetric quality of the assets households acquired during the process of real estate revalorization, on the one hand, and the financial liabilities they amassed in return, on the other. Households' nominal wealth levels were recast downwards following the deflation of the housing bubble, although not the amount of debt they incurred. As noted by Naredo (2009: 123), 'the true problem is that, when savings in the form of housing properties, linked to self-sustained price increases, run the risk of deflating, the opposite holds regarding the amounts of debt contracted to acquire the former'.

Households reacted to their excessive over-indebtedness by sharply reducing their consumption levels from 2008, accumulating, by 2013, a 12 percent reduction since its peak levels of 2008. The necessary counterpart was a sudden increase in their savings rates. As shown in Figure 9.3 below, Spanish households decreased their savings rate in a sustained manner up until 2007, the last year of the expansion phase, when they almost became negative.

Households' saving behavior was sharply reversed in 2008 in order to reduce their excessive leverage levels. Nonetheless, merely taking into consideration the evolution of the savings rate underestimates the actual efforts undertaken by Spanish families, insofar as they were obtained in a social context featuring decreasing households' disposable income and mounting levels of unemployment. The excesses households incurred during the previous decade now had to be paid back under increasingly strenuous conditions. Indeed, the aforementioned reduction in households' aggregate consumption levels was only partially reflected in their lower levels of indebtedness (while households' debt amounted to 150 percent of their net disposable income by 2007, in 2012 their liabilities still stood at 141 percent of the former).

In sum, while ascending levels of household indebtedness, booming employment opportunities, and rising housing prices seemed to go hand in hand during the expansion phase, further propelling each other, as soon as housing prices started to deflate, the relations of mutual reinforcement previously drawn among these processes significantly contributed to enhance their devastating effects. Decreasing family incomes, increasing levels of labor

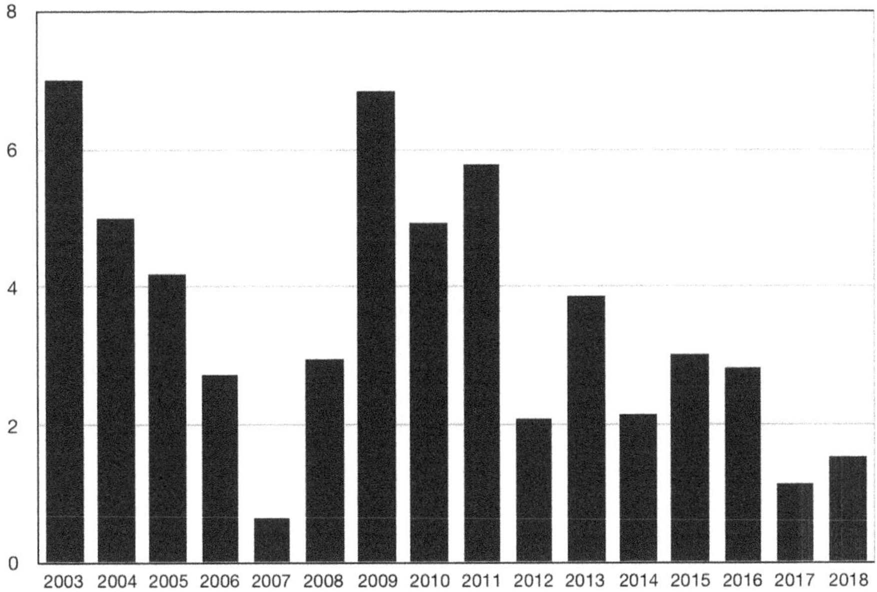

Figure 9.3 Households' savings

precariousness and unemployment, and falling housing prices (which constituted the bulk of households' wealth) greatly complicated the reduction of households' indebtedness levels, requiring in turn increasing efforts to improve their financial position (Carballo-Cruz 2011).

Public finances under strain

During the last years of the expansion phase, public finances had been apparently effortlessly equilibrated while, simultaneously, other EU countries were experiencing serious difficulties in complying with the Stability and Growth Pact's requirements regarding government deficit and public debt levels. Spain was thus presented as the paramount example of the benefits that were to be expected to accrue from the correct implementation of neoliberal policy prescriptions: Prior to the Spanish SSA's implosion, Spain managed to reconcile fiscal surpluses and very low levels of public debt with intense economic and employment growth. However, once the deflation of the housing bubble interrupted the ongoing reproduction of the various synergies hitherto supporting the economic expansion, underlying deficiencies came suddenly to the fore.

While Spain had traditionally been a country with low taxes and a correspondingly small welfare state, an institutional trait dating back to the Francoist period, the long period of growth until 2008 was not used to its full potential to address these deficiencies (Banyuls and Recio 2012). Indeed, despite a timid increase in social expenditures during those years, by 2008 Spain's remained the welfare state with lowest redistributive capacity among the EU-15 countries (Buendía et al. 2018).

Widespread capital gains derived from housing prices revalorization not only helped attenuate social pressures for further welfare state expansion, but also enabled successive downward tax reforms, such as modifications in the personal income tax towards making it less progressive; a reduction of the corporations tax rate; or the suppression of the inheritance tax. Throughout the expansion, a gradual lowering of its tax base made Spain's fiscal balance increasingly dependent upon indirect revenues accruing from real estate activity. Such fiscal prowess was immediately undone with the onset of the crisis: A fiscal surplus of 1.9 percent in 2007, the last year of economic expansion, soon gave way to a fiscal deficit of 11.3 percent in 2009. Concomitantly, public debt levels rapidly escalated. Standing at a markedly low level in 2007 (35.8 percent of GDP, almost half of the eurozone average), it surpassed 100 percent in 2014, by the time an economic recovery was eventually initiated. This behavior of public finances had its roots, in the last instance, in the nature of the previous economic expansion. On the one hand, fiscal revenues plummeted from 2007 onwards (fiscal revenues in relation to GDP had lost 6 percentage points by 2009, EUROSTAT 2020), insofar as indirect taxation linked to the real estate sector collapsed. On the other hand, government spending was abruptly increased as a result of automatic stabilizers (due to mounting unemployment levels), bank bailouts, and the initial Keynesian-inspired response to the crisis until 2010 (the so-called 'Plan-E') (Muñoz de Bustillo and Antón 2013;

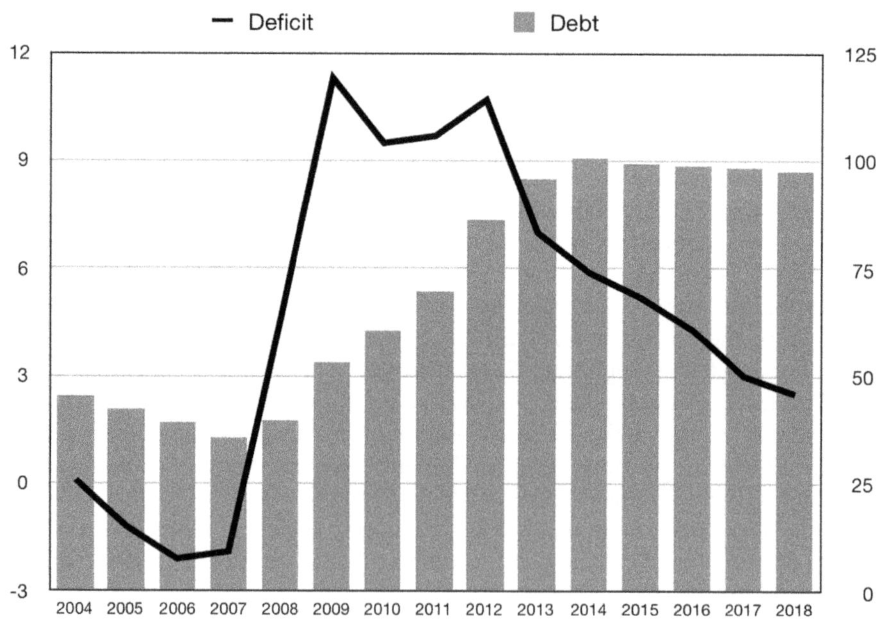

Figure 9.4 Public finances

Buendía 2018b). As a result of, on the one hand, the State having internalized the costs of economic adjustment at the early stages of the crisis, which fostered an increase in the risk premium of Spanish bonds and, on the other, the request of a credit line of up to 100 billion euros from the EU in 2012 to restructure/bail out the banking system, harsh austerity measures were enforced (a detailed account of the chronology and the various measures adopted is provided by Salmon 2017). These included:

> a wage freeze and layoffs in the public sector; a (gradual) increase in retirement age from 65 to 67; an increase in the years of contribution required to access the maxi- mum old-age pension (from 35 to 37); the augmentation of the years used to calculate pensions (from the last 15 to the last 25 years); a hardening in the requirements to access voluntary early retirement; a shift, from 2013, to a defined-contribution pension system, from a defined-benefit system; a reduction in the range of medicines eligible for public subsidy; the out-sourcing of several services in the health-care sector and the erosion of its universalism (by restricting the access of undocumented immigrants); an increase in the price of childcare services; a reduction in, or the elimination of, certain educational services (such as those focused on students with special needs); an increase in the pupil/teacher ratio; an increase in tuition fees and cuts to grants; and privatization in several sectors (such as airports and lotteries).
>
> (Buendía 2018b: 65, see also Banyuls and Recio, 2015)

In sum, a full-scale process of welfare state retrenchment was implemented, with very serious effects both upon the organization of social reproduction, by effecting cuts in public services (especially those more directed towards relieving women of their care responsibilities), and upon the State's capacity of discretionary intervention in capitalist markets. In a sense, whereas the initial counter-cyclical programs were designed to support the Spanish capitalist class, mainly located in the construction, real estate, and financial sectors, the adoption of austerity since 2010 should be understood as the beginning of the State's subservience to the requirements and needs of European financial capital, manifested in the almost exclusive focus on debt repayment (which became the foremost policy priority after a constitutional reform in September 2011). In the absence of both sustained redistributive intervention on the side of the State and the support offered by capital gains from housing prices revaluation, the inherently antagonistic character of Spanish capitalism came abruptly into light. In this context, the only institution that remained in place to avert the worst social effects derived from the implosion of the Spanish SSA was, once again, the Spanish family.

Spanish families on the brink of collapse

Spanish families had been submitted to increasing stress throughout the expansion. A 'familialist' environment, which took for granted the widespread availability of women's unpaid work in order to address care needs, found its reproduction seriously compromised by women's increasing involvement in paid employment. Those potentially unsatisfied care needs had been addressed at the time through, firstly, women's work intensification; secondly, springing low-cost market alternatives in the guise of large swathes of immigrants, many among whom were to be employed in the private household sector; and, thirdly, the support received from family networks, chiefly including women from older generations.

Capitalist crises generally foster a reconfiguration of the public/private divide upon which social reproduction ultimately rests by promoting an intensification of unpaid labor within households (Lux and Wöhl 2015; Bruff and Wöhl 2016). While the peripheral position most women occupy in labor markets makes them particularly vulnerable to the latter's increasing precariousness, falling household incomes together with cuts in public spending tend to result in an intensification of gendered household responsibilities (Gálvez and Rodríguez-Modroño 2016). The Spanish case has been no exception to these dynamics. A 're-privatization of social reproduction' has indeed been attempted, involving a re-domestication of care responsibilities as well as the privatization of previously socialized institutions implicated in social reproduction (Bakker and Gill 2003). Nevertheless, this time was different. Spanish women resisted existing pressures for their re-domestication, insofar as falling family incomes in a context of generalized over-indebtedness forced them to increase their involvement in paid employment in the aftermath of the Great Recession, despite mounting levels of unemployment (Campillo 2018). As had been customary in previous recessions, women's bodies and efforts constituted the ultimate locus where social contradictions have accumulated, and where partial solutions have been attempted (Ezquerra 2012; Fraser 2014).

Despite the generalized impression that male workers had been hit the hardest by unemployment, this has been the case only during the very first moments of the crisis (see above). Public services' budgetary cuts following the implementation of austerity policies from 2010 onwards caused a triple discrimination towards Spanish women (Gálvez and Rodríguez-Modroño 2013; 2016) – firstly, because women make up the majority of public sector workers in those sectors where cuts have been the most intense, such as education, health, or social services; secondly, because women are the main beneficiaries of social transfers and public funding; and, thirdly, because the end result of these austerity programs is to foster a generalized re-privatization of 'care' responsibilities, alleviating public finances through women's increasing efforts. In sum, 'women, particularly the lowest qualified, may have to choose between the devil and the deep blue sea, that is, looking for increasingly precarious and scarce jobs or exiting the labor market and returning to their gender-imposed home-based roles' (González-Gago and Segales-Kirzner 2014: 238).

Nevertheless, existing pressures pushing women back to their 'traditional' domestic roles encountered this time several obstacles (Gálvez and Rodríguez-Modroño 2016). On the one hand, women have tertiary level educational qualifications in higher proportion than men which, together with the tertiarization experienced by the Spanish productive structure in recent decades, have significantly expanded women's employment opportunities relative to past crises. On the other hand, worsening labor conditions in conjunction with generalized over-indebtedness have increased the need for dual-earner households. As a result, women have continuously increased their rates of involvement in paid employment since the onset of the crisis and until 2013. Concomitantly, while rising precariousness and unemployment resulted in an increase in women's work intensity due to increasing fears of losing one's job (López-Andreu and Rubery 2018), they had to take up responsibility for covering the manifold care needs left unsatisfied by welfare state retrenchment.

Inasmuch as contradictions relative to the organization of social reproduction have fallen disproportionally over women's bodies, efforts, and aspirations, the family *qua* social institution ought to be considered to have been the main social institution responsible for the sustainment of social life in the crisis's aftermath, despite their capacity to keep on acting as 'shock absorbers', as they used to in the past, remaining more compromised than ever as a result of rising levels of female participation, the consolidation of non-traditional family arrangements, and the gradual erosion to which traditional gender norms had been submitted in recent times (Caïs and Folguera 2013; Marí-Klose and Moreno-Fuentes 2013). Nevertheless, intense redistributions of resources (monetary and otherwise) within families has been, in many cases, the only source of support many households could have recourse to, especially so in the lower echelons of the social structure. Indeed, class divides tend to be amplified in social environments characterized by a situation of 'implicit familialism' (i.e. where families bear the responsibility for social reproduction without receiving explicit public support in that regard), and especially so in times of recession (Moreno-Colom et al. 2017). On the one hand, while most women from middle-class households have retained their commitment to labor participation, based in the last instance upon outsourcing part of their domestic responsibilities, receding incomes and rising unemployment have nonetheless reduced their capacity to externalize the latter (Hellgren and Serrano 2019). On the other hand, women from lower-class households have been forced to inhabit a continuum of situations of formality and informality, subemployment, unemployment, and inactivity (Sánchez-Mira 2019), as part of the manifold strategies of survival these households had to deploy, ranging from co-habitation with other members of the extended family to practices of 'resource-pooling' in the guise of old-age pensions or unemployment benefits (Deusdad et al. 2016).

In sum, the main institutional blocks sustaining the previous economic expansion underwent a fully-fledged transformation. A sharp reversal in the behavior of all the main social processes is made evident in the brief summary offered here. A social context featuring ascending consumption levels, fiscal surpluses, employment creation, and booming investment levels gave way, all of a sudden, to another one featuring the opposite dynamics, namely, plummeting levels of capital accumulation, vast public deficits, receding consumption levels, massive employment destruction, and so on. While their tendential evolution has been inverted, the interlocking character of the Spanish SSA's main blocks did not fade away, further reinforcing in turn the process of institutional decomposition. The latter could not but contribute to undo the various social consensuses generated during the expansion phase, whose material substratum was now found lacking virtually everywhere.

The development of a 'populist situation'

The sudden disruption of its core internal dynamics threw the precarious nature of the Spanish SSA abruptly into light. In barely a couple of years, the manifold consensuses, social agreements and silent assumptions that had structured social interaction thus far proved incapable of making sense of the current situation. As explored in previous chapters, systemic crises always drag down along with themselves existing social consensuses by depriving them of their socio-material conditions of possibility. Nonetheless, while systemic crises eventually evolve into organic crises, the timing, nature, and scope of such a transition is decisively affected by the institutional form the decaying SSA had taken (Kotz 2015).

Systemic crises derived from Liberal SSAs, unlike those derived from Regulated SSAs, tend to manifest themselves through a sudden and fully-fledged institutional breakdown (Kotz 2010b). On the one hand, the rupture of existing social consensuses gives way to a proliferation of unsatisfied demands generally unrestricted to any specific locus within the social, for it is the whole structure that is shattered at once, rather than just one, or some, among its individual components. Old forms of collective identification cannot help make the new situation intelligible, as the socio-material dynamics acting as their ultimate condition of possibility can no longer be retrieved. As a result, the variety of unsatisfied demands ensuing will be highly heterogeneous. On the other hand, their emergence is to be relatively simultaneous because of the promptitude and abruptness characterizing the institutional breakdown, while the existing order will be particularly ill-suited to properly confront them, itself immersed in a downward spiral of institutional decomposition. In sum, the type of organic crisis experienced can be readily assimilated to what we have termed a 'populist situation', i.e. a social scenario featuring a simultaneous emergence of a wide variety of heterogeneous demands which the existing order is unable to deal with in an orderly and successful manner.

The course events followed after the onset of the Spanish systemic crisis closely conforms to this scheme. While the crisis was initiated in 2008, hegemonic social consensuses, despite lacking their previous foundations, remained virtually unchallenged during its immediate aftermath: The crisis was portrayed, by the media and government authorities alike, as merely a temporary slowdown caused by existing credit restrictions in international markets; the social divisions the decaying SSA had exacerbated had not yet come to the fore; and the State appeared committed not to leave anyone behind. Nevertheless, the Socialist government's sudden embracing of austerity in May 2010 provided a fatal blow to those still-dominant socio-symbolic frameworks, inasmuch as it revealed, firstly, that the state's financial obligations were to take absolute priority over whichever social needs the population had, and, secondly, that the economic crisis was to be the 'new normal' (Charnock et al. 2015). The inability of old narratives and expectations to turn the new situation widely intelligible resulted in generalized disorientation, distress, and astonishment.

To such a situation the 15M or '*indignados*' movement managed to put an end to such a situation. Challenging dominant narratives at the time, the 15M movement introduced a new vocabulary to denounce both the utterly post-political and socially regressive crisis-management strategies deployed by Spanish elites and the dramatic divorce between political elites and their citizenship. Its emergence gave rise to a new wave of contention within the Spanish social formation where a variety of social struggles irrupted into the public arena (Portos 2019b). Despite their inclusion within a common political project being dependent upon a constitutive act of political mediation, they did share some constitutive commonalities: While all these struggles pointed towards the underside of the previous economic expansion, they had been further motivated by how crisis management was being attempted at the time.

'Populist situations', it has been argued, significantly increase the hegemonic depth to be expected from 'populist interventions' in drawing together disparate demands. By early 2014, when the aforementioned cycle of contention was reaching the point of exhaustion, a new political party was born, Podemos, whose carefully designed 'left-populist' strategy succeeded in drawing together these social struggles in its assault on State institutions. Social antagonisms thus left the squares to embark themselves on a new adventure aimed at disrupting the ongoing implementation of austerity policies. Nevertheless, before analyzing in detail this cycle of contention, it is imperative first to offer an account of the transformation of the State along increasingly authoritarian lines, both motivating and responding to the Spanish population's perceive disjunction between politico-economic elites and the rest of the population.

The authoritarian turn of the Spanish State

Two separate stages ought to be identified regarding the crisis management strategies deployed by the Spanish state. The first one, ranging from the onset of the crisis to mid-2010, was characterized by the implementation of a 'timid and naive Keynesianism'. On the one hand, the Socialist government's initial response to the crisis exposed an excessive optimism, close to outright 'negationism', regarding the true causes of the economic breakdown. Displaying a strong belief in the alleged strengths of the Spanish model, the initial turbulences were thought to be deriving exclusively from existing credit restrictions in international markets. While the Spanish banking system had indeed remained relatively unaffected by US toxic financial assets, the government ignored the extent to which the former had been generating their own. On the other hand, consistently with such a diagnosis, the government attempted a timid Keynesian-inspired response along markedly continuist lines. These measures included, among others, a €400 universal rebate in income tax; the elimination of the property tax; a lump-sum payment per newborn child; and, above all, an expansionary, demand-led stimulus plan, the so-called 'Plan-E' (*Plan Español para el Estímulo de la Economía y el Empleo*). The latter, passed in late 2008, consisted of around €13 billion, which was given straight to local authorities to initiate new construction works, with very little control over the actual social interest of the various projects they were to fund (Bellod Redondo 2015). Indeed, such a strategy responded to two main motivations. On the one hand, it aimed at attenuating massive employment destruction by indiscriminately funding construction projects irrespective of their ultimate social and/or economic value. On the other, it aimed at supporting the two economic sectors that were hit the hardest at the initial stages of the crisis, namely, construction and real estate, where, as already noted, the bulk of Spanish economic elites had successfully relocated in the previous years. In the end, this strategy of 'buying consent' through indiscriminate expenditures reflected the influence Spanish elites had in designing policy measures to explicitly fit their needs (Naredo 2010).

The Socialist administration's embracing of austerity in May 2010 marked a turning point regarding the crisis management strategies adopted by the Spanish State. The mildly expansionary measures of the previous two years gave way to a new policy mix enforcing internal devaluation, including measures such as a 5 percent wage cut for public servants; freezing pensions; a significant hardening of the conditions required for retirement; or the elimination of the €2,500 lump-sum payment per newborn child. These were followed by other structural reforms regarding the pension system, the labor market, and a bailout program to support and restructuring of the baking sector (Salmon 2017). While the Zapatero administration's initial response was aimed at reconciling the exigencies posed by domestic capital (implicated in the housing bubble from both the construction/real estate and financial sides) with the need to offer some support to a population submitted to increasing levels of immiseration, from May 2010 signaling to international capital markets its utmost willingness to position debt repayment well above any other obligation it might had contracted became the State's main concern. International financial capital thus replaced domestic capital as the State's chief interlocutor.

In this sense, the Spanish State was turned into what Streeck (2014a; 2014b; 2015) has termed a 'consolidation State', namely, one whose debt repayment obligations take absolute precedence over any other social obligation and where, it follows, international financial capital constitutes itself as, *de facto*, the State's only constituency. States would be required to implement harsh structural reforms not out of the need to address any specific already-existing problem but, rather, in order to show their absolute commitment to comply with financial capital's requirements (Streeck 2014b). In the words of Streeck (2015: 15, original emphasis): 'The consolidation state [firmly internalizes] the primacy of the state's commercial-contractual commitments to its lenders over its public-political commitments to its citizenry. In short, a consolidation state may be described as one whose *commercial market obligations* take precedence over its *political citizenship obligations*.' In sum, it was a matter of proving international financial capital that whichever longings, demands, and expectations the national population might put forward in the future would always be of a second-order priority when the State confronted its debt obligations.

In order to resist the expected social protests, the Spanish State was reconfigured along increasingly authoritarian lines in order to insulate itself from the former. Its mode of operation strongly resembles what Bruff (2014) has termed 'authoritarian neoliberalism', a concept by which he intends to refer to:

> how contemporary capitalism is governed in a way which tends to reinforce and rely upon practices that seek to marginalize, discipline and control dissenting social groups and oppositional politics rather than strive for their explicit consent or co-optation. Such practices include the repeated invocations of 'the market' or 'economic necessity' to justify a wide range of restructurings across various societal sites (e.g. states, households, workplaces, urban spaces), the growing tendency to prioritize constitutional and legal mechanisms rather than democratic debate and participation, the centralization of state powers by the executive branch at the expense of popular participation and other modes of governance, the mobilization of state apparatuses for the repression of oppositional social forces at a range of scales, and the heightened pressures and responsibilities shifted onto households by repeated bouts of crisis and the restructuring of the state's redistributive mechanisms.
>
> (Bruff and Tansel 2019: 234)

A variety of 'authoritarian neoliberal' practices was thus deployed to insulate the State's continuing implementation of austerity from socio-political conflicts, including the increasing constitutionalization of austerity measures in order to isolate them from public debate; moralizing the ultimate responsibilities of the economic breakdown while foreclosing any sort of structural explanation whatsoever; discarding material rewards as a route to secure public support, opting for increasingly punitive strategies instead; and a displacement of social contradictions towards the realm of households and, more crucially, the female body, in response to the ongoing processes of privatization and welfare state retrenchment. While these authoritarian tendencies have permeated Spanish neoliberalism through and through (e.g. Bernat and Whyte 2019), they have nevertheless become more acute since 2010 and, especially, after the Popular Party came back into office in late 2011 with Mariano Rajoy serving as the new president.

Recent developments testify to the increasingly authoritarian nature of the Spanish State in respect of its population since 2010, and especially so since the election of Rajoy as prime minister in 2011 (Clúa-Losada and Ribera-Almandoz 2017: 32–3). Firstly, a reform of the Spanish Constitution was carried forward in 2011, through which the obligation to achieve budgetary stability as well as the pre-eminence of debt repayment over any other type of expenditure were legally inscribed, thus insulating them from political debate and contestation. To add insult to injury, it was agreed upon by the two main parties by then (PSOE and PP) in the midst of August and with no traces of public debate over its alleged social desirability. Secondly, there has been a growing judicialization of politics, as seen in the increasing role played by the Constitutional Court in enforcing austerity measures over Regional Parliaments, where most welfare state entitlements are administered (prominently health, education, and social services). This is coherent with the consolidation state's tendency to achieve budgetary balance by introducing cuts in the area of discretionary, as opposed to mandatory, expenditures (Streeck 2015). Thirdly, the growing use of Royal Decrees to pass legislation, even in the absence of parliamentary opposition, shows a stark trend towards emptying Parliaments of their legislative functions while transferring them to the executive branch of the State, in turn accentuating the latter's democratic deficits (to say the least).[1] Fourthly, the criminalization of political dissent was made explicit with the passing of the so-called 'Gag-Law' (*Ley Mordaza*, Organic Law 4/2015) which, among other measures, enabled the police to conduct indiscriminate personal identity checks as well as to fine citizens when participating in contentious performances such as, for instance, preventing an eviction from taking place (Bruff 2016; Calvo and Portos 2018). Authoritarian neoliberalism's drive to enforce consent through the indiscriminate application of state violence is made paramount in this respect. Finally, the implementation of the two labor reforms of 2010 and 2012, respectively, should also be regarded as part of these increasingly punitive strategies, as they explicitly sought to further individualize labor relations in order to install Hobbesian-like dynamics of competition among workers that would discourage them from partaking in collective action (Banyuls and Recio 2015: 54). In sum, these various practices converged in insulating economic restructuring from public debate and accountability, thus preventing popular struggles from interfering with the State's gradual submission to international finance capital's requirements. In this context, the erasure of observable political differences among the two main parties, together with their lack of responsiveness to popular mobilizations, opened the way for 'relations of equivalence' to emerge among the various social struggles that ensued on the grounds of their shared rejection/dissatisfaction from the existing order (e.g. Laclau 2005a).

Disrupting social consensuses through spreading unsatisfied demands

The government's embracing of austerity in May 2010 meant that, at a symbolic level, the crisis had finally made its entrance into existing hegemonic articulations, leaving the set of social expectations and consensuses developed during the previous expansion indelibly broken. Nonetheless, it took exactly one year for the crisis, whose gravity had only been symbolically recognized in its proper dimension as late as May 2010, to eventually disrupt social consensuses by giving birth to a new social imaginary in the guise of the 15M or '*indignados*' movement. By that time, the systemic crisis had finally turned into an organic one.

The 15M movement was initially sparked by a relatively small anti-austerity demonstration in Madrid on May 15, 2011, called by a recently formed collective named *Democracia Real Ya!* ('Real Democracy Now!'). Harsh police repression at the point where the rally was meant to conclude (Madrid's centric square 'Puerta del Sol') once some of its participants, drawing inspiration from the mobilizations that had taken place at Tahrir Square (Egypt), attempted to camp there, led its participants to call another demonstration the day after. By the 17th, a vast camp had already been formed in the square where thousands of people gathered, while several assemblies and commissions were constituted to discuss various topics, from the economy to the political system, from feminism to environmentalism. In a matter of days, chiefly articulated through social networks, similar dynamics spread all over Spain (see Rodríguez 2016).

The 15M movement was a true event (Badiou 2007; Žižek 2014), radically disrupting the existing state of affairs by opening up new routes of political contestation, while plaguing the social arena with new questions and answers. Nevertheless, however spontaneous it might have looked even to the participants themselves, it benefited from previous rounds of mobilization and a previously existing culture of social movements, chiefly the activist networks developed around the anti-globalization movement and past university struggles (Flesher-Fominaya 2015; Antentas 2015; Portos 2016).

Its influence in Spanish politics can hardly be overstated. A social structure dislocated by the impact of the crisis remained in need of a new narrative capable of inscribing, at a symbolic level, the nature of the current conjuncture, and the 15M movement provided precisely that: 'The 15M movement introduced into the political arena a new critical vocabulary which, starting from a denunciation of the dominant crisis-management strategies at both the national and European arenas, was capable of channeling a systematic objection to Spanish parliamentary democracy' (La Parra-Pérez 2014: 45).

While the movement's refusal to self-identify itself within the Left–Right divide led many to discredit it on the grounds of it being an apolitical movement (e.g. Bauman 2011; Žižek 2012), such interpretation is, in our view, completely misplaced.[2] The 15M rebellion was eminently political insofar as it put forward a new narrative regarding the nature of the current situation which, in turn, enabled various other social requests to enter the political arena by taking the former as their frame of reference. It did so not so much by bringing up new words and concepts but, on the contrary, by succinctly reappropriating several terms, around which mainstream narratives of the 'Spanish normality' had been anchored, in order to give them radically novel meanings (Errejón 2011).

This process of rearticulating what Laclau (1996a) terms 'empty signifiers' is precisely the hegemonic (read political) operation *par excellence*. For instance, against the commonsensical understanding of democracy as meaning little more than voting every four years while silently accepting capitalism as 'the only game in town', demonstrators replied '*Lo llaman democracia y no lo es*' ['They call it democracy, but it is not']. Against the official, moralizing, and incriminatory narrative that Spanish citizens had been living beyond their means, the squares replied '*No es una crisis, es una estafa*' ['It is not a crisis, it is a scam']. In response to the implementation of austerity policies in order to save international capital, they claimed '*No somos mercancías en manos de políticos y banqueros*' ['We are not commodities in the hands of bankers and politicians']. Moreover, they counteracted authoritarian neoliberalism's moralizing and individualizing strategies to placate social dissent by, on the one hand, proving to its participants that what they might have perceived as individual problems resulting from their previous wrong behavior had indeed systemic roots and, on the other, by transforming what otherwise would have been individual strategies of resistance into a collective political subject formed through the very experience of the struggle itself (Espinoza-Pino 2013). In the words of Antentas (2015: 142), 'the *homo indignatus* thus replaced the *homo resignatus*'.

It has been argued that two different 'souls' co-existed within the 15M movement, one more politicized and another with more 'reformist' inclinations (Taibo 2011). In our view, the radicality of the movement cannot be measured through a literal analysis of their self-professed claims: 'The latent meaning of a mobilization can never be read off its literal slogans and proclaimed aims; a political analysis worthy of the name only starts when one probes the over-determination sustaining that meaning' (Laclau 2006: 656). Even those who were demanding a return to a truly meritocratic and equitable form of capitalism by 'purifying' actually existing Spanish capitalism from its alleged excesses (manifested in the ongoing proliferation of corruption scandals prominently affecting the PP), were inadvertently pointing towards the right crux of the matter. Their apparently 'soft' critique of the causes and effects of the economic crisis was nonetheless a tremendously radical one insofar as, had you deprived Spanish capitalism from its corruption-like excesses, you would not have encountered a Nordic type of capitalism but, rather, nothing at all (see Naredo 2019).

While the crowds gathering in the squares were certainly inter-generational, there was nonetheless one social group who stood out among the rest, both in number and in organizational capacity: 'The 15M movement was dominated by the sons of the middle class' (Rodríguez 2016: 34), that is, people in their 20s and 30s who, having been brought up in the midst of the 'Spanish miracle', were suddenly thrown into a reality which they had neither material nor symbolic resources to confront. Two latent contradictions of the Spanish model animated their contestation of the existing order. Firstly, a sharp generational divide regarding labor outcomes, which had been partially attenuated during the expansion phase thanks, prominently, to family support, was now becoming unbearably acute. Secondly, Spain featured one of the highest rates of involvement in tertiary education among EU countries while, nevertheless, the growth path it had adopted strongly and systematically limited the amount of jobs fitting those same qualifications. By condensing the manifold institutional failures and failed promises of the decaying Spanish model in a social figure enjoying significantly high levels of social visibility/recognition, the dramatic situation this generation was living through could interpellate a much broader audience. Rodríguez (2016: 44) explains this in a fragment worthy to be quoted at length:

> What were those boys and girls occupying the squares during the 2011 Spring standing for? [...] [They] represented the discomfort of the central figure of the Spanish social formation. [...] Through their demands for democracy, their outcry against corruption and financial dictatorship, in their sympathy towards, and participation within, the housing movement and, especially, in the unfair image of a truncated future despite having done all that was required (study, effort), the rupture of the elementary social promises that had sustained the weak Spanish social formation was made manifest. The ruins of meritocracy were also the ruins of the middle class and, for the latter, the ruin of the democracy so painfully achieved in 1978.

In sum, the situation they were publicly denouncing was utterly inapprehensible from the perspective of the previously dominant hegemonic frames. The latter, nonetheless, by assigning to them high levels of social visibility, prevented a reading of their claims as merely sectorial demands. Rather, their complaints and aspirations became universal. This is, precisely, Laclau's hegemonic logic at its purest.

While the movement was eventually dissolved, and austerity policies kept on being implemented, a fundamental change was nevertheless accomplished within Spanish contemporary politics. The monopoly Spanish elites had enjoyed over dominant symbolic representations drew to an end, and their capacity to keep on setting the political agenda was severely curtailed. In a sense, the 15M movement helped cement the social legitimacy of a new normality to come. Far from vanishing from the socio-political arena, the events of May sparked a very intense cycle of protests and mobilization through two interrelated channels.

Firstly, the 15M movement consolidated a novel narrative by reference to which further rounds of social contestation were to be framed. The events of May thus acquired a 'mythical' character, in the sense Laclau (1990a: 61) attributes to it: 'Myth is thus a principle of reading of a given situation, [which sutures a] dislocated space through the constitution of a new space of representation, [...] forming a new objectivity by means of the rearticulation of the dislocated elements'. By framing themselves through the worldviews produced and disseminated during the May events, several other social demands were made intelligible to vast segments of the population.

Secondly, new strategic routes were taken in the aftermath of the squares' dissolution which explain the impulse taken by further protests (Portos 2019b).

On the one hand, by shifting downwards its scale of action to the local level, lower degrees of visibility were obtained but, simultaneously, a more locally sensitive and pragmatic approach to political interaction was enabled beyond the eminently pre-figurative type of politics entertained at the squares. On the other hand, the anti-unions stance of the 15M movement's early moments (Antentas 2015) gave way to intermittent collaborations with existing trade unions (chiefly, in organizing the two 2012 general strikes and the 'citizens' tides', see below), whose organizational resources were crucial to extend the peak of protests in the mid-term. In sum, a subsequent cycle of protests ensued, with singular intensity in the years 2012–2013. While this cycle took manifold expressions, we will focus here upon the two we consider to be the most relevant and/or significant, namely, the so-called '*mareas ciudadanas*' ('citizens' tides') and the anti-evictions platform PAH (*Plataforma de Afectados por la Hipoteca*, 'Platform for Mortgage-Affected People').

The 'citizens' tides' were large citizen movements that organized several marches against privatization policies, and austerity politics more broadly, with different colors identifying different sectors of activity. The two most important were the 'white' tide, from the health sector, and the 'green' one, from education, two of the sectors where retrenchment and privatization had been operating the most intensely along austerity-induced lines, although many others had been registered, such as the 'black tide' for public servants, the 'orange tide' for the social care sector, the 'violet tide' for feminist and LGTB collectives, and so on (Portos 2016: 201). The 'white' tide emerged as a response to the ongoing privatization processes of public hospitals and the increasing distress to which public sector workers were submitted as a result of budgetary cuts. The 'green' one, initially spurred by budgetary cuts in education, led to two nationwide strikes as a response to the government's passing of a new Education Act (LOMCE) (Portos 2016; Romanos 2017).

Even though neoliberal pressures towards public services' dismantling had long been present in Spain, especially in regions with right-wing governments (Carmona et al. 2012), the Spanish population stood out among its European counterparts regarding its level of support for welfare state institutions, despite being the one with the lowest redistributive capacity during the previous expansion (Calzada and del Pino 2011; Buendía et al. 2018). Once housing revaluation dynamics were interrupted, ongoing trends of welfare state dismantling could no longer be disguised, thus favoring social contestation. Despite significant differences regarding the organizational means deployed, their programmatic objectives and the actual support they gathered, the various 'tides' did share several commonalities:

> First, they were developed regionally, with weak coordination nationwide [...], second, they were organized through unitary assemblies and represented a true exercise in self-organization; third, official unions [...] played an important role but their leaderships were to a large extent bypassed [...], fourth, rank-and-file unions played a significant role [...] fifth, the

> tides saw the joint mobilization of different worker categories within the same sector.
>
> (Antentas 2017a: 117)

In sum, they represented a process of collective empowerment which, although highly defensive regarding their motivations, did show nonetheless that Spanish elites' political program could be successfully counteracted through collective action.

The other key experience of collective action was the emergence and consolidation of the anti-evictions' platform PAH. The PAH is a social movement comprising several horizontal, autonomous, and non-party-affiliated local assemblies throughout the Spanish territory. Born in Barcelona in 2009, it grew exponentially after the irruption of the 15M movement (Antentas 2017a; de Weerdt and Garcia 2016). While autonomous among themselves, the various assemblies share both programmatic objectives and a repertoire of insurgent practices (Berglund 2018). All PAH assemblies share three non-negotiable demands (García-Lamarca 2017b: 426) – firstly, a retroactive change of the Spanish Mortgage Law, so that outstanding mortgage debt can be cancelled by giving the property to the bank in return; secondly, putting an end to all evictions of families' principal homes; and, thirdly, to transform the many empty buildings in the hands of private banks into social housing dwellings.

Besides public opinion campaigns and other related actions directed towards gaining higher visibility, the PAH makes use of several tactics to alleviate the housing problems suffered by the worst-off (García-Lamarca 2017a). Firstly, collective assemblies are held regularly where social activists share thoughts and experiences with people facing mortgage foreclosures and evictions. Rather than providing ready-made advice, the assemblies aim at empowering those affected by collectively stripping them of fear and guilt, debunking moralizing narratives of victimhood in order to give way to proper political action, one which both displays and assumes the systemic roots of current social problems around housing (Di Feliciantonio 2017). Secondly, a common practice is to try to stop evictions, through assembly participants shielding the building-to-be-evicted with their bodies, blocking the entry to the police. Nonetheless, this is a temporary measure, as PAH activists, together with the affected person, try to secure a better deal with the bank during the extra time gained after the eviction has been successfully postponed. Thirdly, they squat in empty buildings in the hands of banks in order to satisfy the needs for housing of those who lack any other suitable alternative (the so-called '*Obra Social*').

The manifold actions conducted by PAH activists shared a twofold dimension, insofar as they aimed at, on the one hand, offering an immediate material response to the needs of those most affected by ongoing housing repossessions while, on the other, radically affecting the conditions of visibility through which those same problems are collectively framed. In this sense, the activities undertaken by the PAH condense political action at its purest – firstly, because they redraw the very symbolic frames regulating social interaction and material exchanges; secondly, because they promote collective self-empowerment while refusing to introduce new hierarchies within the constitution of political subjects, which, in turn, are given shape by the experience of the collective struggle itself; and, thirdly, by transforming what were initially felt as myriad individual problems into systemic responsibilities, thus highlighting the core systemic contradictions of the Spanish social formation.

By late 2013, however, the climate of social contestation was beginning to recede (Portos 2016; 2019b). While the hegemonic dispute was far from concluded, austerity policies continued to be implemented, and a certain feeling of disillusionment started to disseminate among the movement's most politically active members. In this context marked by receding levels of social contestation, the Spanish political landscape suffered another radical change with the emergence of a new political party, Podemos, which set to alter the existing correlation of forces within the State institutions. Signaling in turn a shift from mostly insurrectional political initiatives to a gradual process of institutionalization, Spanish politics became, in a sense, less Rancièrean and more Laclauian (Rey-Araújo 2018). A new stage of the organic crisis was thus initiated.

The emergence of Podemos: From the squares to the ballot boxes

Podemos was launched in January 2014 by a group of intellectuals and social activists in collaboration with a small anti-capitalist party *Izquierda Anticapitalista*, and it was headed by Pablo Iglesias, a well-known figure thanks to his recurrent TV appearances speaking against austerity. Despite lacking a well-established party structure, the upcoming European elections of May 2014 represented an optimal occasion to enter the Spanish political scene. On the one hand, almost two years had passed since the last nationwide elections, so that the electoral consequences of the new political climate born after the 15M movement were still unknown. On the other hand, the second-order character of these elections made a 'punishment vote' to already-established parties much more likely, while these elections' unique circumscription eased its translation into electoral results (Fernández-Albertos 2015). Unexpectedly, Podemos obtained an 8 percent vote share, being the fourth most voted party.

The irruption of Podemos can hardly be appraised without taking into due consideration the enduring legacy of the 15M movement, as it responded to both the successes and failures of the cycle of social unrest it had sparked. On the one hand, the wave of mobilizations was becoming exhausted, insofar as it had failed thus far to coalesce into organizational means capable of blocking the ongoing implementation of austerity policies. On the other hand, a new social imaginary had emerged from the 15M movement which, by challenging dominant accounts of the crisis and its culprits, left Spanish elites immersed in an unheard-of legitimacy crisis (Antentas 2017b; Sola and Rendueles 2018) while, moreover, a variety of social struggles had thus far been precluded from entering the sphere of political representation. Nevertheless, under no circumstances can Podemos be understood as an implicit and/or straightforward consequence of the '*indignados*' movement. While the latter represented a dislocation to hegemonic configurations of social meaning, forcing their further dissolution and fragmentation while, simultaneously, drawing novel rearticulations among its constituent elements (Errejón 2011), the emergence of Podemos represented an ungrounded decision which, playing upon existing dislocations, imprinted upon them a new shape that could not have been read *a priori* from the dislocated structure itself (see Laclau 1990a).

Certainly, many parallels can be drawn between the 15M movement and the initial practices of Podemos, such as their unashamedly pointing to political-economic elites as the main culprits of the crisis, an accusation which Podemos encapsulated through the term '*la casta*'; an emphasis upon corruption as the main malaise pervading the political system; a resignification of 'democracy' as lying beyond mere electoral contests, thus foregrounding a new political identity anchored around a novel understanding of 'citizenship' in lieu of class antagonism (Gerbaudo 2017); and a reception of the 'horizontalist' drives of the 15M movement in the guise of the so-called '*Círculos*', which were to constitute Podemos's local cells or nodes. However, important departures from the legacy of the 15M comprise, prominently, the ultimately top-down nature of Podemos's intervention and, above all, the decision to enter the sphere of political representation itself.

Podemos's initial strategy represented a paramount example of 'left-wing populism' (e.g. Kioupkiolis 2016; Ferrada-Stoehrel 2017; Rendueles and Sola 2018; García-Agustín and Briziarelli 2018). Podemos attempted to dichotomize the social field by advancing a popular identity ('*el pueblo*', '*la gente*'), defined in opposition to the political-economic oligarchic elites ('*la casta*'). While the latter was a relatively well-defined term, the former was constitutively vague and imprecise, so that the possibilities of incorporating disaffected subjects into such 'chains of equivalence' could be maximized in return. The antagonistic relation between these two poles was over-stressed in order to prevent already-existing political cleavages and loyalties from acquiring prevalence when drawing future political alignments. This way, Podemos aimed at incorporating manifold existing disaffections with the existing social order into a new political project capable not only of giving them due recognition but, crucially, of advancing them all.

Accordingly, Podemos stubbornly refused to position itself in the left–right divide. Far from giving in to post-political narratives about the end of political cleavages, Podemos aimed at putting forward a new dichotomous partition that, by forcing a disidentification from old identity positions, fostered the emergence of a new social bloc through such a rearrangement of the socio-symbolic field. Perhaps paradoxically, 'Podemos adopted a Left-wing populist strategy precisely by avoiding any reference to populism and to the Left' (Rendueles and Sola 2018: 36). Nevertheless, not only did Podemos's voters prominently identify themselves as left-wing, but they were also perceived as such by the general electorate (Fernández-Albertos 2015). While the majoritarian profile among its 2014 voters matched the dominant profile in the 15M demonstrations (i.e. young, well-educated, politically active urban voters), as long as Podemos's electoral base was enlarging, those more intensely affected by the economic crisis (or, at least, those self-perceived as such) gradually joined in (Fernández-Albertos 2015; Rendueles and Sola 2018).

Podemos's initial 'left-wing populist intervention' confronted the vast majority of the population with the existing institutional order *as such*. It was not only a matter of political/economic elites illegitimately using their own prerogatives to their own benefit but, rather, of a whole institutional order self-consciously designed to protect the interests of the ruling elites (Franzé 2018), so that, Podemos contended, the various demands it voiced were unattainable within the contours of the existing order. In sum, it was a confrontation between, on the one hand, the existing institutional order and, on the other, the manifold social positions which, because they had been expelled from/by such institutional order, found themselves compelled to subvert it. While hegemonic articulations equated parliamentary capitalism with the only democracy conceivable and attainable, embedded in de-politicizing and apro-blematic narratives of social interaction (which we had referred to as *CT*), Podemos re-framed it as a system of oligarchic rule which had sequestered democracy for the benefit of the elites. It was not only a matter of illicit conducts undertaken by the political-economic establishment but, rather, of a given institutional order which promoted the latter in the first instance. During 2014, Spanish elites were mainly on the defensive. On the one hand, Podemos's left-wing populist intervention was met by already-established parties with an eminently institutionalist-technocratic discourse, mixed with paternalist tones. On the other, they gradually made use of accusations portraying Podemos as a serious threat/danger to liberal democracy (Miró 2019; Rendueles and Sola 2018; Franzé 2018). Confronted by highly disoriented political rivals, Podemos's mixture of discursive novelty and audacity saw it soaring in the polls all throughout 2014, with the December 2015 general elections on the horizon. Nevertheless, the structural conditions favoring populist interpellations were starting, albeit slowly, to recede.

The imperfect restoration of the old order

The resumption of economic growth in 2014 put a provisional end to five consecutive years of socio-economic decay. Supported by several tailwinds, such as very low interest rates derived from the ECB's 'quantitative easing' policy, the recovery of global demand, a depreciating euro, or the drastic reduction experienced by oil prices (Rosnick and Weisbrot 2015; Cárdenas et al. 2018), the economic expansion enabled a gradual amelioration of some of the Spanish SSA's core imbalances (e.g. households' leverage, public debt levels, or the weight of the real estate sector within the productive structure). Nevertheless, the core defining features of Spanish capitalism remain firmly in place, as internal devaluation could not but reinforce its overall logic – a 'low-road' pattern of socio-economic development was maintained, while the structural power of Spanish capital over co-existing social groups has been reinforced.

Concomitantly, the socio-political field has been partially pacified. While recovering capitalist activity and employment opportunities have definitely played a non-negligible role, it is the internal dynamics of the hegemonic struggle itself which accounts for its relative stabilization, within which Podemos's abandonment of its initial antagonistic stance towards the existing order represents the most relevant phenomenon. Nevertheless, despite the initial de-institutionalizing impetus having partially faded away, there have been important developments within the socio-political field, such as the exacerbation of the conflict over Catalan independence, the emergence of a new radical-right party (VOX), and a resurgent feminist movement enjoying, at the moment, unheard-of vitality. As soon as the current economic expansion succumbs to its fragile bases, it will come to the fore the extent to which the hegemonic struggle remains far from resolved.

A new economic upturn, old vulnerabilities

The year 2014 marked the beginning of a new economic expansion. While net exports had already been growing since 2010, by 2014 all components of aggregate demand but public consumption were finally following suit. Animated by the recovery experienced by its main trade partners, resurgent capitalist investment and households' consumption pushed forward GDP growth (Álvarez et al. 2019; Cárdenas et al. 2018). Employment, whose pro-cyclical character had been accentuated by the 2010 and 2012 labor reforms, immediately followed suit. Capital investment, the ultimate engine of the previous expansion, has been the component of aggregate demand that registered the highest rates of annual growth since 2013, to reach 20.4 percent of GDP in 2018 (although very far from the 30.4 percent it reached in 2007). Nonetheless, its internal composition has undergone significant changes, reflecting the absence of sustained real estate self-revaluation during these years: While in 2007 more than two-thirds of total investment consisted in housing and other constructions, by 2018 such proportion was reduced to below 50 percent. Conversely, investment in machinery and equipment went from representing a quarter in 2007, to one-third of total investment in 2018. Hence, whereas by 2018 the latter had already reached previous 2008 levels in volume terms, the former remained 36 percent below (INE 2020b). Therefore, construction-related investments no longer represent the main driver of economic growth – in 2018, it merely accounted for 5.6 percent of GDP while employing slightly more than 1.2 million workers (in 2007, those figures stood at 10.5 percent and 2.5 million, respectively) (INE 2020b; 2020a). Nevertheless, despite speculative dynamics in the real estate sector no longer paralleling those featured during the previous economic expansion, housing remains to date a prominent locus of ongoing rent-extraction practices and, by extension, a location where contradictions pertaining to social reproduction continue to accumulate.

Table 9.1 Annual rates of growth of GDP components

	1995–2008	*2008–2010*	*2010–2013*	*2013–2018*
Households' consumption	3.29	−1.69	−2.96	2.42
Public consumption	4.37	2.84	−2.12	1.02
GFC	5.21	−11.62	−7.31	5.78
Exports	5.89	−1.39	4.45	4.40
Imports	7.45	−6.85	−2.25	4.88
GDP	3.50	−1.82	−1.74	2.70

Source: INE (2020a)

After the Great Recession, the widespread prevalence of low wages, labor precariousness, and, especially, households' over-indebtedness, precluded the continuation of the previous model based on extracting rents from households through mortgage payments. Moreover, banks were left with thousands of empty dwellings and non-performing loans (insofar as the Spanish Mortgage Law prescribes foreclosing the property when the debtor fails to re-pay its mortgage) which they desperately needed to sell in order to obtain the liquidity required to pay off their respective debts (Yrigoy 2019). In order to rescue a domestic financial system overexposed to the real estate collapse, the State intervened actively in both areas. Firstly, it promoted the re-capitalization of the banking system through supporting several mergers among financially distressed entities (Vives-Miró 2018). Secondly, it helped banks to get rid of their 'toxic assets' through the creation of a 'bad bank' named SAREB (Gabarre 2019). Thirdly, the State re-regulated the rental market to allow hedge funds to enter the Spanish rental market through Real Estate Investment Trusts (REIT), in order to create demand for the Spanish banks' assets. REITs were granted various tax exemptions while, at the same time, existing regulations protecting tenants' rights have been derogated (Gabarre 2019; Yrigoy 2020).

Once the appropriate regulations had been rolled out, hedge funds could successfully enter the Spanish housing market, in the guise of REITs, by buying empty properties from private banks, the SAREB, and real estate developers (Yrigoy 2020). Having eased previous restrictions preventing sustained rental price increases, rental housing did rapidly become an increasingly profitable investment niche for quantitative easing–induced international pools of liquidity. Soaring rental prices in the main Spanish cities rapidly ensued (Gabarre 2019; Yrigoy 2020; Vives-Miró 2018). In sum, while before 2008 financial expropriation through housing was prominently accomplished through mortgage payments accruing to domestic banks, nowadays it takes the prominent form of rental payments accruing to transnational financial institutions (Yrigoy 2020). Nonetheless, this new model of financial expropriation finds its capacity to push forward aggregate demand and employment, through synergies developed around real estate dynamics, severely curtailed. The main anchoring point of the pre-2008 Spanish model, therefore, is now missing.

The adoption of austerity policies, nonetheless, has not given rise to an alternative growth path. While internal devaluation in the aftermath of the Great Recession was indeed successful in reducing labor costs, in turn helping recover firms' profit margins, the latter were not used to finance investment expenditures aimed at fostering a more productive use of labor power but, rather, to reduce firms' excessive leverage levels in a context of private over-indebtedness (Cárdenas et al. 2018; Álvarez et al. 2019; Pérez and Matsaganis 2019). The correction of balance of payments' disequilibria thus came not from an improvement in Spain's external price competitiveness but from a sharp contraction of import demand resulting from the collapse experienced by domestic demand. Indeed, the bulk of Spanish exports remain concentrated nowadays in medium-technology products and the primary sector, while the proportion of goods with high-technological content remains significantly low (Gracia and Paz 2018). Moreover, while public spending in R&D has been drastically reduced as a result of austerity policies, in turn enlarging the already-significant difference in that regard with the countries of the European 'core', foreign capital has further increased its presence in the most technologically advanced sectors (Sánchez Iglesias 2016). Therefore, far from leading to a technological upgrading of the Spanish productive structure, the implementation of austerity has reinforced Spain's peripheral position within the EU, remaining very dependent upon importing energy inputs, technology, and capital goods (Gracia and Paz 2018). Nonetheless, the widespread reduction of labor costs did certainly play a role in further enhancing the traditional specialization of the Spanish economy in the tourist sector: Tourist entries experienced an upsurge since 2008 of more than 25 million (López and Rodríguez 2019).

In sum, the current recovery has reinforced the previous 'low-road' pattern of sectorial specialization. Looking at the new employment that has been created since 2013, the sectors showing greater dynamism have been Administrative activities, Retail, Hostelry, and Construction, reflecting the extent to which Spain's productive specialization in low-quality services, prominently linked to construction and tourism, has been further reinforced. Nonetheless, despite the sustained reduction experienced by labor costs, the recent upsurge in employment has not sufficed to regain its pre-crisis levels: In the last quarter of 2019, the employed population remains almost 700,000 people below its previous 2008 levels, while the unemployment rate remains at 14.1 percent (16 percent for women).

Moreover, legislative changes directed towards de-centralizing and individualizing labor relations since 2008 have further reinforced the latter's antagonistic character, in turn underpinning the extensive pattern of diachronic expansion which Spanish capitalism had already been practicing during previous decades. On the one hand, average real hourly wages have remained stagnant throughout the current expansion (actually, they have not increased in the slightest since 1995). On the other hand, the traditional dualism of the Spanish labor market has not been eliminated. In 2019, 26 percent of

Table 9.2 Employment growth, in absolute terms and as percentage of total employment growth, and real hourly wage growth, per sector of activity

	2008–2013			*2013–2018*		
	Absolute	*% Δ Total*	*Δ Real Hourly Wages*	*Absolute*	*% Δ Total*	*Δ Real Hourly Wages*
Agriculture	−81.1	−2.4	−9.3	59	2.9	−4.0
Extractive industries	−20.2	−0.6	11.4	−3.5	−0.2	−1.1
Energy supply	−1.5	0.0	1.7	−5.6	−0.3	7.0
Water supply	32.6	1.0	−3.9	19.3	1.0	8.7
Manufacturing	−815.6	−24.0	0.0	177.7	8.8	−0.6
Construction	−1406.3	−41.4	−0.8	192.3	9.5	−6.0
Retail	−493.9	−14.6	−2.5	178.5	8.9	2.5
Transport and storage	−172.5	−5.1	−2.8	109.6	5.4	2.3
Hostelry	−167.8	−4.9	−1.5	298.7	14.8	−3.1
Information and communications	−39	−1.1	−1.6	87.5	4.3	−3.5
Financial activities	−44.4	−1.3	−3.2	−11.3	−0.6	−3.1
Real estate activities	−59.2	−1.7	−10.4	56.6	2.8	7.1
Professional activities	−122	−3.6	0.3	136.6	6.8	5.0
Administrative activities	−94.4	−2.8	−2.6	263.1	13.1	−1.3
Public administration	111.1	3.3	−15.8	83.4	4.1	2.2
Education	6.1	0.2	−9.3	104	5.2	5.6
Health	37.1	1.1	−8.0	166.7	8.3	2.5
Entertainment activities	−11	−0.3	−11.6	71.9	3.6	−2.8
Other services	30.3	0.9	2.7	66	3.3	1.1
Household activities	−81.6	−2.4	1.8	−36.6	−1.8	9.5
TOTAL	−3393.3	100.0	−2.6	2013.9	100	−0.1

Source: INE (2020a; 2020c)

wage-earners had a temporary contract, whereas more than half of those who had a part-time job had one involuntarily (i.e. because they could not find a full-time job) (INE 2020a). The self-professed objective of the 2010 and 2012 labor reforms was to reduce the labor market's markedly dual character (Muñoz de Bustillo and Esteve 2017). Nonetheless, even though the level of protection enjoyed by permanent workers has been significantly downgraded, a variety of even more precarious work arrangements has been enabled by those same reforms (Pérez and Matsaganis 2018). Indeed, by further individualizing labor relations while increasing the employers' prerogatives to have recourse to both internal and external flexibility at will, myriad situations of exclusion have been consolidated, resulting in 'an increasing picture of social diversification and a continuum of increasing inequalities' (Banyuls and Recio 2017: 144). In sum, the austerity-induced labor reforms have not promoted a profound restructuring of Spanish capitalism along more competitive lines, nor have they managed to reduce the duality of its labor market. Quite to the contrary, they have served to further accentuate the antagonistic and socially regressive character of Spanish capitalism by increasing capital's prerogatives in the workplace and beyond (López-Andreu 2019).

In sum, institutional transformations in the aftermath of the Great Recession contributed to reinforce the core features of the Spanish SSA – the dominance of capital over co-existing social groups in the domestic arena, on the one hand, and a 'low-road' pattern of productive specialization, on the other. This last expansion has nonetheless benefited from the operation of several contingent factors, such as a reduction of crude oil prices whilst still being very dependent upon energy imports; a marked increase in tourist visitors, itself partly a result of the terrible conjunctural situation experienced by North African countries on the Mediterranean coast; very low interest rates as a result of the ECB's 'quantitative easing' policy; or the recovery of external demand coming from Spain's main trade partners. Nevertheless, at the end of 2019 aggregate employment remains distant from its pre-crisis level, whereas it took until 2017 for GDP to reach its pre-crisis level in volume terms (INE 2020b; 2020a).

Therefore, while the Spanish SSA's main vulnerabilities definitely persist, its capacity to overcome them, at least temporarily, appears severely curtailed. The 1995–2008 expansion, despite being built upon worrisome foundations, did manage to conceal them for a relatively long time thanks to the idiosyncratic interplay among several dynamics whose repetition seems to be highly unlikely. Firstly, private debt, especially that corresponding to non-financial corporations, remains at very high levels despite having been reduced ever since the onset of the Great Recession. While very low interest rates supported by sustained economic growth permitted its gradual reduction over time, a more restrictive monetary policy that resulted in a sudden hike of interest rates would prove detrimental to private agents' capacity for repayment. Moreover, public debt levels have stabilized at around 100 percent of GDP, which seriously compromises the Spanish State's capacity to bail out the private sector in the next recession in case that was needed.

Secondly, the antagonistic character of capital–labor relations has been reinforced. The job protection enjoyed by permanent workers has been significantly eroded, thus compromising one of the key elements enabling families, through internally redistributing available resources among its members, to ameliorate the harsh conditions enjoyed by workers participating in the external segments of the labor market. Moreover, the pro-cyclical evolution of employment has been reinforced, as the share of temporary contracts indicates, so that, as soon as aggregate demand starts to recede, unemployment will more likely soar up again.

Thirdly, internal devaluation has strengthened the seemingly exhausted 'low-road' pattern of sectorial specialization while maintaining the Spanish economy's dependent pattern of external insertion. The diachronic reproduction of this model thus requires the systematic repression of real wages in order not to undo the meagre improvements in external competitiveness it manages to deliver. However, insofar as domestic demand remains the main driver of growth (Álvarez et al. 2019), wage containment will seriously limit the reproduction of the current model in the absence of 'atypical' process that might enable domestic demand to be expanded in the face of widespread wage stagnation. However, neither can families stop their current de-leveraging, nor can wealth effects push aggregate demand forward as they did in the past. In sum, the current recovery the Spanish SSA is experiencing at the moment retains the main weaknesses that had haunted it in the past, while its capacity to give rise to social processes able to postpone the eventual manifestation of the former over time appears dramatically compromised. Nevertheless, despite not having promoted a significant improvement of the Spanish SSA's main features, this period of economic expansion, however precarious, played a crucial role in reinstituting old expectations, allegiances and loyalties towards the existing order. The latter, in turn, proved detrimental to Podemos's aspirations of radically transforming existing socio-political alignments.

Cooling down social discontent

Following its electoral appearance in the May 2014 European elections, the forces of the establishment, espousing a mixture of paternalism and inflamed demagoguery, were unable to stop Podemos's soaring evolution in electoral polls. Preparing itself for the several electoral contests to be held in the upcoming year, Podemos celebrated its founding congress in November 2014. There, the tension between 'verticalism' and 'horizontalism', intrinsic to every populist movement, was reflected in the two main contending positions (Kioupkiolis 2016). On the one hand, the sector led by, among others, Pablo Iglesias and Iñigo Errejón, advocated for consolidating a classical party structure, highly verticalized and with strong prerogatives granted to the General Secretary. Lacking both experienced cadres and a well-established organizational culture, building up an 'electoral war machine' free from internal disputes and collective decision-making processes, was argued to represent a necessary condition to suddenly enter successfully into the electoral arena (Errejón 2014). On the other hand, the competing sector advocated instead for a more horizontal and less hierarchical structure, with mechanisms designed to incentivize active involvement by rank and file members into the organization's decision-making process, in line with what Kitschelt (2006) has termed a 'movement-party' (Martín 2015). The position commanded by Pablo Iglesias obtained a clear majority. Podemos was thus officially born, and a centralized political strategy ensued which understood politics as basically electoral work, where communication strategies took prevalence over programmatic discussion, and whose ultimate goal was to alter the existing balance of forces within the State apparatuses (Antentas 2017b). Over time, such highly vertical and centralized organization ended up becoming an increasingly self-enclosed communicative network with few ties to civil society beyond recurrent TV appearances (Briziarelli 2018), a factor which severely complicated its own long-term survival in case an immediate access to State institutions did not eventually materialize.

While Podemos entered 2015 leading most electoral polls (Fernández-Albertos 2015), its insurrectionary stance towards the existing order in the guise of a 'left-wing populist intervention' gradually faded away throughout the year. On the one hand, the socio-symbolic terrain was less conducive to populist interventions, as economic growth and recovering employment opportunities gradually reinstated the allegiances and loyalties of many towards the existing order, while receding social mobilization in the streets left Podemos increasingly isolated in impugning the latter. On the other hand, from January 2015 onwards, Podemos gradually abandoned its previous wholesale condemnation of the existing order to adopt a softer stance, where 'although an "us" and a "them" persisted, the latter was embodied more in the *political behavior* of the caste and less in the 1978 institutions' (Franzé 2018: 59, original emphasis). Insofar as the existing institutional order was no longer understood to stand in antagonistic relation towards the 'people' Podemos represented, the demands the latter voiced were no longer framed as incompatible with the former. Hence, the wholesale replacement of the institutional environment structuring social co-existence was no longer demanded, just the replacement of the dominant political elites. Therefore, Podemos no longer stood in opposition to the existing order but, rather, gradually became an internal element of it, however idiosyncratic its ultimate aspirations might have been.

Moreover, Podemos's aspirations of 'transversality' led it to abandon the most socially transformative proposals it had initially embraced (such as the implementation of basic income schemes, or the cancellation of illegitimate debt), in favor of emphasizing notions *a priori* more entrenched in the dominant common sense, such as reducing the systemic critique of its early moments to a critique of corruption-like excesses; an embracing of a meritocratic rhetoric too reminiscent of a neoliberally inspired 'culture of winners'; downplaying the '*pueblo*'–'*casta*' opposition in favor of another one anchored around the divide 'new politics'–'old politics'; or its reticence to engage with existing class realities and the intrinsically antagonistic nature of Spanish capitalism. Podemos's eventual vindication of social democracy thus testified to its abandonment of its initial populist stance. Several factors motivated the latter.

Firstly, a new electoral competitor emerged in the guise of *Ciudadanos*, a nominally liberal, business-sponsored party which embraced several of Podemos's claims while emptying them of transformative potential (Rodríguez-Teruel and Barrio 2016; Antentas 2017b). Embracing an anti-corruption discourse while arguing for a 'soft and sensible' change, it had a strong appeal to the most conservative layers of the middle and working classes. The 'new versus old politics' cleavage it promoted thus blocked Podemos's aspiration of building a transversal movement against the *statu quo*:

> This revealed two things: on the one hand, it highlighted the political limits of mass discomfort and the 15M legacy in terms of political consciousness; on the other hand, it showed that Podemos' policy of using 'empty signifiers' with little programmatic precision favored its contenders' attempts to give them another meaning.
>
> (Antentas 2017b: 481)

Podemos, by concealing the systemic character of the corruption it denounced, thus left the door open for a new party with equally young leaders, embracing a corruption-free and democratic regeneration rhetoric capable of confronting Podemos in the very symbolic arena the latter had contributed to bring forward.

Secondly, a renewed attack from the forces of the establishment put Podemos in the defensive for the first time. From early 2015 onwards, Podemos's indictment of the existing order was no longer countered through a post-political technocratic stance (Miró 2019). Rather, the establishment forces assumed and reinforced the very antagonistic divide initially drawn by Podemos to load it with markedly pejorative and apocalyptic connotations. Podemos was now pictured as a threat not only to the existing order but to democratic politics *tout court*: 'the signifier populism […] had come to condense all the anxieties of the Spanish political elites, thus becoming an omnipresent point of reference in opposition to which traditional political actors based their democratic credentials' (Miró 2019: 122). The signifier 'populism' thus served to link Podemos to other threats and accusations, some of them with a long history in acting as a 'constitutive outside' for previously dominant hegemonic formations, such as ETA's terrorist activity or communism, some others recently imported into the Spanish socio-symbolic arena, such as the party's alleged links with countries such as Iran or Venezuela (Labio-Bernal 2018). No longer capable of generating a material common ground through which to secure the consent of subordinate social groups, the PP government resorted to a highly technocratic management of economic affairs in conjunction with an overt politicization of the social order's constitutive outside (Borriello 2017).

Lastly, Podemos's discursive shift was further motivated by the need to confront the successive elections predating the national ones, to be celebrated at the end of 2015. In May 2015 local and (some) regional elections were held. A self-perceived inability to build up electoral lists that were in full agreement with the political line devised by the party leadership, together with a marked fear to take controversial decisions which could affect in the future its state-wide image, favored the choice of not running at the local level, choosing instead to be integrated in multi-party electoral alliances, so-called '*confluencias*' (Rodón and Hierro 2016). This choice turned out to be highly successful, insofar as these various local *coallitios* managed to win the local elections in many among the country's biggest cities, such as Madrid, Barcelona, Valencia, Zaragoza, and A Coruña, although at the expense of empowering majors unsubmitted to Podemos's internal hierarchies (Rodríguez-Teruel et al. 2016). In the regional elections Podemos's vote share was lower than expected: It did not surpass the PSOE in any region (Rodón and Hierro 2016). The Catalan regional elections celebrated in October 2015 delivered similar results. In a very polarized scenario around Catalunya's self-determination, Podemos's coalition candidacy did not reach 10 percent of the vote share.

In this context, expectations over the 2015 general elections (December) were certainly low. Nonetheless, Podemos emerged as the third force in the Spanish political system, very close to the PSOE and well above Ciudadanos (Medina and Correa 2016). On the one hand, it benefited from entering into coalitions with other forces in various regions, such as Catalunya, Valencia, and Galicia, where Podemos obtained its best results. On the other, Podemos advanced a self-fulfilling narrative of electoral recovery (so-called '*remontada*') which managed to polarize the electoral campaign while also presenting Podemos, again, as an emerging 'outsider'.

The results obtained did not enable a straightforward government formation and, for the first time in the short history of Spanish democracy, the most voted party did not manage to reach an agreement with other parliamentary forces to establish a government. The relevance played by the Catalan conflict as well as the existing dispute between Podemos and PSOE caused an irresolvable parliamentary blockage (Medina and Correa 2016). The necessity to repeat elections was made obvious. In preparing for the next elections, in June 2016, the main novelty was the constitution of a joint candidacy between Podemos and the traditional left-wing party *Izquierda Unida* (itself a coalition led by the Communist Party). In order to finally overtake the Socialist Party, an even more moderate discourse was advanced, aiming at not frightening potential voters who had aligned themselves previously with its, now, only rival on the Left.

Contrary to the initial expectations, the joint candidacy of Podemos and Izquierda Unida, saw its aspirations of finally overtaking the PSOE truncated, as it lost close to 1,100,000 votes compared to the 2015 general elections. In this regard, while the reticence of some of its past electorate to support the new joint candidacy played an important role, being led to either the ranks of abstentionist or towards the Socialist Party (Simón 2016), the discursive stance eventually adopted, almost univocally aimed at securing the support of previous Socialist voters, might have had the unintended effect of de-mobilizing its own electoral base. This time, the Socialist Party, after having accomplished an internal *coup d'état* to its own general secretary, did support the conformation of another right-wing government headed by PP's leader Mariano Rajoy (Lancaster 2017). At this point, the cycle of social contestation initiated in 2011 with the emergence of the 15M movement found here a provisional end point. Nevertheless, political instability persisted.

The Rajoy government lasted only until June 2018. Following the publication of the final verdict of the so-called *Gürtel Case* (one of the greatest cases among the seemingly endless list of corruption scandals linked to the PP's inherently kleptocratic mode of government), which found the PP guilty of having benefited from illegal financing during the last three decades, the PSOE promoted a motion of no confidence against Rajoy. Supported by Podemos and an array of regional and/or nationalist parties, the PSOE formed a minority government headed by its General Secretary Pedro Sánchez. This government was short-lived as well. Being unable to pass the national budget in Parliament due to the rejection of Catalan secessionist parties (who had supported PSOE in the previous motion of no confidence) forced the government to call new elections in April 2019. The Socialist Party stood clearly as the most voted party. Nevertheless, Podemos insistence in forming part of the new government, and PSOE's stark reticence to let that happen, led to new elections in November 2019. This time, despite the election results not showing stark differences with regard to the previous elections in April, a joint cabinet between Podemos and PSOE was eventually constituted (Camas and Ferrándiz 2020). Podemos's eventual accession to government, even though it is a coalition government, thus represents the end of the long journey, initiated back in 2014, where the self-professed heirs of the 15M set themselves the goal to enter the State institutions. Nevertheless, other important socio-political developments have recently taken place which, in turn, indicate that the hegemonic struggle is far from concluded.

The main novelty affecting the Spanish party system in 2019 was the emergence first, and then consolidation, of an extreme-right party: VOX. Despite the term being widely used in the mainstream media, VOX cannot be considered a populist party, insofar as no traces of attempting to build a 'people' through a top-down opposition to Spanish elites are found in its discourse, but, rather, constitutes an example of right-wing authoritarian nationalism (De Cleen and Stavrakakis 2017). Indeed, VOX has not managed so far to significantly re-draw the main axes of socio-political alignment operating in Spain: According to post-electoral studies, Vox's voters are mostly people self-defined as right-wing, discontent with the various corruption scandals linked to the PP and, above all, the situation in Catalunya (Vampa 2020; Turnbull-Dugarte 2019; Camas and Ferrándiz 2020)

VOX's discursive intervention has been articulated around three main axes – firstly, a harsh anti-immigration stance, advocating for the deportation of illegal or crime-convicted immigrants, and for an end to social policies catering to their needs; secondly, a strong anti-feminist message, by opposing abortion rights, a ban on same-sex marriage, or gender violence protection policies; and, thirdly, an unabashedly reactionary and authoritarian version of Spanish nationalism, defined in opposition to Spain's peripheral nationalisms and, especially, the Catalan pro-independence movement (Turnbull-Dugarte 2019). Thus, the emergence of VOX has been partly a response to two of the most relevant social mobilizations Spain has witnessed in recent years, namely, the Catalan pro-independence movement and the recent mainstreaming of feminism.

Regarding the former, it must be noted that secessionism had traditionally been a relatively marginal position within the Catalan nationalist movement. Nevertheless, from the mid-2000s, the pro-independence movement started to acquire momentum. On the one hand, new grassroots forms of social mobilization, autonomous from the main Catalan nationalist parties, started to emerge. On the other hand, the bid for Catalan independence increasingly adopted a democratic imaginary by framing itself as a struggle for 'the right to decide' (Miró 2020). Within this social context, the Constitutional Court announced it had nullified several parts of the Catalan Statute of Autonomy, which had been previously ratified by referendum in 2006 (della Porta and Portos 2020). Such a decision represented a dislocation to the 'social imaginary' (Laclau 1990a) that had articulated Catalan nationalism thus far, namely, that increasing self-government for Catalunya could be achieved *within* the 1978 Spanish Constitution (Miró 2020). The year 2012 marked a definitive turning point regarding the social projection of Catalan secessionism. On the one hand, the *Assemblea Nacional Catalana* (ANC, National Catalan Assembly) was born, a civil organization with no explicit party linkages whose only goal was to struggle for Catalunya's independence. On the other, following a massive pro-independence demonstration on September 11 (Catalunya's national day), the then President of the Catalan Autonomous Community, Artur Mas, officially took up the quest of organizing an independence referendum.

At the time, of course, Catalunya was living through a 'populist situation' analogous to that affecting the rest of the country. In this context, secessionist political forces succeeded in launching a populist intervention through which 'the good and naïve Catalan people [were pitched] against the oppressive and corrupt Spanish State' (Barrio et al. 2018: 1000), thus turning the 'independence' into an 'empty signifier' (Laclau 1996b) through which disparate dissatisfaction with the existing order could have been voiced, framed, and articulated (Miró 2020). Moreover, its social appeal was further enhanced by presenting the struggle for independence, on the one hand, as a matter of social justice in relation to the allegedly unfair redistributive policies of the Spanish State and, on the other, as an inherently democratic struggle in relation to the 'right to vote' (della Porta et al. 2020). In the years that followed, support for the independence oscillated between 40 percent and 50 percent of the population, with a marked cross-class character (della Porta and Portos 2020).

In the November 2012 elections, pro-independence political forces obtained a clear majority, and set themselves to organize the aforementioned referendum, to be celebrated in 2014. The latter, following the prohibition dictated by the Spanish Constitutional Court, turned out to be merely a citizen mobilization in favor of the right to decide. Following the September 2015 snap elections, where the pro-independence forces obtained an absolute majority, the Catalan government adopted for the first time the achievement of Catalan independence as its main goal. An independence referendum was set to be celebrated on October 1, 2017. Even though the Constitutional Court had prohibited its celebration, it was successfully self-organized by the civil society. Despite brutal police repression, up to 2.3 million people deposited their vote. On October 10, facing the refusal of the central government to negotiate with the Catalan government, the latter proclaimed Catalunya's independence only to suspend it eight seconds later. On October 27, the Spanish executive suspended Catalunya's independence, and three days later, Carles Puigdemont, then president of Catalunya, left Catalunya and was exiled in Brussels. Other members of the Catalan government followed suit, while those who remained in Spanish territory were imprisoned and had to face a trial. The Spanish Supreme Court announced the final verdict on October 14, 2019, where 9 out of 12 accused were found guilty of sedition, and were sentenced to prison for between 9 and 13 years.

For its part, the Spanish feminist movement gained an unprecedented level of media coverage and diffusion with the organization a 24-hour women's strike on March 8, 2018 (to be repeated back again in 2019). The various attempts to re-domesticate women in the aftermath of the 2008 crisis had been resisted, on the one hand, by women's continuing, and increasing, participation in paid employment and, on the other, through a particular cycle of feminist social contention (Lombardo 2017). Indeed, since the cycle of contention sparked by the 15M movement started to recede from 2014 onwards (Portos 2019b), an autonomous cycle of feminist contention endured. Thereafter, feminism has been the only social movement capable of sustaining massive and expanding social mobilizations to date (Campillo 2019), becoming in turn one of the main vectors of politicization for younger generations (Portos 2019a). While this cycle of contention, which culminated in the 2018 and 2019 women's strikes, has been mainly articulated around the defense of the 'right to choose' and against the multifarious forms of gender violence experienced by women, over the years the politicization of 'care work' has gained increasing attention (Campillo 2018). Within an eminently 'familialist' environment such as Spain's, the systemic consequences to be expected from the widespread politicization of the gendered organization of social reproduction can hardly be overstated. This cycle comprised several milestones.

Firstly, following the announcement of the PP's Minister of Justice to pass a new bill significantly restricting the right to abortion in 2012, the feminist movement organized frequent mass demonstrations in several Spanish cities until 2014, when the new law was finally overthrown, and the Minister of Justice was forced to resign. These mobilizations chiefly included the so-called *Tren de la Libertad* ['Liberty Train'], when several marches coming from all over the country converged in a state-wide march in Madrid in February 2014, gathering together tens of thousands of people. Secondly, fed by the social networks that had developed during the aforementioned demonstrations, the so-called '7N platform' emerged as a state-wide organization aimed at broadening the legal definition of gender violence in order to recognize, among other demands, the structural character of gender violence, its multifarious forms beyond intimate-partner violence, and the necessary public responsibility in protecting victims (Campillo 2018). Two state-wide marches took place in Madrid on November 7, 2015 and 2016, gathering an unprecedented level of support from diverse organizations and political parties. A State Pact against Gender Violence was finally approved in Parliament in November 2017, including several of the aforementioned demands.

Lastly, the culmination thus far of these increasing mobilizations has been the state-wide women's strike that took place on March 8, 2018. Building upon already-existing networks, local commissions coordinated state-wide were created in virtually all cities and towns to prepare for the upcoming labor, care, education, and consumption strike (Campillo 2019). The strike managed to receive impressive media coverage as it obtained the explicit support of leftist parties (Podemos, Izquierda Unida), some minority unions (CGT, CNT), and several professional women's associations (judges, journalists), while other relevant actors, such as the PSOE or the two main union confederations, distanced themselves from the strike, while calling for a two-hour stoppage. While previous rounds of feminist mobilization in Spain had mainly revolved around issues related to gender violence and women's rights over their bodies, this time demands related to the situation of migrant women, or the gendered distribution of reproductive labor, were placed center stage (Campillo 2019). Despite media coverage centering upon the wage inequalities and gender violence, having called for a 'care labor strike' turned the gendered domestic division of labor into an explicit public issue (García et al. 2010). The ultimate pillar sustaining social reproduction in the Spanish social formation had thus finally come to light. Women have taken up the public space to denounce not only the myriad inequalities they suffered, but also the systemic relevance carried by the latter. Future attempts to displace social contradictions onto women's bodies will more likely be contested to an extent they have not been in the past. 'If they stop, the world stops', and even more so in a 'familialist' environment such as Spain.

Notes

1 Despite enjoying an absolute majority in Parliament, the Rajoy government passed the 33.8 percent of its legislation by Royal Decrees (Clúa-Losada and Ribera-Almandoz 2017: 33).

2 'Far from being depoliticized or apolitical, the indignados rebellion showed an unusual degree of politicization, albeit one that was contradictory. It would be erroneous to interpret "they don't represent us" in a depoliticized sense, as an "anti-politics" criticism. In reality, it was a politicized criticism of politics as it exists today' (Antentas 2015: 146).

Concluding comments

At the time of writing these lines (end of March 2020), I find myself confined at home due to the COVID-19 outbreak. It has been two weeks already and, to date, it is impossible to know with a minimum degree of certainty what will happen in the near future. Most probably, once these pages can eventually see the light, the broad contours of the general scenario will most likely have settled down. Nevertheless, although the dramatic consequences the outbreak will have can already be glimpsed now, the extent and intensity with which the pandemic will spread over the world, the type of response the Spanish government and, by extension, the EU will offer to it, the intensity with which the world economy will be shattered, or how geopolitical relations will be affected in turn remains unknown.

As I was bringing this work to an end, the Spanish economy was in the midst of a capitalist expansion. Nonetheless, there is absolutely no doubt that an intense economic recession will ensue, whose consequences are likely to be quite dramatic in terms of employment losses, defaults on private debt, and, regrettably, thousands of human lives. The gradual recovery of capitalist activity initiated back in 2014 did certainly serve to provide a minimum of relief to those who had suffered the harshest consequences of the Great Recession, first, and the adoption of austerity, later on, as well as to partially correct and/or ameliorate some of the core disequilibria that had developed during the long phase of expansion leading to the Great Recession.

Nevertheless, the highly regressive manner in which the crisis management was conducted from 2010 onwards ended up blocking the possibility of accomplishing a profound transformation of the Spanish SSA. Instead, its core defining features have been further reinforced and, in consequence, its main vulnerabilities remained firmly in place. This, in turn, is likely to exacerbate the socio-economic effects of the pandemic. Firstly, the Spanish labor market is now even more precarious than it was prior to the Great Recession. Singularly, its archetypical duality has not been eradicated, insofar as, as of late 2019, more than a quarter of those involved in paid employment were on fixed-term contracts. Once again, the effects of the economic crisis on unemployment will be further exacerbated by the persistent pervasiveness of temporary contracts throughout the Spanish labor market. Secondly, Spanish capitalism had further reinforced its 'low-road' pattern of sectorial specialization, as manifested in the disproportionate weight that low-quality services and, especially those linked to tourism, keep on displaying within the Spanish productive structure. The interruption (or, at least, sharp reduction) of new tourist entries will leave its impoverished productive structure without one of its traditional anchoring points. Moreover, its exiguous industrial base makes the Spanish productive structure significantly ill-suited to respond to current social and productive needs without having recourse to imports from international markets, thus furthering its exposure to external disequilibria. Thirdly, the private sector and, especially, non-financial firms, remain highly indebted, so that, in the absence of profound public intervention in this regard in order to ensure the wide-spread availability of abundant liquidity, a long interruption of economic activity is likely to compromise their respective capacity of repaying their outstanding debts and, by extension, a system-threatening proliferation of defaults. Fourthly, the social consequences of the sharp budgetary cuts that had been effected on the welfare state in general, and on the social services and the public health care system in particular, are now coming to the fore in a dramatically acute manner. Lastly, inasmuch as the public sector had been forced to bail out the private sector in the aftermath of the Great Recession, its capacity to refloat the economic appears at the moment much more severely compromised than it was a decade ago. Moreover, the overreliance of public finances upon indirect sources of taxation linked to consumption, on the one hand, and upon the direct taxation of labor incomes, on the other hand, will further aggravate the strains to which public finances are probably going to be submitted.

In sum, Spanish capitalism will have to face an economic crisis which will inevitably bring to the fore the extent to which several among its core internal imbalances have not only failed to be properly addressed but, rather, further exacerbated. Certainly, the outbreak of the pandemic had little to do with the dominance of capitalism at a world scale. Nevertheless, the way the former impacts upon the organization of social reproduction is indeed intimately related to the extent to which it continues to be mediated by the imperatives of capitalist profitability. The dominance of capitalism within a given social formation means that the ongoing reproduction of the latter is ultimately subject to the successful reproduction of the former, so that, inasmuch as the pandemic provides a fatal blow to capitalist self-reproduction, the very sustainment of social life might be put at serious risk.

The various potential scenarios the current pandemic might give rise to in the near future will be, in the last instance, the end result of the relative balance of forces at stake. In the absence of a radical transformation of the current correlation of forces within the European Union, on the one hand, and in the domestic arena, on the other, one can hardly conceive any future scenario where ample latitudes of the social will remain impervious to the effects of the ensuing economic recession. Rather, its dislocatory effects ought to be expected to pervade the whole social structure in a very short time span albeit, certainly, with different degrees of intensity. Whether the current crisis will give rise to a new progressive 'common sense', one which acknowledges, firstly, the necessity of protecting the public health care system from commodifying pressures; secondly, the utter incompatibility, especially in times of capitalist crisis, between the continuing reproduction of the logic of capital profitability, on the one hand, and that of social reproduction, on the other; and, thirdly, the indelibly essential character of those manifold labors and activities which had so far been mostly neglected, undervalued, and underpaid on the grounds of them being 'unskilled', is yet undecided. Otherwise, as long as that ends up not being the case, the resolution of capitalist imbalances will most likely be secured at the expense of consolidating a new socially regressive scenario featuring widening social differentials, mounting impoverishment and a reinforcement of the power of capital in structuring social life. I hope that, by the time these pages finally see the light, it is the first scenario which is incipiently taking shape.

Bibliography

Aalbers, Manuel B. 2017. "The Variegated Financialization of Housing." *International Journal of Urban and Regional Research* 41 (4): 542–554.

Acha, Omar. 2019. "From Marxist to Post-Marxist Populism: Ernesto Laclau's Trajectory within the National Left and Beyond." *Historical Materialism* 28 (1): 1–32.

Aglietta, Michel. 1979. *A Theory of Capitalist Regulation. The U.S. Experience*. London: New Left Books.

Albarracín, Jesús. 1991. "La Extracción Del Excedente y El Proceso de Acumulación." In *La Reestructuración Del Capitalismo En España, 1970–1990*, edited by Miren Etxezarreta, 313–348. Barcelona: Icaria.

Alonso, Luis Enrique, Gomer Betancor, and Roberto Cilleros. 2015. "Nuevos y Novísimos Movimientos Sociales. Una Aproximación al Activismo Social En La España Actual." In *España 2015. Situación Social*, edited by Critóbal Torres, 1126–1148. Madrid: CIS.

Alonso, Luis Enrique, Carlos Fernández-Rodríguez, and Rafael Ibáñez-Rojo. 2015. "From Consumerism to Guilt: Economic Crisis and Discourses about Consumption in Spain." *Journal of Consumer Culture* 15 (1): 66–85.

Alonso, Luis Enrique, Carlos Fernández-Rodríguez, and Rafael Ibáñez-Rojo. 2017. "'I Think the Middle Class Is Disappearing': Crisis Perceptions and Consumption Patterns in Spain." *International Journal of Consumer Studies* 41: 389–396.

Althusser, Louis. 1969. *For Marx*. London: Verso.

Althusser, Louis. 1990. "Theory, Theoretical Practice and Theoretical Formation: Ideology and Ideologial Struggle." In *Philosophy and the Spontaneous Philosophy of the Scientists*, 1–42. London: Verso.

Althusser, Louis. 1994. "Ideology and Ideological State Apparatuses (Notes towards and Investigation)." In *Mapping Ideology*, edited by Slavoj Žižek, 100–140. London: Verso.

Althusser, Louis, and Étienne Balibar. 2009. *Reading Capital*. London: Verso.

Álvarez, Ignacio, Fernando Luengo, and Jorge Uxó. 2013. *Fracturas y Crisis En Europa*. Madrid: Clave Intelectual.

Álvarez, Ignacio, Jorge Uxó, and Eladio Febrero. 2019. "Internal Devaluation in a Wage-Led Economy. The Case of Spain." *Cambridge Journal of Economics* 43 (2): 335–360.

Antentas, Josep Maria. 2015. "Spain: The Indignados Rebellion of 2011 in Perspective." *Labor History* 56 (2): 136–160.

Antentas, Josep Maria. 2017a. "Spain: From the Indignados Rebellion to Regime Crisis (2011–2016)." *Labor History* 58 (1): 106–131.

Antentas, Josep Maria. 2017b. "Podemos and the Spanish Political Crisis." *Labor History* 58 (4): 468–489.

Anxo, Dominique, Colette Fagan, Inmaculada Cebrián, and Gloria Moreno. 2007. "Patterns of Labour Market Integration in Europe – a Life Course Perspective on Time Policies." *Socio-Economic Review* 5 (2): 233–260.

Arditi, Benjamin. 2010. "Review Essay: Populism Is Hegemony Is Politics? On Ernesto Laclau's On Populist Reason." *Constellations* 17 (3): 488–497.

Arts, WIL, and John Gelissen. 2002. "Three Worlds of Welfare Capitalism or More? A State-of-the-Art Report." *Journal of European Social Policy* 12 (2): 137–158.

Badiou, Alain. 2007. *Being and Event.* New York: Continuum.

Bakir, Erdogan, and Al Campbell. 2015. "Is Over-Investment the Cause of the Post-2007 U.S. Economic Crisis?" *Review of Radical Political Economics* 47 (4): 550–557.

Bakker, Isabella, and Stephen Gill. 2003. *Power, Production and Social Reproduction. Human In/Security in the Global Political Economy.* Basingstoke: Palgrave Macmillan.

Balibar, Etienne. 1993. "The Non-Contemporaneity of Althusser." In *The Althusserian Legacy*, edited by E. Ann Kaplan and Michael Sprinkler, 1–16. London and New York: Verso.

Bank of Spain. 2020a. *Financial Accounts.*

Bank of Spain. 2020b. *Survey of Household Finances.*

Banyuls, Josep, Fausto Miguélez, Albert Recio, Ernest Cano, and Raúl Lorente. 2009. "The Transformation of the Employment System in Spain: Towards a Mediterranean Neoliberalism?" In *European Employment Models in Flux: A Comparison of Institutional Change in Nine European Countries*, edited by Gerhard Bosch, Steffen Lehndorff, and Jill Rubery, 247–269. Basingstoke: Palgrave Macmillan.

Banyuls, Josep, and Albert Recio. 2012. "Spain. The Nightmare of Mediterranean Neoliberalism." In *A Triumph of Failed Ideas. European Models of Capitalism in Crisis*, edited by Steffen Lehndorff, 199–218. Brussels: ETUI.

Banyuls, Josep, and Albert Recio. 2015. "A Crisis Inside the Crisis: Spain under a Conservative Neoliberalism." In *Divisive Integration. The Triumph of Failed Ideas – Revisited*, edited by Steffen Lehndorff, 39–68. Brussels: ETUI.

Banyuls, Josep, and Albert Recio. 2017. "Labour Segmentation and Precariousness in Spain. Theories and Evidence." In *Making Work More Equal. A New Labour Market Segmentation Approach*, edited by Damian Grimshaw, Colette Fagan, Gail Hebson, and Isabel Tavora, 129–149. Manchester: Manchester University Press.

Baran, Paul A., and Paul Sweezy. 1966. *Monopoly Capital. An Essay on the American Economic and Social Order.* New York: Monthly Review Press.

Barceló, Alfons. 1998. *Economía Política Radical.* Madrid: Síntesis.

Barrio, Astrid, Oscar Barberà, and Juan Rodríguez-Teruel. 2018. "'Spain Steals from Us!' The 'Populist Drift' of Catalan Regionalism." *Comparative European Politics* 16 (6): 993–1011. https://doi.org/10.1057/s41295-018-0140-3.

Barros, Sebastián. 2006. "Espectralidad e Inestabilidad Institucional. Acerca de La Ruptura Populista." *Estudios Sociales* 30 (Primer Semestre): 145–162.

Bauman, Zygmunt. 2011. "El 15-M es emocional, le falta pensamiento." *El País*, October 17, 2011, https://elpais.com/diario/2011/10/17/cultura/1318802401_850215.html.

Bellod Redondo, José Francisco. 2015. "Plan E: la estrategia keynesiana frente a la crisis en España." *Revista de Economía Crítica* 20: 4–22.

Bentolila, Samuel, and Juan J. Dolado. 1994. "Labour Flexibility and Wages. Lessons from Spain." *Economic Policy* 9 (18): 53–99.

Benton, Ted. 1984. *The Rise and Fall of Structural Marxism. Althusser and His Influence.* New York: Macmillan Education.

Berglund, Oscar. 2018. "Contesting Actually Existing Austerity." *New Political Economy* 23 (6): 804–818.

Bernardi, Fabrizio. 2005. "Public Policies and Low Fertility: Rationales for Public Intervention and a Diagnosis for the Spanish Case." *Journal of European Social Policy* 15 (2): 123–138.

Bernat, Ignasi, and David Whyte. 2019. "Postfascism in Spain: The Struggle for Catalonia." *Critical Sociology* 46 (4–5): 761–776.

Best, Beverley. 2014. "Speculating Without Hedging." *Critical Discourse Studies* 11 (3): 272–287.

Bettio, Francesca, and Janneke Plantenga. 2004. "Comparing Care Regimes in Europe." *Feminist Economics* 10 (1): 85–113.

Bettio, Francesca, Annamaria Simonazzi, and Paola Villa. 2006. "Change in Care Regimes and Female Migration: The 'Care Drain' in the Mediterranean." *Journal of European Social Policy* 16 (3): 271–285.

Bettio, Francesca, and Paola Villa. 1998. "A Mediterranean Perspective on the Breakdown of the Relationship between Participation and Fertility." *Cambridge Journal of Economics* 22 (2): 137–171.

Bhattacharya, Tithi, ed. 2017a. "How Not to Skip Class: Social Reproduction of Labor and the Global Working Class." In *Social Reproduction Theory. Remapping Class, Recentering Oppression*, edited by Tithi Bhattacharya, 68–93. London: Pluto Press.

Bhattacharya, Tithi, ed. 2017b. "Introduction." In *Social Reproduction Theory. Remapping Class, Recentering Oppression*, 1–20. London: Pluto Press.

Bidet, Jacques. 2019. "Marxism and Left Populism in Southern Europe Today." *International Critical Thought* 9 (3): 365–375.

Biglieri, Paula, and Gloria Perello. 2011. "The Names of the Real in Laclau's Theory: Antagonism, Dislocation, and Heterogeneity." *Filozofski Vestnik* 32 (2): 47–64.

Borriello, Arthur. 2017. "'There Is No Alternative': How Italian and Spanish Leaders' Discourse Obscured the Political Nature of Austerity." *Discourse & Society* 28 (3): 241–261.

Boucher, Geoff. 2009. *The Charmed Circle of Ideology. A Critique of Laclau and Mouffe, Butler and Žižek.* Melbourne: Re.Press.

Boucher, Geoff. 2019. "Tensions in the Post-Althusserian Project: Descriptive Indeterminacy and Normative Uncertainty." In *Discourse, Culture and Organization. Inquiries into Relational Structures of Power*, edited by Tomas Martilla, 299–322. Cham: Palgrave Macmillan.

Bowles, Samuel, and Herbert Gintis. 1986. *Democracy and Capitalism. Property, Community, and the Conditions of Modern Social Thought.* Routledge & Kegan Paul.

Bowles, Samuel, David M. Gordon, and Thomas Weisskopf. 1983. *Beyond the Waste Land: A Democratic Alternative to Economic Decline.* New York: Anchor Books.

Bowles, Samuel, David M. Gordon, and Thomas E. Weisskopf. 1986. "Power and Profits: The Social Structure of Accumulation and the Profitability of the Postwar U. S. Economy." *Review of Radical Political Economics* 18 (2): 132–167.

Bowles, Samuel, David M. Gordon, and Thomas E. Weisskopf. 1989. "Business Ascendancy and Economic Impasse: A Structural Retrospective on Conservative Economics, 1979–87." *The Journal of Economic Perspectives* 3 (1): 107–134.

Bowles, Samuel, David M. Gordon, and Thomas Weisskopf. 1990. *After the Waste Land: Democratic Economics for the Year 2000.* New York: Routledge.

Boyer, Robert. 2010. "The Rise of CEO Pay and the Contemporary Social Structure of Accumulation in the United States." In *Contemporary Capitalism and Its Crises: Social Structure of Accumulation Theory for the 21st Century*, edited by Terrence McDonough, Michael Reich, and David M. Kotz, 215–238. Cambridge: Cambridge University Press.

Braverman, Harry. 1974. *Labor and Monopoly Capital: The Degradation of Work in the Twentieth Century*. New York: Monthly Review Press.

Bray, Michael. 2015. "Rearticulating Contemporary Populism: Class, State, and Neoliberal Society." *Historical Materialism* 23 (3): 27–64.

Bray, Michael. 2018. "*Populisms as Social Reproduction Struggles: An Approach to the Question of 'Left Populism'*." Paper presented at the Historical Materialism Conference, November 2018, London.

Brenner, Robert. 2006. *The Economics of Global Turbulence*. London: Verso.

Briziarelli, Marco. 2018. "Podemos' Twofold Assault on Hegemony: The Possibilities of the Post-Modern Prince and the Perils of Passive Revolution." In *Podemos and the New Political Cycle. Left-Wing Populism and Anti-Establishment Politics*, edited by Óscar García-Agustín and Marco Briziarelli, 97–122. Cham: Palgrave Macmillan.

Brown, Wendy. 1995. *States of Injury: Power and Freedom in Late Modernity*. Princeton, NJ: Princeton University Press.

Bruff, Ian. 2014. "The Rise of Authoritarian Neoliberalism." *Rethinking Marxism* 26 (1): 113–129.

Bruff, Ian. 2016. "Neoliberalism and Authoritarianism." In *The Handbook of Neoliberalism*, edited by Simon Springer, Kean Birch, and Julie MacLeavy, 107–117. London and New York: Routledge.

Bruff, Ian, and Cemal Burak Tansel. 2019. "Authoritarian Neoliberalism: Trajectories of Knowledge Production and Praxis." *Globalizations* 16 (3): 233–244.

Bruff, Ian, and Stefanie Wöhl. 2016. "Constitutionalizing Austerity, Disciplining the Household: Masculine Norms of Competitiveness and the Crisis of Social Reproduction in the Eurozone." In *Scandalous Economics: Gender and the Politics of Financial Crises*, edited by Aida A. Hozic and Jacqui True. Oxford: Oxford University Press.

Buendía, Luis. 2018a. "A Perfect Storm in a Sunny Economy: A Political Economy Approach to the Crisis in Spain." *Socio-Economic Review*. https://doi.org/10.1093/ser/mwy021.

Buendía, Luis. 2018b. "The Spanish Economic 'Miracle' That Never Was." In *Crisis in the Eurozone Periphery*, edited by Owen Parker and Dimitris Tsarouhas, 51–72. London: Palgrave Macmillan.

Buendía, Luis, Ricardo Molero-Simarro, and F. Javier Murillo. 2018. "The Distributive Pattern of the Spanish Economy." In *The Political Economy of Contemporary Spain. From Miracle to Mirage*, edited by Luis Buendía and Ricardo Molero-Simarro, 124–149. London and New York: Routledge.

Bukharin, Nikolai. 1973. *Imperialism and World Economy*. New York: Monthly Review Press.

Bustelo, Pablo. 1994. "El Enfoque de La Regulación En Economía: Una Propuesta Renovadora." *Cuadernos de Relaciones Laborales* 4: 149–163.

Butler, Judith. 1990. *Gender Trouble: Feminism and the Subversion of Identity*. New York: Routledge.

Caïs, Jordi, and Laia Folguera. 2013. "Redefining the Dynamics of Intergenerational Family Solidarity in Spain." *European Societies* 15 (4): 557–576.

Callinicos, Alex. 1976. *Althusser's Marxism*. London: Pluto Press.

Callinicos, Alex. 1993. "What Is Living and What Is Dead in the Philosophy of Althusser." In *The Althusserian Legacy*, edited by Ann E. Kaplan and Michael Sprinker, 39–50. London: Verso.
Callinicos, Alex. 2007. *Social Theory. A Historical Introduction*. Cambridge: Polity.
Calvo, Kerman, and Martín Portos. 2018. "Panic Works. The 'Gag Law' and the Unruly Youth in Spain." In *Governing Youth Politics in the Age of Surveillance. The Criminalization of Political Dissent*, edited by J. Bessant and M. Grasso, 33–47. Abingdon: Routledge.
Calzada, Inés, and Eloísa del Pino. 2011. "Are Spaniards Different? European Convergence and Regional Divergence in the Evaluation of the Welfare State." In *The Spanish Welfare State in the European Context*, edited by Ana M.Guillen and Margarita Leon, 139–161. Burlington, VT: Ashgate.
Camas, Francisco, and José Pablo Ferrándiz. 2020. *Radiografía de unas Elecciones No Deseadas. 10 Notas Sobre El 10N*. Madrid: Catarata.
Campillo, Inés. 2018. "Economic Boom, Recession and Recovery in Spain: The Permanent Care Crisis and Its Effects on Gender Equality. The Search for Feminist Alternatives." *Rosa Luxemburg Stiftung*.
Campillo, Inés. 2019. "'If We Stop, the World Stops': The 2018 Feminist Strike in Spain." *Social Movement Studies* 18 (2): 252–258.
Cano, Ernest. 2007. "La Extensión de la Precariedad Laboral como Norma Social." *Sociedad y utopía: Revista de ciencias sociales* 29: 117–138.
Carballo-Cruz, Francisco. 2011. "Causes and Consequences of the Spanish Economic Crisis: Why the Recovery Is Taken So Long?" *Panoeconomicus* 58 (3): 309–328.
Carbó, Rosa, Marc Pradel Miquel, María Luisa Duarte, and Tomás Herreros Sala. 2005. "La Ultima Oleada de Movilizaciones (2002–2004)." In *La Política En La Red. Anuario de Movimientos Sociales*, edited by Pedro Ibarra and Elena Grau, 34–52. Barcelona: Icaria.
Cárdenas, Luis, Paloma Villanueva, Ignacio Álvarez, and Jorge Uxó. 2018. "Peripheral Europe beyond the Troika. Assessing the 'Success' of Structural Reforms in Driving the Spanish Recovery." *Forum for Macroeconomic and Macroeconomic Polices, Hans-Böckler-Stiftung* 40.
Carmona, Pablo, Beatriz García, and Almudena Sánchez. 2012. *Spanish Neocon. La Revuelta Neoconservadora En La Derecha Española*. Madrid: Traficantes de Sueños.
Castles, Francis G., and Maurizio Ferrera. 1996. "Home Ownership and the Welfare State: Is Southern Europe Different?" *South European Society and Politics* 1 (2): 163–185.
Charnock, Greig, Thomas Purcell, and Ramón Ribera-Fumaz. 2014. *The Limits to Capital in Spain. Crisis and Revolt in the European South*. Houndmills: Palgrave Macmillan.
Charnock, Greig, Thomas Purcell, and Ramón Ribera-Fumaz. 2015. "The Limits to Capital in Spain: The Roots of the 'New Normal.'" *Critique: Journal of Socialist Theory* 43 (2): 173–188.
Clúa-Losada, Mónica, and Olatz Ribera-Almandoz. 2017. "Authoritarian Neoliberalism and the Disciplining of Labour." In *States of Discipline. Authoritarian Neoliberalism and the Contested Reproduction of Capitalist Order*, edited by Cemal Burak Tansel, 29–46. London and New York: Rowman and Littlefield Int.
Conde-Ruiz, J. Ignacio, Florentino Felgueroso, and J. Ignacio García-Pérez. 2011. "Reforma Laboral 2010: Una Primera Evaluación y Propuests de Mejora." *Revista de Economía Aplicada* 19 (57): 147–180.

Coq-Huelva, Daniel. 2013. "Urbanisation and Financialisation in the Context of a Rescaling State: The Case of Spain." *Antipode* 45 (5): 1213–1231.

Coutrot, Thomas. 2008. "The American Radicals: A Subversive Current at the Heart of the Empire." In *Critical Companion to Critical Marxism*, edited by Jacques Bidet and Stathis Kouvelakis, 255–266. Leiden and Boston: Brill.

Creighton, C. 1999. "The Rise and Decline of the 'Male Breadwinner Family' in Britain." *Cambridge Journal of Economics* 23 (5): 519–541.

Crouch, Colin. 2009. "Privatised Keynesianism: An Unacknowledged Policy Regime." *The British Journal of Politics & International Relations* 11 (3): 382–399.

Crouch, Colin, Wolfgang Streeck, Robert Boyer, Bruno Amable, Peter A. Hall, and Gregory Jackson. 2005. "Dialogue on 'Institutional Complementarity and Political Economy.'" *Socio-Economic Review* 3 (2): 359–382.

Dahlberg, Lincoln. 2014. "Capitalism as a Discursive System? Interrogating Discourse Theory's Contribution to Critical Political Economy." *Critical Discourse Studies* 11 (3): 257–271.

Daly, Glyn. 2004. "Radical(Ly) Political Economy. Luhmann, Postmarxism and Globalization." *Review of International Political Economy* 11 (1): 1–32.

De Cleen, Benjamin. 2019. "The Populist Political Logic and the Analysis of the Discursive Construction of 'the People' and 'the Elite'." In *Imagining the Peoples of Europe: Populist Discourses across the Political Spectrum*, edited by Jan Zienkowski and Ruth Breeze, 19–42. Amsterdam: John Benjamins Publishing Company.

De Cleen, Benjamin, and Yannis Stavrakakis. 2017. "Distinctions and Articulations: A Discourse Theoretical Framework for the Study of Populism and Nationalism." *Javnost – The Public* 24 (4): 301–319.

Delgado, Luisa Elena. 2015. *La Nación Singular. Fantasías de La Normalidad Democrática Española (1996–2011)*. Madrid: Siglo XXI.

della Porta, Donatella, Francis O'Connor, and Martín Portos. 2020. "The Framing of Secessionism in the Neo-Liberal Crisis. The Scottish and Catalan Cases." In *Between Democracy and Law. The Amorality of Secession*, 153–170. London and New York: Routledge.

della Porta, Donatella, and Martín Portos. 2020. "A Bourgeois Story? The Class Basis of Catalan Independentism." *Territory, Politics, Governance*. doi:10.1080/21622671.2020.1737208.

Deusdad, Blanca A., Dolors Comas-d'Argemir, and Sophia F. Dziegielewski. 2016. "Restructuring Long-Term Care in Spain: The Impact of The Economic Crisis on Social Policies and Social Work Practice." *Journal of Social Service Research* 42 (2): 246–262.

De Weerdt, Julie, and Marisol Garcia. 2016. "Housing Crisis. The Platform of Mortgage Victims (PAH) Movement in Barcelona and Innovations in Governance." *Journal of Housing and the Built Environment* 31 (3): 471–493.

Di Feliciantonio, Cesare. 2017. "Social Movements and Alternative Housing Models: Practicing the 'Politics of Possibilities' in Spain." *Housing, Theory and Society* 34 (1): 38–56.

Diskin, Jonathan. 1992. "An Essay on Post-Marxism, Democracy and Class." *Review of Radical Political Economics* 24 (2): 139–145.

Diskin, Jonathan, and Blair Sandler. 1993. "Essentialism and the Economy in the Post-Marxist Imaginary: Reopening the Sutures." *Rethinking Marxism* 6 (3): 28–48.

Doeringer, Peter B., and Michael J. Piore. 1971. *Internal Labor Markets and Manpower Analysis*. Lexington, MA: D.C. Heath and Company.

Edwards, Richard. 1979. *Contested Terrain: The Transformation of the Workplace in the Twentieth Century*. New York: Basic Books.

Edwards, Richard, Michael Reich, and David M. Gordon, eds. 1975. *Labor Market Segmentation*. Lexington, MA: D.C. Heath and Company.

Elliot, Gregory. 1993. "Althusser's Solitude." In *The Althusserian Legacy*, edited by E. Ann Kaplan and Michael Sprinkler, 17–38. London and New York: Verso.

Elliot, Gregory. 2006. *Althusser. The Detour of Theory*. Leiden and Boston: Brill.

Engels, Friedrich. 1890a. "Letter to Conrad Schmidt, London, October 27, 1890," 1890. https://www.marxists.org/archive/marx/works/1890/letters/90_10_27.htm.

Engels, Friedrich. 1890b. "Letter to J. Bloch, London, September 21, 1890," 1890. https://www.marxists.org/archive/marx/works/1890/letters/90_09_21.htm.

Engels, Friedrich. 1894. "Letter to Borgius, London, January 25, 1894," 1894. https://www.marxists.org/archive/marx/works/1894/letters/94_01_25a.htm.

Engels, Friedrich. 1978. *Anti-Dühring, o La Revolución de La Ciencia de Eugenio Dühring*. Madrid: Ayuso.

Errejón, Iñigo. 2011. "El 15-M como discurso contrahegemónico." *Encrucijadas – Revista Crítica de Ciencias Sociales* 2: 120–145.

Errejón, Iñigo. 2014. "Vamos a Construir Una Maquinaria de Guerra Electoral," 2014. https://www.publico.es/actualidad/construir-maquinaria-guerra-electoral.html.

Esping-Andersen, Gøsta. 1990. *The Three Worlds of Welfare Capitalism*. Oxford: Polity Press.

Esping-Andersen, Gøsta. 1999. *Social Foundations of Post-Industrial Economies*. New York: Oxford University Press.

Espinoza-Pino, Mario. 2013. "Politics of Indignation: Radical Democracy and Class Struggle beyond Postmodernity." *Rethinking Marxism* 25 (2): 228–241.

Estrada, Ángel, Juan Francisco Jimeno, and José Luis Malo de Molina. 2009. "La Economía Española en la UEM. Los Diez Primeros Años." *Documentos ocasionales – Banco de España*.

Etchemendy, Sebastián. 2004. "Revamping the Weak, Protecting the Strong, and Managing Privatization: Governing Globalization in the Spanish Takeoff." *Comparative Political Studies* 37 (6): 623–651.

Etxezarreta, Miren. 1991. "La Economía Política Del Proceso de Acumulación." In *La Reestructuración Del Capitalismo En España, 1970–1990*, edited by Miren Etxezarreta, 31–94. Barcelona: Icaria.

EUROSTAT (2020). *Government Finance Statistics*.

Ezquerra, Sandra. 2012. "Acumulación por desposesión, género y crisis en el estado español." *Revista de Economía Crítica* 14: 124–147.

Fassin, Eric. 2018. "Left-Wing Populism. A Legacy of Defeat." *Radical Philosophy* 2 (June): 79–93.

FBBVA. 2020. *El Stock y los Servicios del Capital en España y su Distribución Territorial y Sectorial (1964–2016)*. Valencia: Fundación BBVA-IVIE.

Febrero, Eladio, Ignacio Álvarez, and Jorge Uxó. 2019. "Current Account Imbalances or Too Much Bank Debt as the Main Driver of Gross Capital Inflows? Spain During the Great Financial Crisis." *Journal of Economic Issues* 53 (4): 1126–1151.

Fernández, Rafael, and Clara García. 2018. "Wheels within Wheels within Wheels: The Importance of Capital Inflows in the Origin of the Spanish Financial Crisis." *Cambridge Journal of Economics* 42 (2): 331–353.

Fernández-Albertos, José. 2015. *Los Votantes de Podemos. Del Partido de Los Indignados al Partido de Los Excluídos*. Madrid: Catarata.

Fernández-Rodríguez, Carlos, Rafael Ibáñez-Rojo, and Miguel Martínez-Lucio. 2016. "Austerity and Collective Bargaining in Spain: The Political and Dysfunctional Nature of Neoliberal Deregulation" *European Journal of Industrial Relations* 22 (3): 267–280.
Fernández-Savater, Amador. 2012. "El Nacimiento de Un Nuevo Poder Social." *Hispanic Review* 80 (4): 667–681.
Fernández-Savater, Amador. 2013. "La Cultura de La Transición y El Nuevo Sentido Común." *Eldiario.Es*, June 14, 2013. https://www.eldiario.es/interferencias/Cultura_de_la_Transicion-segunda_transicion_6_113798632.html.
Ferrada-Stoehrel, Rodrigo. 2017. "The Regime's Worst Nightmare: The Mobilization of Citizen Democracy. A Study of Podemos' (Aesthetic) Populism and the Production of Affect in Political Discourse." *Cultural Studies* 31 (4): 543–579.
Ferrera, Maurizio. 1996. "The 'Southern Model' of Welfare in Social Europe." *Journal of European Social Policy* 6 (1): 17–37.
Ferrera, Maurizio. 2010. "The Southern Countries." In *The Oxford Handbook of the Welfare State*, edited by Francis G. Castles, Stephan Leibfried, Jane Lewis, Herbert Obinger, and Christopher Pierson, 616–629. Oxford: Oxford University Press.
Flaquer, Lluis. 2001. "Is There a Southern European Model of Family Policy?" In *Families and Family Policies in Europe. Comparative Perspectives*, 15–33. Brussels: Peter Lang.
Flesher-Fominaya, Cristina. 2007. "Autonomous Movements and the Institutional Left: Two Approaches in Tension in Madrid's Anti-Globalization Network." *South European Society and Politics* 12 (3): 335–358.
Flesher-Fominaya, Cristina. 2015. "Debunking Spontaneity: Spain's 15-M/Indignados as Autonomous Movement." *Social Movement Studies* 14 (2): 142–163.
Formenti, Carlo. 2017. *La Variante Populista. Lucha de Clases en el Neoliberalismo*. Barcelona: El Viejo Topo.
Franzé, Javier. 2018. "The Podemos Discourse: A Journey from Antagonism to Agonism." In *Podemos and the New Political Cycle. Left-Wing Populism and Anti-Establishment Politics*, edited by Óscar García-Agustín and Marco Briziarelli, 49–74. Cham: Palgrave Macmillan.
Fraser, Nancy. 2014. "Behind Marx's Hidden Abode." *New Left Review* 86: 55–72.
Fraser, Nancy. 2015. "Legitimation Crisis? On the Political Contradictions of Financialized Capitalism." *Critical Historical Studies* 2 (2): 157–189.
Freud, Sigmund. 1976. *The Interpretation of Dreams*. Harmondsworth: Penguin Books.
Gabarre, Manuel. 2019. *Tocar Fondo. La Mano Invisible Detrás de La Subida Del Alquiler*. Madrid: Traficantes de Sueños.
Gálvez, Lina, and Paula Rodríguez-Modroño. 2013. "El empleo de las mujeres en la España democrática y el impacto de la Gran Recesión." *Areas: Revista internacional de ciencias sociales* 32: 105–123.
Gálvez, Lina, and Paula Rodríguez-Modroño. 2016. "A Gender Analysis of the Great Recession and 'Austericide' in Spain." *Revista Crítica de Ciências Sociais* 111: 133–152.
Gálvez, Lina, Paula Rodríguez-Modroño, and Mónica Domínguez-Serrano. 2011. "Work and Time-Use by Gender. A New Clustering of European Welfare Systems." *Feminist Economics* 17 (4): 125–157.
García, Beatriz, Nuria Alabao, and Marisa Pérez. 2010. "Spain's Feminist Strike." *New Left Review* 110: 35–37.
García-Agustín, Óscar, and Marco Briziarelli. 2018. "Left-Wing Populism and the Assault on the Establishment." In *Podemos and the New Political Cycle. Left-Wing Populism and Anti-Establishment Politics*, edited by Óscar García-Agustín and Marco Briziarelli, 281–294. Cham: Palgrave Macmillan.

García-Lamarca, Melissa. 2017a. "From Occupying Plazas to Recuperating Housing: Insurgent Practices in Spain." *International Journal of Urban and Regional Research* 41 (1): 37–53.

García-Lamarca, Melissa. 2017b. "Creating Political Subjects: Collective Knowledge and Action to Enact Housing Rights in Spain." *Community Development Journal* 52 (3): 421–435.

Garzón, Eduardo, Bibiana Medialdea, and Antonio Sanabria. 2018. "The Spanish Financial Sector: Debt Crisis and Bailout." In *The Political Economy of Contemporary Spain. From Miracle to Mirage*, edited by Luis Buendía and Ricardo Molero-Simarro, 77–97. London and New York: Routledge.

Geras, Norman. 1987. "Post-Marxism?" *New Left Review* 163: 40–82.

Gerbaudo, Paolo. 2017. "The Indignant Citizen. Anti-Austerity Movements in Southern Europe and the Anti-Oligarchic Reclaiming of Citizenship." *Social Movement Studies* 16 (1): 36–50.

Gibson-Graham, J.K. 1996. *The End of Capitalism (as We Knew It). A Feminist Critique of Political Economy*. Cambridge: Basil Blackwell.

Gillespie, Michael D. 2013. "The Economic Deterioration of the Family: Historical Contingencies Preceding the Great Recession." *American Journal of Economics and Sociology* 72 (2): 329–360.

Glynos, Jason, and David R. Howarth. 2007. *Logics of Critical Explanation in Social and Political Theory*. New York: Routledge.

Gómez Uranga, Mikel. 1991. "La Internacionalización de La Economía Española: Un Proceso Acelerado." In *La Reestructuración Del Capitalismo En España, 1970–1990*, edited by Miren Etxezarreta, 465–500. Barcelona: Icaria.

González i Calvet, Josep. 1991. "Transformación Del Sector Público e Intervención En La Economía." In *La Reestructuración Del Capitalismo En España, 1970–1990*, edited by Miren Etxezarreta, 177–238. Barcelona: Icaria.

González-Gago, Elvira, and Marcelo Segales-Kirzner. 2014. "Women, Gender Equality and the Economic Crisis in Spain." In *Women and Austerity. The Economic Crisis and the Future for Gender Equality*, edited by Maria Karamessini and Jill Rubery, 228–247. London and New York: Routledge.

Gordon, David M. 1980. "Stages of Accumulation and Long Economic Cycles." In *Processes of the World System*, edited by T.K. Hopkins and Immanuel Wallerstein, 9–45. Beverly Hills, CA: Sage.

Gordon, David M., Richard Edwards, and Michael Reich. 1982. *Segmented Work, Divided Workers*. Cambridge: Cambridge University Press.

Gordon, David M., Thomas Weisskopf, and Samuel Bowles. 1987. "Power, Accumulation and Crises: The Rise and Demise of the Postwar Social Structure of Accumulation." In *The Imperiled Economy: Macroeconomics from a Left Perspective*, edited by Robert Cherry and Thomas Michl, 43–58. New York: URPE.

Gracia, Manuel, and María José Paz. 2018. "Spain's External Insertion. Peripheral or Not?" In *The Political Economy of Contemporary Spain. From Miracle to Mirage*, edited by Luis Buendía and Ricardo Molero-Simarro, 49–76. London and New York: Routledge.

Gramsci, Antonio. 2013. *Antología. Selección, Traducción y Notas de Manuel Sacristán*. Madrid: Akal.

Guillén, Ana M. 2010. "Defrosting the Spanish Welfare State: The Weight of Conservative Components." In *A Long Goodbye to Bismarck?* edited by Bruno Palier, 183–206. Amsterdam: Amsterdam University Press.

Hall, Peter A., and David Soskice. 2001. "An Introduction to Varieties of Capitalism." In *Varieties of Capitalism. The Institutional Foundations of Comparative Advantage*, edited by Peter A. Hall and David Soskice, 1–69. Oxford: Oxford University Press.

Hamza, Agon. 2017. "Re-Reading Capital 150 Years After. Some Philosophical and Political Challenges." *Continental Thought & Theory. A Journal of Intellectual Freedom* 1 (4): 153–176.

Hansen, Alan D. 2008. "*Laclauian Discourse Theory and the Problem of Institutions*." Paper Presented at the second Global International Studies Conference. Ljubljana.

Harrison, Oliver. 2014. *Revolutionary Subjectivity in Post-Marxist Thought. Laclau, Negri, Badiou*. Burlington: Ashgate.

Hellgren, Zenia, and Inmaculada Serrano. 2019. "Financial Crisis and Migrant Domestic Workers in Spain. Employment Opportunities and Conditions during the Great Recession." *International Migration Review* 53 (4): 1209–1229.

Hernández Marco, Jose Luis. 2012. "La Economía Durante La Etapa de Los Gobiernos Socialistas." In *Historia Económica de España*, edited by Agustín González Enciso and Juan Manuel Matés Barco, 795–818. Barcelona: Ariel.

Hilferding, Rudolf. 1980. *Finance Capital*. London: Routledge and Kegan Paul.

Hirschman, Albert O. 1970. *Exit, Voice and Loyalty: Responses to Decline in Firms, Organizations and States*. Cambridge, MA: Harvard University Press.

Howarth, David. 2013. *Poststructuralism and After. Structure, Subjectivity and Power*. Basingstoke: Palgrave Macmillan.

Ibáñez, Zyab, and Margarita León. 2014. "Resisting Care Crisis at What Cost? Migrant Care Workers in Private Households." In *Migration and Care Labour. Theory, Policy and Politics*, edited by Bridget Anderson and Isabel Shutes, 110–129. Basingstoke: Palgrave Macmillan.

INE. 2020a. *Spanish National Accounts*.

INE. 2020b. *Survey of Living Conditions*.

INE. 2020c. *Labor Force Survey*.

INE. 2020d. *Continuous Population Register Statistics*.

Jacobs, Thomas. 2019. "Poststructuralist Discourse Theory as an Independent Paradigm for Studying Institutions: Towards a New Definition of 'Discursive Construction' in Institutional Analysis." *Contemporary Political Theory* 18 (3): 379–401.

Jaffee, David. 2019. "The Current Crisis of US Neoliberal Capitalism and Prospects for a New 'Social Structure of Accumulation'." *Review of Radical Political Economics* 51 (2): 193–210.

Jessop, Bob. 2019. "Critical Discourse Analysis in Laclau and Mouffe's Post-Marxism." *Simbiótica* 6 (2): 8–30.

Juste, Rubén. 2017. *IBEX 35. Una Historia Herética Del Poder*. Madrid: Capitan Swing.

Kalleberg, Arne L. 2009. "Precarious Work, Insecure Workers: Employment Relations in Transition." *American Sociological Review* 74 (1): 1–22.

Karamessini, Maria. 2008. "Still a Distinctive Southern European Employment Model?" *Industrial Relations Journal* 39 (6): 510–531.

Katsambekis, Giorgos, and Alexandrod Kioupkiolis. 2019. "Introduction. The Populist Radical Left in Europe." In *The Populist Radical Left in Europe*, edited by Giorgos Katsambekis and Alexandros Kioupkiolis, 1–20. Abingdon: Routledge.

Kemeny, Jim. 1981. *The Myth of Home Ownership*. London: Routledge.

Kioupkiolis, Alexandros. 2016. "Podemos: The Ambiguous Promises of Left-Wing Populism in Contemporary Spain." *Journal of Political Ideologies* 21 (2): 99–120.

Kitschelt, Herbert. 2006. "Movement Parties." In *Handbook of Party Politics*, edited by Richard Katz and William J. Crotty, 278–290. London: Sage.
Kondratiev, Nikolai D. 1935. "The Long Waves in Economic Life." *Review of Economic Statistics* 17 (6): 105–115.
Kotz, David M. 1994a. "Interpreting the Social Structure of Accumulation Approach." In *Social Structures of Accumulation: The Political Economy of Growth and Crisis*, edited by David M. Kotz, Terrence McDonough, and Michael Reich, 50–71. Cambridge: Cambridge University Press.
Kotz, David M. 1994b. "Regulation Theory and the Social Structure of Accumulation Approach." In *Social Structures of Accumulation: The Political Economy of Growth and Crisis*, edited by David M. Kotz, Terrence McDonough, and Michael Reich, 85–98. Cambridge: Cambridge University Press.
Kotz, David M. 2002. "Globalization and Neoliberalism." *Rethinking Marxism* 14 (2): 64–79.
Kotz, David M. 2003a. "Neoliberalism and the US Economic Expansion in the 1990s." *Monthly Review* 54 (11): 15–33.
Kotz, David M. 2003b. "Neoliberalism and the Social Structure of Accumulation Theory of Long-Run Capital Accumulation." *Review of Radical Political Economics* 35 (3): 263–270.
Kotz, David M. 2006. "Institutional Structure or Social Structures of Accumulation." In *Growth and Crisis: Social Structure of Accumulation Theory and Analysis*, edited by Terrence McDonough, Michael Reich, David M. Kotz, and María Alejandra González-Pérez, 50–57. Galway: SSRC and CISC at the National University of Ireland.
Kotz, David M. 2009. "Economic Crises and Institutional Structures: A Comparison of Regulated and Neoliberal Capitalism in the U.S." In *Heterodox Macroeconomics: Keynes, Marx and Globalization*, edited by Jonathan Goldstein and Michael Hillard, 176–188. London and New York: Routledge.
Kotz, David M. 2010a. "Financialization and Neoliberalism." In *Relations of Global Power: Neoliberal Order and Disorder*, edited by Gary Teeple and Stephen McBride, 1–18. Toronto: University of Toronto Press.
Kotz, David M. 2010b. "The Final Conflict. What Can Cause a System-Threatening Crisis of Capitalism." *Science and Society* 74 (3): 362–379.
Kotz, David M. 2013a. "Social Structures of Accumulation, the Rate of Profit, and Economic Crises." In *Capitalism on Trial. Explorations in the Tradition of Thomas E. Weisskopf*, edited by Robert Pollin and Jeanette Wick-Lim, 335–349. Cheltenham: Edward Elgar.
Kotz, David M. 2013b. "The Current Economic Crisis in the United States: A Crisis of Over-Investment." *Review of Radical Political Economics* 45 (3): 284–294.
Kotz, David M. 2015. "Capitalism and Forms of Capitalism: Levels of Abstraction in Economic Crisis Theory." *Review of Radical Political Economics* 47 (4): 541–549.
Kotz, David M. 2017. "Social Structure of Accumulation Theory, Marxist Theory, and System Transformation." *Review of Radical Political Economics* 49 (4): 534–542.
Kotz, David M., and Deepankar Basu. 2019. "Stagnation and Institutional Structures." *Review of Radical Political Economics* 51 (1): 5–30.
Kotz, David M., and Terrence McDonough. 2010. "Global Neoliberalism and the Contemporary Social Structure of Accumulation." In *Contemporary Capitalism and Its Crises: Social Structure of Accumulation Theory for the 21st Century*, edited by Terrence McDonough, Michael Reich, and David M. Kotz, 93–120. Cambridge: Cambridge University Press.

Kotz, David M., and Martin H. Wolfson. 2004. "Deja Vu All Over Again: The 'New' Economy in Historical Perspective." *Labor Studies Journal* 28 (4): 25–44.

La Parra-Pérez, Pablo. 2014. "Revueltas Lógicas: El Ciclo de Movilización Del 15M y La Práctica de La Democracia Radical." *Journal of Spanish Cultural Studies* 15 (1–2): 39–57.

Labio-Bernal, Aurora. 2018. "Anti-Communism and the Mainstream Online Press in Spain: Criticism of Podemos as a Strategy of a Two-Party System in Crisis." In *The Propaganda Model Today: Filtering Perception and Awareness*, edited by Joan Pedro-Carañana, Daniel Broudy, and Jeffery Klaehn, 125–141. London: University of Westminster Press.

Laclau, Ernesto. 1979. *Politics and Ideology In Marxist Theory. Capitalism, Fascism, Populism*. London: Verso.

Laclau, Ernesto. 1990a. *New Reflections on the Revolution of Our Time*. London: Verso.

Laclau, Ernesto. 1990b. "Theory, Democracy, Socialism." In *New Reflections on the Revolution of Our Time*, 197–248. London: Verso.

Laclau, Ernesto. 1996a. "Deconstruction, Pragmatism, Hegemony." In *Deconstruction and Pragmatism*, edited by Chantal Mouffe, 47–68. London and New York: Routledge.

Laclau, Ernesto. 1996b. *Emancipation(s)*. London: Verso.

Laclau, Ernesto. 1996c. "Why Do Empty Signifiers Matter to Politics?" In *Emancipation (s)*, 36–46. London: Verso.

Laclau, Ernesto. 1996d. "The Death and Resurrection of the Theory of Ideology." *Journal of Political Ideologies* 1 (3): 201–220.

Laclau, Ernesto. 2000a. "Constructing Universality." In *Contingency, Hegemony, Universality. Contemporary Dialogues on the Left*, edited by Judith Butler, Ernesto Laclau, and Slavoj Žižek, 281–307. London: Verso.

Laclau, Ernesto. 2000b. "Identity and Hegemony: The Role of Universality in the Constitution of Political Logics." In *Contingency, Hegemony, Universality. Contemporary Dialogues on the Left*, edited by Judith Butler, Ernesto Laclau, and Slavoj Žižek, 44–89. London: Verso.

Laclau, Ernesto. 2000c. "Structure, History and the Political." In *Contingency, Hegemony, Universality. Contemporary Dialogues on the Left*, by Judith Butler, Ernesto Laclau, and Slavoj Žižek, 182–212. London: Verso.

Laclau, Ernesto. 2005a. *On Populist Reason*. London: Verso.

Laclau, Ernesto. 2005b. "Populism: What's in a Name?" In *Populism and the Mirror of Democracy*, edited by Francisco Panizza, 32–49. London: Verso.

Laclau, Ernesto. 2006. "Why Constructing a People Is the Main Task of Radical Politics." *Critical Inquiry* 32 (4): 646–680.

Laclau, Ernesto, and Chantal Mouffe. 1987. "Post-Marxism Without Apologies." *New Left Review* I (166): 79–106.

Laclau, Ernesto, and Chantal Mouffe. 2001. *Hegemony and Socialist Strategy: Towards a Radical Democratic Politics*. London: Verso.

Lancaster, Thomas D. 2017. "The Spanish General Elections of 2015 and 2016. A New Stage in Democratic Politics?" *West European Politics* 40 (4): 919–937.

Leitner, Sigrid. 2003. "Varieties of Familialism: The Caring Function of the Family in Comparative Perspective." *European Societies* 5 (4): 353–375.

Lenin, V.I. 1917. "Imperialism. The Highest Stage of Capitalism." https://www.marxists.org/archive/lenin/works/1916/imp-hsc/.

León, Margarita, and Emmanuele Pavolini. 2014. "'Social Investment' or Back to 'Familism': The Impact of the Economic Crisis on Family and Care Policies in Italy and Spain." *South European Society and Politics* 19 (3): 353–369.

Lewis, William. 2005. "The Under-Theorization of Hegemony in 'Hegemony and Socialist Strategy'." *Borderlands E-Journal* 4 (2).

Lipietz, Alain. 1979. *Crise et Inflation. Pourquoi?*Paris: François Maspero.

Lipietz, Alain. 1987. "Rebel Sons: The Regulation School." *French Politics and Society* 5 (4).

Lipietz, Alain. 1993. "From Althusserianism to 'Regulation Theory.'" In *The Althusserian Legacy*, edited by E. Ann Kaplan and Michael Sprinkler, 99–138. London and New York: Verso.

Lippit, Victor D. 1997. "The Reconstruction of a Social Structure of Accumulation in the United States." *Review of Radical Political Economics* 29 (3): 11–21.

Lippit, Victor D. 2005. *Capitalism*. London and New York: Routledge.

Lippit, Victor D. 2010. "Social Structure of Accumulation Theory." In *Contemporary Capitalism and Its Crises: Social Structure of Accumulation Theory for the 21st Century*, edited by Terrence McDonough, Michael Reich, and David M. Kotz, 45–71. Cambridge: Cambridge University Press.

Lippit, Victor D. 2014. "The Neoliberal Era and the Financial Crisis in the Light of SSA Theory." *Review of Radical Political Economics* 46 (2): 141–161.

Lombardo, Emanuela. 2017. "Austerity Politics and Feminist Struggles in Spain: Reconfiguring the Gender Regime?" In *Gender and the Economic Crisis in Europe. Politics, Institutions and Intersectionality*, edited by Johanna Kantola and Emanuela Lombardo, 209–230. Cham: Palgrave Macmillan.

López, Isidro, and Emmanuel Rodríguez. 2010. *Fin de Ciclo. Financiarización, Territorio y Sociedad de Propietarios En La Onda Larga Del Capitalismo Hispano (1959–2010)*. Madrid: Traficantes de Sueños.

López, Isidro, and Emmanuel Rodríguez. 2019. "Del Discurso de La Recuperación a Una Nueva Crisis Política." *Viento Sur* 162: 97–108.

López-Andreu, Martí. 2019. "Employment Institutions under Liberalization Pressures: Analysing the Effects of Regulatory Change on Collective Bargaining in Spain." *British Journal of Industrial Relations* 57 (2): 328–349.

López-Andreu, Martí, and Jill Rubery. 2018. "Austerity and Women's Employment Trajectories in Spain and the UK: A Comparison of Two Flexible Labour Markets." *Economic and Industrial Democracy*, March.

López-Andreu, Martí, and Joan Miquel Verd. 2016. "Employment Instability and Economic Crisis in Spain: What Are the Elements That Make a Difference in the Trajectories of Younger Adults?" *European Societies* 18 (4): 315–335.

López-Andreu, Martí, and Joan Miquel Verd. 2020. "The Impact of Neoliberal Policies During the Great Recession on Youth Transition Regimes in Spain and the UK." *Critical Sociology*. Forthcoming.

Lux, Julia, and Stefanie Wöhl. 2015. "Gender Inequalities in the Crisis of Capitalism. Spain and France Compared." In *New Directions in Comparative Capitalisms Research*, edited by Matthias Ebenau, Ian Bruff, and Christian May, 101–117. London: Palgrave Macmillan.

Mandel, Ernest. 1995. *Long Waves of Capitalist Development. A Marxist Interpretation*. London: Verso.

Marchart, Oliver. 2007. *Post-Foundational Political Thought. Political Difference in Nancy, Lefort, Badiou and Laclau*. Edinburgh: Edinburgh University Press.

Marí-Klose, Pau, and Francisco Javier Moreno-Fuentes. 2013. "The Southern European Welfare Model in the Post-Industrial Order." *European Societies* 15 (4): 475–492.

Martín, Irene. 2015. "Podemos y otros Modelos de Partido-movimiento." *Revista Española de Sociología* 24.

Martínez, Guillem, ed. 2012. *CT o La Cultura de La Transición: Crítica a 35 Años de Cultura Española*. Barcelona: DeBolsillo.

Marx, Karl (1977 [1859]) *A Contribution to the Critique of Political Economy*. Moscow: Progress Publishers. https://www.marxists.org/archive/marx/works/1859/critique-pol-economy/preface.htm.

Marx, Karl and Frederick Engels (2010 [1848]) *The Communist Manifesto*. London: Bookmarks Publications.

Mateo, Juan Pablo. 2019. *The Theory of Crisis and the Great Recession in Spain*. Cham: Palgrave Macmillan.

Mateo, Juan Pablo, and Miguel Montanyà. 2018. "The Accumulation Model of the Spanish Economy: Profitability, the Real Estate Bubble, and Sectorial Imbalances." In *The Political Economy of Contemporary Spain. From Miracle to Mirage*, edited by Luis Buendía and Ricardo Molero-Simarro, 20–48. London and New York: Routledge.

Maura, Eduardo. 2018. *Los 90. Euforia y Miedo En La Modernidad Democrática Española*. Madrid: Akal.

Mavroudeas, Stavros. 2006. "Social Structures of Accumulation, Regulation Approach and Stages Theory." In *Growth and Crisis.: Social Structure of Accumulation Theory and Analysis*, edited by Terrence McDonough, Michael Reich, David M. Kotz, and María Alejandra González-Pérez, 200–216. Galway: SSRC and CISC at the National University of Ireland.

McDonough, Terrence. 1994a. "Social Structure of Accumulation Theory, Contingent History and Stages of Capitalism." In *Social Structures of Accumulation: The Political Economy of Growth and Crisis*, edited by David M. Kotz, Terrence McDonough, and Michael Reich, 72–84. Cambridge: Cambridge University Press.

McDonough, Terrence. 1994b. "The Construction of Social Structures of Accumulation in US History." In *Social Structures of Accumulation: The Political Economy of Growth and Crisis*, edited by David M. Kotz, Terrence McDonough, and Michael Reich, 101–132. New York: Cambridge University Press.

McDonough, Terrence. 2003. "What Does Long Wave Theory Have to Contribute to the Debate on Globalization?" *Review of Radical Political Economics* 35 (3): 280–286.

McDonough, Terrence. 2010. "The State of the Art of Social Structure of Accumulation Theory." In *Contemporary Capitalism and Its Crises: Social Structure of Accumulation Theory for the 21st Century*, edited by Terrence McDonough, Michael Reich, and David M. Kotz, 23–44. Cambridge: Cambridge University Press.

McDonough, Terrence. 2011. "Social Structures of Accumulation: A 'Punctuated' View of Embeddedness." *American Journal of Economics and Sociology* 70 (5): 1234–1247.

McDonough, Terrence. 2015. "Social Structures of Accumulation. A Marxist Comparison of Capitalisms?" In *New Directions in Comparative Capitalisms Research. Critical and Global Perspectives*, edited by Matthias Ebenau, Ian Bruff, and Christian May, 118–133. London: Palgrave Macmillan.

McDonough, Terrence, and Emlyn Nardone. 2006. "Social Structures of Accumulation, the Regulation Approach and the European Union." *Competition & Change* 10 (2): 200–212.

McDonough, Terrence, Michael Reich, and David M. Kotz. 2010. "Introduction." In *Contemporary Capitalism and Its Crises: Social Structure of Accumulation Theory for the 21st Century*, edited by Terrence McDonough, Michael Reich, and David M. Kotz, 1–19. Cambridge: Cambridge University Press.

Medina, Iván, and Patricia Correa. 2016. "The 2015 Spanish Election: The Times They Are a' Changing." *Regional & Federal Studies* 26 (3): 407–417.

Miklitsch, Robert. 1995. "The Rhetoric of Post-Marxism. Discourse and Institutionality in Laclau and Mouffe, Resnick and Wolff." *Social Text* 45 (Winter): 167–196.

Milanovic, Branko. 2016. *Global Inequality. A New Approach for the Age of Globalization.* Cambridge, MA: Harvard University Press.

Mingione, Enzo. 1995. "Labour Market Segmentation and Informal Work in Southern Europe." *European Urban and Regional Studies* 2 (2): 121–143.

Miró, Joan. 2017. "Las Tensiones del Populismo en el Poder. Pueblo e instituciones en la Teoría de Ernesto Laclau." *Inguruak* 62: 19–38.

Miró, Joan. 2019. "Beyond Populism and Institutionalism: Anti-Populism and the Management of Austerity in Spain." *Constellations* 26 (1): 116–131.

Miró, Joan. 2020. "The Tensions of Populism in Power. A Discursive-Theoretical Analysis of the Catalan Secessionist Push (2006–2017)." *Distinktion. Journal of Social Theory.* Forthcoming.

Montag, Warren. 2013. *Althusser and His Contemporaries. Philosophy's Perpetual War.* Durham and London: Duke University Press.

Montag, Warren. 2018. "The Last Instance. Resnick and Wolff at the Point of Heresy." In *Knowledge, Class and Economics. Marxism without Guarantees*, edited by Theodore Burczak, Robert Garnett, and Richard McIntyre, 171–175. Abingdon: Routledge.

Montes, Pedro. 1993. *La Integración En Europa: Del Plan de Estabilización a Maastricht.* Madrid: Trotta.

Moreno, Luis. 2004. "Spain's Transition to New Risks. A Farewell to 'Superwoman'." *Documentos de Trabajo CSIC.*

Moreno, Luis, and Amparo Serrano. 2011. "Europeanization and Spanish Welfare: The Case of Employment Policy." In *The Spanish Welfare State In European Context*, edited by Ana M. Guillen and Margarita Leon, 39–58. Burlington, VT: Ashgate.

Moreno-Caballud, Luis. 2015. *Cultures of Anyone. Studies on Cultural Democratization in the Spanish Neoliberal Crisis.* Liverpool: Liverpool University Press.

Moreno-Colom, Sara, Carolina Recio, Teresa Torns, and Vicente Borràs. 2017. "Long-Term Care in Spain: Difficulties in Professionalizing Services." *Journal of Women & Aging* 29 (3): 200–215.

Moreno Mínguez, Almudena. 2007. *Familia y Empleo de La Mujer En Los Regímenes de Bienestar Del Sur de Europa.* Madrid: Centro de Investigaciones Sociologicas.

Moseley, Fred. 2013. "Comment on Kotz, Skillman, and Thompson." In *Capitalism on Trial. Explorations in the Tradition of Thomas E. Weisskopf*, edited by Robert Pollin and Jeanette Wick-Lim, 381–384. Cheltenham: Edward Elgar.

Mouffe, Chantal. 2005. *On the Political.* New York: Routledge.

Mouffe, Chantal. 2017. "Interview with Chantal Mouffe: 'We Urgently Need to Promote a Left-Wing Populism'." 2017. https://www.versobooks.com/blogs/3341-chantal- mouffe-we-urgently-need-to-promote-a-left-populism.

Mouffe, Chantal. 2018. *For a Left Populism.* London: Verso.

Mouzelis, Nicos. 1988. "Marxism or Post-Marxism?" *New Left Review* 167: 107–123.

MTMUA. 2020. *Statistical Information.* Ministry of Transport, Mobility and Urban Agenda.

Muñoz de Bustillo, Rafael, and José-Ignacio Antón. 2013. "Those Were the Days, My Friend. The Public Sector and the Economic Crisis in Spain." In *Public Sector Shock. The Impact of Policy Retrenchment in Europe*, edited by Daniel Vaughan-Whitehead, 511–543. Cheltenham: Edward Elgar.

Muñoz de Bustillo, Rafael, and Fernando Esteve. 2017. "The Neverending Story. Labour Market Deregulation and the Performance of the Spanish Labour Market."

In *Myths of Employment Deregulation. How It Neither Creates Jobs nor Reduces Labour Market Segmentation*, 61–80. Brussels: ETUI.

Nardone, Emlyn, and Terrence McDonough. 2010. "Global Neoliberalism and the Possibility of Transnational State Structures." In *Contemporary Capitalism and Its Crises: Social Structure of Accumulation Theory for the 21st Century*, edited by Terrence McDonough, Michael Reich, and David M. Kotz, 168–193. Cambridge: Cambridge University Press.

Naredo, José Manuel. 1996. *La Burbuja Inmobiliario-Financiera En La Coyuntura Económica Reciente (1985–1995)*. Madrid: Siglo XXI de España.

Naredo, José Manuel. 2009. "La Cara Oculta de la Crisis: El Fin del Boom Inmobiliario y sus Consecuencias." *Revista de economía crítica* 7: 118–133.

Naredo, José Manuel. 2010. "Entrevista." *El Blog de José Fariña* (blog). July 23, 2010. https://elblogdefarina.blogspot.com/2010_07_01_archive.html.

Naredo, José Manuel. 2019. *Taxonomía Del Lucro*. Madrid: Siglo XXI.

Naredo, José Manuel, and Antonio Montiel. 2011. *El Modelo Inmobiliario Español y Su Culminación En El Caso Valenciano*. Barcelona: Icaria.

Naredo, José Manuel, Oscar Carpintero Redondo, and Carmen Marcos. 2008. *Patrimonio Inmobiliario y Balance Nacional de la Economía Española (1995–2007)*. Madrid: Fundacion Cajas de Ahorros.

Nieto, Maximiliano. 2006. "Tendencias de la Rentabilidad y la Acumulación en el Capitalismo Español (1954–2003)." *Revista de Economía Institucional* 8 (15): 185–206.

Norton, Bruce. 1988. "The Power Axis: Bowles, Gordon, and Weisskopf's Theory of Postwar U.S. Accumulation." *Rethinking Marxism* 1 (3): 6–43.

OECD. 2020. *Households' Savings (indicator)*.

O'Hara, Phillip Anthony. 1995. "Household Labor, the Family, and Macroeconomic Instability in the United States: 1940s–1990s." *Review of Social Economy* 53 (1): 89–120.

O'Hara, Phillip Anthony. 2006. *Growth and Development in the Global Political Economy*. New York: Routledge.

Overbeek, Henk. 2002. "Neoliberalism and the Regulation of Global Labor Mobility." *The Annals of the American Academy of Political and Social Science* 581 (1): 74–90.

Panizza, Francisco. 2011. "¿De Qué Hablamos Cuando Hablamos de Populismo? «¡Más Populista Será Tu Abuela!»." *RECSO* 2 (2): 15–38.

Panizza, Francisco, and Romina Miorelli. 2013. "Taking Discourse Seriously: Discursive Institutionalism and Post-Structuralist Discourse Theory." *Political Studies* 61 (2): 301–318.

Pareja-Eastaway, Montserrat, and Teresa Sánchez-Martínez. 2017. "Social Housing in Spain: What Role Does the Private Rented Market Play?" *Journal of Housing and the Built Environment* 32 (2): 377–395.

Pérez, Sofía A. 1999. "From Labor to Finance: Understanding the Failure of Socialist Economic Policies in Spain." *Comparative Political Studies* 32 (6): 659–689.

Pérez, Sofía A., and Manos Matsaganis. 2018. "The Political Economy of Austerity in Southern Europe." *New Political Economy* 23 (2): 192–207.

Pérez, Sofía A., and Manos Matsaganis. 2019. "Export or Perish: Can Internal Devaluation Create Enough Good Jobs in Southern Europe?" *South European Society and Politics* 24 (2): 259–285.

Pérez-Orozco, Amaia. 2014. *Subversión Feminista de La Economía. Aportes Para Un Debate Sobre El Conflicto Capital-Vida*. Madrid: Traficantes de Sueños.

Piketty, Thomas. 2014. *Capital in the Twenty-First Century*. Cambridge, MA: Harvard University Press.

Piore, Michael J., and Charles Sabel. 1984. *The Second Industrial Divide. Possibilities for Prosperity*. New York: Basic Books.

Polanyi, Karl. 1957. *The Great Transformation*. Boston: Beacon Press.

Pontusson, Jonas. 2013. "Unionization, Inequality and Redistribution." *British Journal of Industrial Relations* 51 (4): 797–825.

Portos, Martín. 2016. "Taking to the Streets in the Shadow of Austerity: A Chronology of the Cycle of Protests in Spain, 2007–2015." *Partecipazione e Conflitto* 9 (1): 181–210.

Portos, Martín. 2019a. "Divided We Stand, (Oftentimes) United We Fight: Generational Bridging in Spain's Feminist Movement and the Cycle of Anti-austerity Mobilizations." *American Behavioral Scientist*, 1–22.

Portos, Martín. 2019b. "Keeping Dissent Alive under the Great Recession: No-Radicalisation and Protest in Spain after the Eventful 15M/Indignados Campaign." *Acta Politica* 54 (1): 45–74.

Poulantzas, Nicos. 1974. *Fascism and Dictatorship: The Third International and the Problem of Fascism*. London: New Left Books.

Prieto, Carlos, and Fausto Miguélez. 2009. "Trasformaciones del Empleo, Flexibilidad y Relaciones Laborales en Europa." *Política y Sociedad* 46 (1): 275–287.

Ramiro, Pedro, and Erika González. 2019. *A Dónde Va El Capitalismo Español*. Madrid: Traficantes de Sueños.

Rancière, Jacques. 1999. *Dis-Agreement*. Minneapolis, MN: University of Minnesota Press.

Rancière, Jacques. 2004a. "The Distribution of the Sensible." In *The Politics of Aesthetics*. London: Bloomsbury.

Rancière, Jacques. 2004b. *The Politics of Aesthetics*. London: Bloomsbury.

Rancière, Jacques. 2007. *On the Shores of Politics*. New York: Verso.

Rancière, Jacques. 2014. *Hatred of Democracy*. London: Verso.

Recio, Albert. 2009. "Rasgos del Nuevo Poder Oligárquico en España: Viejas y Nuevas Caras de la Oligarquía Española." In *Economía, Poder y Megaproyectos*, edited by Federico Aguilera Klink and José Manuel Naredo, 125–152. Madrid: Fundación César Manrique.

Recio, Albert. 2010. "Capitalismo Español. La Inevitable Crisis de un Modelo Insostenible." *Revista de Economía Crítica* 9: 198–222.

Recio, Albert, and Jordi Roca. 1998. "The Spanish Socialists in Power: Thirteen Years of Economic Policy." *Oxford Review of Economic Policy* 14 (1): 139–158.

Reich, Michael. 1993. "Radical Economics in Historical Perspective." *Review of Radical Political Economics* 25 (3): 43–50.

Reich, Michael. 1997. "Social Structure of Accumulation Theory: Retrospect and Prospect." *Review of Radical Political Economics* 29 (3): 1–10.

Rendueles, César, and Jorge Sola. 2018. "The Rise of Podemos: Promises, Constraints, and Dilemmas." In *Podemos and the New Political Cycle. Left-Wing Populism and Anti-Establishment Politics*, edited by Óscar García-Agustín and Marco Briziarelli, 25–48. Cham: Palgrave Macmillan.

Resnick, Stephen, and Richard D. Wolff. 1987. *Knowledge and Class. A Marxian Critique of Political Economy*. Chicago and London: University of Chicago Press.

Retamozo, Martín. 2014. "Populismo En América Latina: Desde La Teoría Hacia El Análisis Político. Discurso, Sujeto e Inclusión En El Caso Argentino." *Colombia Internacional* 82: 221–258.

Retamozo, Martín. 2017. "La Teoría Del Populismo de Ernesto Laclau: Una Introducción." *Estudios Políticos* 41: 157–184.

Rey-Araújo, Pedro M. 2018. "Tensiones y Confluencias En Las Obras de Jacques Rancière y Ernesto Laclau." *Revista Española de Investigaciones Sociológicas* 162: 111–128.
Rey-Araújo, Pedro M. 2019. "Un Análisis Discursivo del Neocaciquismo Inmobiliario. El Caso de Jesús Gil En Marbella." *Revista Española de Sociología* 28 (2): 305–322.
Rey-Araújo, Pedro M., and Melchor Fernández. 2019. "La Distribución Del Tiempo Discrecional En España." *Revista Internacional de Sociología* 77 (1).
Rodón, Toni, and María José Hierro. 2016. "Podemos and Ciudadanos Shake up the Spanish Party System: The 2015 Local and Regional Elections." *South European Society and Politics* 21 (3): 339–357.
Rodríguez, Emmanuel. 2015. *Por Qué Fracasó La Democracia En España La Transición y El Régimen Del '78*. Madrid: Traficantes de Sueños.
Rodríguez, Emmanuel. 2016. *La Política En El Ocaso de La Clase Media. El Ciclo 15M – Podemos*. Madrid: Traficantes de Sueños.
Rodríguez-Alonso, Raquel, and Mario Espinoza-Pino. 2017. *De La Especulación al Derecho a La Vivienda. Más Allá de las Contradicciones del Modelo Inmobiliario Español*. Madrid: Traficantes de Sueños.
Rodriguez-Cabrero, Gregorio. 2011. "The Consolidation of the Spanish Welfare State (1975–2010)." In *The Spanish Welfare State In European Context*, edited by Ana M. Guillen and Margarita Leon, 17–38. Burlington, VT: Ashgate.
Rodríguez-Teruel, Juan, and Astrid Barrio. 2016. "Going National: Ciudadanos from Catalonia to Spain." *South European Society and Politics* 21 (4): 587–607.
Rodríguez-Teruel, Juan, Astrid Barrio, and Oscar Barberà. 2016. "Fast and Furious: Podemos' Quest for Power in Multi-Level Spain." *South European Society and Politics* 21 (4): 561–585.
Romanos, Eduardo. 2017. "Late Neoliberalism and Its Indignados: Contention in Austerity Spain." In *Late Neoliberalism and Its Discontents in the Economic Crisis. Comparing Social Movements in the European Periphery*, edited by Donatella della Porta, Massimiliano Andretta, Tiago Fernandes, Francis O'Connor, Eduardo Romanos, and Markos Vogiatzoglou. London: Palgrave Macmillan.
Rosenberg, Samuel. 2010. "Labor in the Contemporary Social Structure of Accumulation." In *Contemporary Capitalism and Its Crises: Social Structure of Accumulation Theory for the 21st Century*, edited by Terrence McDonough, Michael Reich, and David M. Kotz, 195–214. Cambridge: Cambridge University Press.
Rosnick, David, and Mark Weisbrot. 2015. "Has Austerity Worked in Spain?" Center for Economic and Policy Research Working Paper.
Ruiz-Gálvez, María Eugenia, and Lucia Vicent. 2018. "The Spanish Labor Market: On the Path of Flexibility and Wage Devaluation." In *The Political Economy of Contemporary Spain. From Miracle to Mirage*, edited by Luis Buendía and Ricardo Molero-Simarro, 98–123. London and New York: Routledge.
Rustin, Michael. 1988. "Absolute Voluntarism: Critique of a Post-Marxist Concept of Hegemony." *New German Critique* 43: 146–173.
Salmon, Keith. 2017. "A Decade of Lost Growth: Economic Policy in Spain through the Great Recession." *South European Society and Politics* 22 (2): 239–260.
Sánchez-Cuenca, Ignacio. 2012. *Años de Cambios, Años de Crisis. Ocho Años de Gobiernos Socialistas, 2004–2011*. Madrid: Los Libros de la Catarata.
Sánchez Iglesias, Eduardo. 2016. *Empresas Transnacionales, Capitalismo Español y Periferia Europea*. Madrid: Los Libros de la Catarata.

Sánchez-Mira, Nuria. 2019. "Work-Family Arrangements and the Crisis in Spain. Balkanized Gender Contracts?" *Gender, Work & Organization*. Forthcoming.

Saraceno, Chiara, and Wolfgang Keck. 2010. "Can We Identify Intergenerational Policy Regimes in Europe?" *European Societies* 12 (5): 675–696.

Schumpeter, Joseph A. 1939. *Business Cycles. A Theoretical, Historical, and Statistical Analysis of the Capitalist Process*. New York: McGraw-Hill.

Schwartz, Herman, and Leonard Seabrooke. 2008. "Varieties of Residential Capitalism in the International Political Economy: Old Welfare States and the New Politics of Housing." *Comparative European Politics* 6 (3): 237–261.

Serrano-Pascual, Amparo, Alba Artiaga-Leiras, and Eduardo Crespo. 2019. "El Género de Los Cuidados. Repertorios Emocionales y Bases Morales de La Microsolidaridad." *Revista Española de Investigaciones Sociológicas* 166: 153–168.

Sevilla-Sanz, Almudena, Jose Ignacio Gimenez-Nadal, and Cristina Fernández. 2010. "Gender Roles and the Division of Unpaid Work in Spanish Households." *Feminist Economics* 16 (4): 137–184.

Simón, Pablo. 2016. "The Challenges of the New Spanish Multipartism: Government Formation Failure and the 2016 General Election." *South European Society and Politics* 21 (4): 493–517.

Simonazzi, Annamaria. 2009. "Care Regimes and National Employment Models." *Cambridge Journal of Economics* 33 (2): 211–232.

Sola, Jorge, and César Rendueles. 2018. "Podemos, the Upheaval of Spanish Politics and the Challenge of Populism." *Journal of Contemporary European Studies* 26 (1): 99–116.

Sotiris, Panagiotis. 2019. "Is a 'Left Populism' Possible?" *Historical Materialism* 27 (2): 3–39.

Standing, Guy. 2011. *The Precariat. The New Dangerous Class*. London: Bloomsbury Academic.

Stavrakakis, Yannis. 2000. "On the Emergence of Green Ideology. The Dislocation Factor in Green Politics." In *Discourse Theory and Political Analysis. Identities, Hegemonies and Social Change*, edited by David Howarth, Aletta J. Norval, and Yannis Stavrakakis, 100–118. Manchester: Manchester University Press.

Stavrakakis, Yannis, and Giorgos Katsambekis. 2014. "Left-Wing Populism in the European Periphery: The Case of SYRIZA." *Journal of Political Ideologies* 19 (2): 119–142.

Streeck, Wolfgang. 2014a. *Buying Time. The Delayed Crisis of Democratic Capitalism*. London: Verso.

Streeck, Wolfgang. 2014b. "The Politics of Public Debt: Neoliberalism, Capitalist Development and the Restructuring of the State." *German Economic Review* 15 (1): 143–165.

Streeck, Wolfgang. 2015. "The Rise of the European Consolidation State." *MPIfG Discussion Paper* 15 (1): 1–28.

Streeck, Wolfgang. 2016. *How Will Capitalism End?*London: Verso.

Sweezy, Paul. 1968. *The Theory of Capitalist Development*. New York: Monthly Review Press.

Tabb, William K. 2010. "Financialization in the Contemporary Social Structure of Accumulation." In *Contemporary Capitalism and Its Crises: Social Structure of Accumulation Theory for the 21st Century*, edited by Terrence McDonough, Michael Reich, and David M. Kotz, 145–167. Cambridge: Cambridge University Press.

Taibo, Carlos. 2011. *Nada Será Como Antes. Sobre El Movimiento 15M*. Madrid: La Catarata.

Thomassen, Lasse. 2005. "Antagonism, Hegemony and Ideology after Heterogeneity." *Journal of Political Ideologies* 10 (3): 289–309.
Tobío, Constanza. 2013. "Estado y familia en el cuidado de las personas: Sustitución o complemento." *Cuadernos de Relaciones Laborales* 31 (1): 17–38.
Toharia, Luis, Jesús Cruz Villalón, Cecilia Albert Verdú, and Francisco Javier Calvo Gallego. 2005. *El Problema de La Temporalidad En España: Un Diagnóstico.* Madrid: Ministerio de Trabajo y Asuntos Sociales.
Torfing, Jacob. 1998. *Politics, Regulation and the Modern Welfare State.* Basingstoke: Palgrave Macmillan.
Torfing, Jacob. 1999. *New Theories of Discourse. Laclau, Mouffe, and Žižek.* Malden, MA: Blackwell.
Torns, Teresa, Pilar Carrasquer, Sara Moreno, and Vicent Borràs Català. 2013. "Career Paths in Spain. Gendered Division of Labour and Informal Employment." *Revue Interventions Économiques* 47.
Townshend, Jules. 2003. "Discourse Theory and Political Analysis: A New Paradigm from the Essex School?" *The British Journal of Politics and International Relations* 5 (1): 129–142.
Trifiletti, Rossana. 1999. "Southern European Welfare Regimes and the Worsening Position of Women." *Journal of European Social Policy* 9 (1): 49–64.
Turnbull-Dugarte, Stuart J. 2019. "Explaining the End of Spanish Exceptionalism and Electoral Support for Vox." *Research & Politics* 6 (2): 1–8.
Vampa, Davide. 2020. "Competing Forms of Populism and Territorial Politics. The Cases of Vox and Podemos in Spain." *Journal of Contemporary European Studies.* Forthcoming.
Veltmeyer, Henry. 2000. "Post-Marxist Project: An Assessment and Critique of Ernesto Laclau." *Sociological Inquiry* 70 (4): 499–519.
Vives-Miró, Sonia. 2018. "New Rent Seeking Strategies in Housing in Spain after the Bubble Burst." *European Planning Studies* 26 (10): 1920–1938.
Wallace, Michael, and David Brady. 2010. "Globalization or Spatialization? The Worldwide Spatial Restructuring of the Labor Process." In *Contemporary Capitalism and Its Crises: Social Structure of Accumulation Theory for the 21st Century*, edited by Terrence McDonough, Michael Reich, and David M. Kotz, 121–144. Cambridge: Cambridge University Press.
Weisskopf, Thomas. 1981. "The Current Economic Crisis in Historical Perspective." *Socialist Review* 57: 9–53.
Weisskopf, Thomas E., Samuel Bowles, and David M. Gordon. 1985. "Two Views of Capitalist Stagnation: Underconsumption and Challenges to Capitalist Control." *Science & Society* 49 (3): 259–286.
Wigger, Angela. 2017. "Understanding the Competition-Crisis Nexus: Revisiting U.S. Capitalist Crises." *Rethinking Marxism* 29 (4): 556–573.
Wolfson, Martin H. 2003. "Neoliberalism and the Social Structure of Accumulation." *Review of Radical Political Economics* 35 (3): 255–262.
Wolfson, Martin H., and David M. Kotz. 2010. "A Reconceptualization of Social Structure of Accumulation Theory." In *Contemporary Capitalism and Its Crises: Social Structure of Accumulation Theory for the 21st Century*, edited by Terrence McDonough, Michael Reich, and David M. Kotz, 72–90. Cambridge: Cambridge University Press.
Wood, Ellen Meiksins. 1986. *The Retreat from Class: A New "True" Socialism.* London: Verso.

Yrigoy, Ismael. 2019. "The Role of Regulations in the Spanish Housing Dispossession Crisis: Towards Dispossession by Regulations?" *Antipode* 52 (1): 316–336.

Yrigoy, Ismael. 2020. "The Political Economy of Rental Housing in Spain: The Dialectics of Exploitation(s) and Regulations." *New Political Economy*. Forthcoming.

Žižek, Slavoj. 1990. "Beyond Discourse Analysis." In *New Reflections on the Revolution of Our Time*, edited by Ernesto Laclau, 249–260. London: Verso.

Žižek, Slavoj. 2000. "Class Struggle or Postmodernism? Yes, Please!" In *Contingency, Hegemony, Universality*, edited by Judith Butler, Ernesto Laclau, and Slavoj Žižek, 90–136. London: Verso.

Žižek, Slavoj. 2006a. "Against the Populist Temptation." *Critical Inquiry* 32 (3): 551–574.

Žižek, Slavoj. 2006b. *The Parallax View*. Cambridge, MA: MIT Press.

Žižek, Slavoj. 2008. *The Ticklish Subject. The Absent Centre of Political Ontology*. London: Verso.

Žižek, Slavoj. 2012. *The Year of Dreaming Dangerously*. London: Verso.

Žižek, Slavoj. 2014. *Event. A Philosophical Journey through a Concept*. New York: Melville House.

Index

For Product Safety Concerns and Information please contact our EU
representative GPSR@taylorandfrancis.com
Taylor & Francis Verlag GmbH, Kaufingerstraße 24, 80331 München, Germany

www.ingramcontent.com/pod-product-compliance
Ingram Content Group UK Ltd.
Pitfield, Milton Keynes, MK11 3LW, UK
UKHW022132190926
475702UK00013B/1776

9780367567224